ARE THE LIPS A GRAVE?

ARE THE LIPS A GRAVE?

A Queer Feminist on the Ethics of Sex

Lynne Huffer

Columbia University Press New York

Columbia University Press
Publishers Since 1893
New York   Chichester, West Sussex
cup.columbia.edu

Library of Congress Cataloging-in-Publication Data
Huffer, Lynne
    Are the lips a grave? : a queer feminist on the ethics of sex / Lynne Huffer.
        pages cm
    Includes bibliographical references and index.
    ISBN 978-0-231-16416-0 (cloth: alk. paper)—ISBN 978-0-231-16417-7 (pbk.: alk. paper)—
ISBN 978-0-231-53577-9 (e-book)
    1. Feminist theory.   2. Queer theory.   3. Sex.   4. Ethics.   I. Title.

HQ1190.H84 2013
306.7601—dc23

                                                                        2013004397

Columbia University Press books are printed on permanent and durable acid-free paper.
This book is printed on paper with recycled content.
Printed in the United States of America
c 10 9 8 7 6 5 4 3 2 1
p 10 9 8 7 6 5 4 3 2
Cover Image: Jennifer Yorke, *Venus*, 2012, collage on paper
References to websites (URLs) were accurate at the time of writing. Neither the author nor
Columbia University Press is responsible for URLs that may have expired or changed since the
manuscript was prepared.

Contents

Acknowledgments

This book feels a bit like a palimpsest of my life over the past fifteen years. It is difficult to reconstruct all the exchanges that helped me to transform a loosely related set of ideas into something coherent. But let me attempt to acknowledge those who have accompanied me on the travels I trace here.

First and foremost, I want to thank Cynthia Willett, Shannon Winnubst, Gyan Pandey, and Ruby Lal for their incisive readings of the entire manuscript. Cindy's intellectual friendship has been one of the most enriching I've enjoyed in my twenty-five years of teaching and writing. Our conversations about the ethics of eros in particular have pushed me to be both more rigorous and more creative in my thinking about what such a concept might mean. Cindy's generosity and philosophical brilliance have made this a better book than it would have been without her. Shannon offered support, critique, wisdom, and especially humor exactly where they were needed. I am also grateful to Gyan and Ruby, my dear Emory writer's group members, who asked crucial questions along the way and inspired me to keep writing even when I was convinced I had nothing of interest to say. A special thanks to my artist book collaborator Jennifer Yorke for offering her collage, *Venus,* as an image for the cover.

I also want to thank the numerous friends and colleagues who have contributed to the improvement of some of the parts that make up the whole of the book. Chapter 1 began as a keynote lecture for a 2009 symposium on Irigaray at Emory University, and I want to thank the organizers, Emily Parker and Stefanie Speanburg, for inviting me to present my ideas there. A slightly different version of chapter 1 was originally published in *GLQ*, and I am especially grateful to former *GLQ* editors Ann Cvetkovich and Annamarie Jagose, as well as the two anonymous readers, for their rigorous review of the essay. I also want to thank Penelope Deutscher for her early encouragement and her insights into how to think Irigaray with Foucault. I am grateful to the Women's Caucus for the Modern Languages for honoring the *GLQ* essay with the 2011 Modern Language Association Florence Howe Award for Feminist Scholarship in English.

I began writing the argument that became chapter 2 while I was teaching at Rice University in the early 2000s, and I want to acknowledge the colleagues there who helped me along the way, especially Elizabeth Long, Susan Lurie, Helena Michie, Betty Joseph, Carol Quillen, Rachel Zuckert, and the members of the Feminist Inquiries Reading Group. In thinking about the arguments of chapter 3, both Michael Moon and Thomas Foster offered insights into queer culture, Foucault, and the history of sexual practices for which I am deeply grateful. A special word of thanks goes to Michael for his friendship and collegial support at Emory.

I am also grateful to Martha Fineman and the Feminism and Legal Theory Project at the Emory Law School for providing the occasion to begin exploring the issues that resulted in chapter 4. A special thanks to the participants of the October 2006 Storytelling and the Law conference at the Emory Law School whose questions and insights spurred me to develop the argument I presented there. I am also grateful to Catherine Smith for our conversations about race, sexuality, and the law, both as they relate to this chapter and to my arguments in chapter 7. I want to thank Jonathan Goldberg for his helpful reading of an earlier version of chapter 4 as well as for his friendship and ongoing support of my work. I also want to acknowledge his leadership at Emory in his position as director of Studies in Sexualities. A special word of thanks to Elizabeth Wilson for fabulous conversations about norms, the repressive hypothesis, and intersectionality. Emory has proven to be a fruitful environment for thinking and practicing a queer feminism.

Chapter 5 benefited from stimulating conversations with Anne Garretta about Violette Leduc and chapter 6 was enriched by ongoing dialogue with Elisabeth Ladenson about lesbianism in Proust. I am deeply grateful to Tamara Jones for allowing me to share some of her life story in chapter 7; special thanks to Serene Jones for her insights into the feminist theological issues I raise there, and to Leslie Harris for crucial conversations about the history of race in the U.S. I also want to acknowledge Catherine Smith, Jennifer Holladay, and their daughter Zoe for their inspiration and friendship. Chapter 8 began as an invited talk at Cerisy-la-Salle in 2008, and I want to thank Martine Delvaux for including me in the conference she organized there, "Femmes, Création, Poétique." I'd like to thank the members of the MLA Committee on the Status of Women in the Profession for inviting me to speak about work-life balance on an MLA panel in December 2010. That invitation prompted me to think about "Queer Lives in the Balance," the topic of my afterword. I also gained enormously from conversations with Carla Freeman about work, social reproduction, and affective labor in a neoliberal economy.

A number of scholars continue to inspire me to think and write about Foucault. I am especially grateful to Amy Allen, Penelope Deutscher, James Faubion, Laura Hengehold, Kyle Jensen, Mark Jordan, Colin Koopman, Kyoo Lee, Ladelle McWhorter, Mary Beth Mader, Jana Sawicki, and Shannon Winnubst for stimulating work and ongoing exchanges. A special word of appreciation goes to the organizers of PhiloSOPHIA: A Feminist Society, which has become an especially important site for me for queer feminist reflections on the ethics of sex.

I want to express my appreciation to Emory University and former Dean Robert Paul for providing the leave time to complete the book manuscript during the 2010–2011 academic year. I am extremely grateful to my colleagues and students in the Women's, Gender, and Sexuality Studies Department at Emory: I could not ask for a more collegial and supportive department. I also want to thank Cecelia Cancellaro, my agent, for her efforts in helping me to transform a set of essays into a book and find it a home. This is the second time I have worked with Columbia University Press and, once more, the home is a happy one. I am especially grateful to Wendy Lochner and Christine Dunbar for their editorial efforts.

Finally, I'd like to thank my family and my heart friends (you know who you are), both near and far, who have seen me disappear into the vortex of writing more times than they'd like to count. I'm grateful to them all, including the furry ones and the feathery ones. To Tamara: more than anyone, you have lived through this book in countless ways. Thank you for all you've done to help us create a queer feminist life to be cherished.

ARE THE LIPS A GRAVE?

I am restoring to our silent and apparently immobile soil its rifts, its instability, its flaws; and it is the same ground that is once more stirring under our feet.

—Michel Foucault, 1966

Introduction
Claiming a Queer Feminism

This book is a weave of voices: a crazy cat's cradle, some might say, of my own decades-old thinking about sex. Each of its chapters tells a different story about contemporary sexual lives that unfold in a variety of spaces: in classrooms and academic journals; at political rallies; in deserts, courtrooms, and grocery stores; in archives, sex clubs, and bedrooms. Taken together, the chapters trace the shifting trajectory not only of my thinking but also of an intellectual field. The result is a journey—sometimes zigzagging, sometimes twisted—through a land I call queer feminism.

On the most basic level, the book is motivated by a simple question: what does queer feminism have to offer now? Some readers may think that contemporary scholarship on sexuality has nothing new to say, that sexual thinking has turned into business as usual. They may argue that not only have feminist and queer studies been institutionalized as discrete fields of knowledge—through everything from doctoral degrees to an academic publishing niche to a canonical list of greatest hits—but also that many of the concepts generated by feminist and queer thinkers over the past thirty years have seeped into the lingua franca of culture at large. And they may wonder, rightly: what *does* queer feminism bring to sexual thinking and practice today that is surprising and transformative?

The chapters of this book respond to that question in a genealogical excavation of queer feminism's ground. I call that ground, as shorthand, modern Western subjectivity. To be sure, each of the terms I've deployed in that shorthand—*modern, Western, subjectivity*—compresses into coherence a set of fraught assumptions about history, geography, and the human that deserve interrogation and critique. And, indeed, over the course of the book I will bring some conceptual clarity and experiential texture to the epistemological, ethical, and political formation named by that shorthand. In doing so, I hope to restore to our soil, as Foucault puts it in the epigraph, "its rifts, its instability, its flaws": to make queer feminism stir once more under our feet.[1]

A Genealogical Approach to Queer Feminism

Before introducing the themes of the book, let me say a word about the philosophical perspective that informs my genealogical approach to queer feminism. The Foucauldian term *genealogy* has become pervasive in contemporary critical discourse, although it is often used, contra Foucault, to denote the tracing of influence or lines of filiation. Foucault distinguishes genealogy from the continuities that characterize history writing: genealogy eschews the search for origins and reconfigures the past as disparate, discontinuous, and radically contingent. Although many perceive a distinct break between Foucault's genealogical approach of the 1970s and his earlier archeological period, this sense of rupture has been overstated. It is clear that Foucault's object of analysis remains the same throughout his life: "discourse in its archival form."[2] Distinguishing himself from the linguistic structuralists to whom he is repeatedly compared, Foucault insists that his "object is not language but the archive, which is to say, the accumulated existence of discourses."[3] Foucault is less interested in language as a formal system than he is in "the fact that words were spoken."[4] In his 1977 essay, "Lives of Infamous Men," he emphasizes that "real lives were 'enacted' [*jouées*] in these few sentences."[5] He also asserts in a 1967 interview that his "archeology owes more to Nietzschean genealogy than to structuralism properly so called."[6]

I want to stress that Foucault's genealogies are embedded in his archeologies and vice versa: although archeology formally precedes genealogy, the former exhibits features of the latter. I want to further insist, as does

Foucault, that his genealogies must be understood in an explicitly Nietz-schean sense. As Deleuze makes clear in his 1962 book, *Nietzsche and Philosophy*, what Nietzsche brings to philosophy is the problem of critique in terms of values. "The problem of critique," Deleuze writes, "is that of the value of values, of the evaluation from which their value arises, thus the problem of their *creation*."[7] Deleuze continues: "Nietzsche creates the new concept of genealogy. The philosopher is a genealogist rather than a Kantian tribunal judge or a utilitarian mechanic" (2). In his critique of the value of values, the genealogist exposes the creation of values as a problem of origin. Deleuze writes: "Genealogy means both value of origin and the origin of values" (2). Rather than positing an unexamined ground—either "the 'high' idea of foundation which leaves values indif-ferent to their own origin" or "the idea of a simple causal derivation or smooth beginning which suggests an indifferent origin" (2)—"genealogy signifies the *differential* element of values from which their value itself derives" (2, emphasis added).

In my focus on queer feminist ethics, I want to accentuate this Nietz-schean inflection of the term *genealogy* as it relates to what Foucault calls power-knowledge.[8] Foucault's genealogical critique of power-knowledge interrogates the value of its value, the evaluation by which it arises, and the problem of its creation. In that critique, he exposes, as does Nietzsche, the unacknowledged *moral* values that undergird modern science: ratio-nality and morality go hand in hand.[9] With regard to our reconstruction of the past as a rational-moral practice, Foucault demonstrates that all the things we take for granted when we think about history—causality, origins or sources, influence, thinking of the past as depth—are linked to moral premises.

Importantly, this does not mean that Foucault's Nietzschean critique of the premises of morality is a nihilistic denial of morality itself, as many have charged. As Nietzsche puts it in *Daybreak*: "I deny morality as I deny alchemy, that is, I deny their premises."[10] Denying alchemy does *not* mean denying that people believed they were transforming base met-als into gold; it does not mean that alchemy had no historically specific social value. So too with morality: denying morality does *not* mean that people do not act morally or that morality has no social value. But deny-ing morality, like denying alchemy, *does* mean questioning the premises of the beliefs and actions we attach to the moral systems that have gone unquestioned.[11]

My genealogical approach in this book is indebted to Irigaray as well. As I detail in chapter 1, reading Foucault and Irigaray together helps me to reframe queer feminism in ways that I hope will be useful to both feminists and queer theorists. In their different approaches, specifically to genealogy, Foucault and Irigaray nonetheless hold in common a Nietzschean suspicion of origin that is worth pursuing further. Throughout her work, Irigaray shares with Foucault an aim to dismantle the rational-moral premises of Western thought. In that dismantling, Irigaray both draws on and disrupts genealogy understood in the usual, non-Nietzschean sense, as kinship or filiation. In doing so, like many twentieth-century antifoundationalist philosophers, Irigaray brings attention to the metaphysics of presence that both produces origin as the source of truth and masks the violence of that production. Irigaray names that violence by invoking an always already dead maternal body. If Western metaphysics both produces and masks the constitutive absence at its source, Irigaray argues that this constitutive absence is sexed: Western culture is founded on the murder of the mother and the absence of a maternal genealogy at the level of the symbolic. As Margaret Whitford puts it, "there is no maternal genealogy."[12] In light of this absence, women are always residual and derivative: they can only appear as defective copies of men or as the objects of exchange that secure masculine homosocial bonds.

Irigaray's critique of the sexed violence that undergirds Western metaphysics allows me to reframe genealogy in specifically feminist terms that would be difficult to tease out of Foucault alone. The absence of a maternal genealogy means that the mother-daughter relation remains unsymbolized. And, as Whitford points out, this lacuna produced by the vertical lines of patriarchal filiation creates problems for the feminist project of constructing a female sociality or horizontal relations among women. Put more pragmatically, the maternal absence at the source of our symbolic system exposes the aggressions that rupture our most cherished feminist myths of female solidarity. As Whitford explains, it reveals "the discrepancy between the idealization of women's nature found in some early feminist writing and the actual hostilities and dissensions engendered within the women's movement itself."[13]

Irigaray's diagnosis of the genealogical absence that produces sexual difference thus underscores an important theme of this book: the ethical failures, hostilities, and especially betrayals that besiege relations among women. As I show in chapter 7 in particular, these historically inscribed failures are irresolvable; our betrayals are not simply the result of tactical mistakes or false consciousness or blindness to the complex multiplicity of oppressions. They are, rather, the abject residue of an ideal we repeatedly fail to achieve. That ideal of female harmony without exclusion is a function of the metaphysics of presence Irigaray exposes as both violent and deceptive. In this sense, Irigaray's diagnosis of the founding of Western culture in the murder of the mother adds a feminist dimension to the Foucauldian conception of genealogy that will be useful for elaborating a queer feminist ethics.

In their mutual critique of the rational-moral foundations of Western knowledge, Foucault and Irigaray allow me to link genealogy to a postmoral ethics that has both diagnostic and constructive functions. As diagnosis, it challenges, à la Nietzsche, the premises of a society of normalization Foucault explicitly links to the human sciences.[14] As I will show shortly, the network that connects morality, power-knowledge, and disciplinary power helps to explain some of the problems that have arisen within gender and sexuality studies as knowledge projects with emancipatory aims. In its constructive dimension, the ethics I elaborate exploits the unstable epistemic foundations of morality as we know it in order to rearticulate ethics as eros. If eros is a term we can't quite pin down, I want to harness that strangeness for the relational ethics it might offer.

I mentioned in the opening of this introduction that, as a genealogical excavation of queer feminism's ground, this book focuses on how that ground falsely secures a modern subject. Both Foucault and Irigaray recognize the centrality of sexuality to that subject-making project. Indeed, as I detail in the book's chapters, contemporary experiences of sexuality, including queer feminist ones, are the most visible layer of a historical sedimentation that binds sexuality to morality in the very constitution of the modern subject. And, while other thinkers (most notably, Foucault) have made this point, its relevance to queer feminism has yet to be explored. Indeed, possibilities for a renewed queer feminism emerge precisely out of this philosophical insight into the historical convergence that 1) makes the modern Western subject a specifically sexual subject and 2) makes modern Western sexual subjectivity a function of rationalist morality. This book is thus not merely an attempt to flesh out the contours of a contemporary queer feminism. It is also, crucially, a genealogical retraversal of the fissured ground of morality on which our sexual lives are played out.

The Queer Split from Feminism

That retraversal opens a lens onto the book's more local and more immediate concern: an oft-noted, aegis-creating, persistently repeated splitting of queers away from feminists. That differentiation-through-splitting, initiated from within feminism by sexual thinkers like Gayle Rubin (1984) and Eve Kosofsky Sedgwick (1990), has been reaffirmed by feminist and queer theorists alike, although many have repeatedly cautioned against the reductionism of a binary opposition between a queer attention to sexuality and a feminist focus on gender.[15] Nonetheless, in many of its theoretical and institutional forms, the queer feminist split is more than an illusion. Such a split was most recently and explicitly reasserted in Janet Halley's 2006 *Split Decisions: How and Why to Take a Break from Feminism*, which tells one formerly feminist but now queer theorist's tale about leaving feminism in ways that repeat queer theory's most oft-told origin stories.[16]

While many thinkers share a commitment to the queer feminism I describe in this book, it is clear that many others do not. More specifically, the queer feminism I invoke might seem to go against the grain of some of the more radically antifoundationalist strands of queer theory.[17] However, while the restored queer feminism I'm claiming appears, at first glance, to require that we commit to unwavering feminist beliefs in women's identity and shared moral values—beliefs that make many queer theorists squirm—this particular picture of feminism is not the only one available to us. I hope to restore to our contemporary conversations about sex an antifoundationalist feminist tradition whose queerness has been eclipsed, somewhat paradoxically, with the rise of queer theory. In that eclipse, queer feminism has receded behind the line-drawing opposition Halley stages as frumpy, sex-phobic feminists pitted against their kinky, stylish queer cousins. As Annamarie Jagose and others have argued, an important antifoundationalist strand of feminist thinking needs to be brought back into this reductive picture. "Careful consideration of the anti-foundationalist impulse in feminist theory," Jagose writes, "promotes an alternative relation in which feminism is both an historical source of inspiration for queer thought and its present-tense interlocutor."[18] Along similar lines, Robyn Wiegman asks: "why should queer theory get all the theoretic thrill?"[19]

Halley's arguments are representative of the kind of reductive queer portrait of feminism both Jagose and Wiegman decry. The feminism Halley describes is a foundationalist one whose humorless pieties include a belief in the universal domination of women by men, an obsessive concern for women's sexual victimization, and a political strategy to harness the regulatory apparatuses of the state to alleviate those sexual harms. Halley's rejection of this "governance feminism" (SD 20) includes, interestingly, a critique of what she calls feminism's "convergentist" (SD 81) tendencies: the drive to coalesce under one feminist umbrella an array of positions that complicate gender as a single category of analysis. Rejecting these "hybrid convergentist feminist" (SD 88) positions, which attempt to think together the myriad differences of race, class, sexuality, and nation that threaten to separate women from one another, Halley argues instead for the critical power of "divergentist" positions valuing discontinuity and dispersal.[20] If an antisexist stance that is critical of pornography is at odds with a sex-positive, porn-friendly queer politics, divergentism says: let the separation dividing them remain. Importantly, Halley describes the convergentist feminist politics that would attempt to bridge such differences as a "*moral* project" (SD 89), which makes theory "normative" (SD 89). The implication of her argument is that divergentism is ethically and politically superior to convergentism because it is open-ended, non-normative, and less prone to abuses of power than feminism's regulatory governance project: "divergence in left-of-center thinking about sexuality and power," she writes, "can not only get us some conceptual gains that seem unavailable from convergence; it can also get us analyses that seem crucial to responsible involvement in governance" (SD 34).

Arguing, as I am, for a restored queer feminism, Halley would most likely disagree with what might appear to be a convergentist impulse driving this book. I both welcome that disagreement and want to reframe Halley's terms. As Jacques Rancière reminds us, disagreement is the place where politics starts.[21] But disagreement is not the same as divergence, nor is agreement or consensus the same as convergence. Rather, disagreement happens precisely in those times and places *where divergent positions converge*: in Rancière's terms, convergence in a common world (without a consensus) is the beginning of the *contestation* that not only makes politics possible but also differentiates politics from policing.[22] Rancière's rethinking of politics as disagreement makes the stark either/or choice Halley offers seem unhelpfully dualistic: either you're divergentist or you're convergentist, and never the twain shall meet. Following Sedgwick in her pursuit of nondualism, I want to suggest that, while Halley's dualism has certainly served a purpose by exposing queer theory's divergentist impulses as an explanation for its divergence from feminism, that either/or frame is no longer useful.[23] Indeed, Halley's binary frame threatens to produce the same kind of closing down of thinking she attributes to the convergentist position. Finally, at the heart of Halley's concerns is a worry about moralism that for her comes to characterize not only feminism but convergentism itself. This worry not only reduces numerous varieties of feminism to the moral bullying of a governance feminism that "wants to rule the world" (SD 60) but also fails to examine the problem of morality as a historical formation inextricably linked to the very thing Halley celebrates as kinky sexuality: modern queer perversions Foucault famously historicizes in his critique of the repressive hypothesis in *History of Sexuality*, volume 1. Although Halley's book is replete with denunciations of antiqueer moralisms of various kinds, her analysis falls short of the kind of genealogical examination of the relationship between sexuality and morality that is constitutive of the queer itself.

My commitment to queer feminism is only convergentist in a contestatory, rift-restoring sense. In epistemological and moral terms, this means I want to follow the cracks: I want to pursue the fissures that characterize genealogical work and that make politics as disagreement possible. In political terms, I want to seek convergence in fractured common worlds, whatever those worlds might be: not only departments, conferences, and classrooms but also kitchens, bedrooms, and social media sites. I seek that ruptured convergence where disagreement keeps the political from degenerating into a moralizing form of critical policing that Wiegman identifies as "an accusatory discourse of incipient complicity."[24] Because this queer feminism is simultaneously convergentist and rift restoring, it differs significantly from Halley's insistence on line drawing, decision making, splitting, and break taking. This difference between us is not an argument about right versus wrong: I am not proposing a more correct theory than hers about the truth of sexuality. Indeed, one thing Halley and I share is a recognition of the irresolvable ambiguities that characterize sexual life. The difference between us—between committing to queer feminism and taking a queer break from feminism—stems from a difference in our tactics. As an intervention into the problems that plague us, a queer feminist genealogy seems, in my view, more theoretically and politically promising as a form of resistance than a queer decision to split from feminism. Indeed, the very different activist agendas that frame contemporary queer and feminist politics suggest that the break Halley theorizes has in fact already happened on the ground and that such a break has produced what many view today as a stagnant, compromised, or moribund sexual politics. Politically and ethically, queers need feminists and feminists need queers.

Returning to the philosophical stage on which these differences are played out, my antifoundationalist approach to queer feminism insists on the critical value of genealogically excavating the tensions that bind sexuality to morality. In this sense, the book's explicit stakes are primarily ethical, although my interests remain political as well. Following Nietzsche, whose retraversal of the land of morality in *On the Genealogy of Morals* is paradigmatic for a genealogical thinking that extends, through Deleuze's book on Nietzsche, to Foucault and Irigaray, this book's retraversal of feminism and queer theory produces a transvaluation of sexual values rather than simply their rejection.[25] Addressing sexuality as a moral experience in modernity, I situate ethics as the fraught terrain over which queer feminist battles have been fought. I do so, specifically, by reflecting on the elaboration of queer theory in the 1990s and 2000s as a response, corrective, or alternative to the feminist thought that had developed over the previous two decades.

Focusing on this tension between queers and feminists, one of the book's most insistent claims is that the recurring drama of a queer split from feminism is driven by this ethical tension. Exploring in detail some of the contours of that split, each chapter clarifies the specific conceptual, aesthetic, and political problems that have plagued queer and feminist thinking and practice. Taken together, the chapters argue for more concerted attention to the specifically ethical stakes of queer versus feminist conceptions of sexual practices, laws, norms, and artistic production. Folding together the feminist with the queer, I call not only for a new approach to sexual thinking but, just as crucially, for a new conception of ethics.

From Sexual Subjectivity to an Ethics of Eros

In rethinking ethics I draw on and extend my previous work on feminist and queer ethics in *Maternal Pasts, Feminist Futures* (1998) and in *Mad for Foucault* (2010). In *Maternal Pasts* I used Irigaray to critique nostalgia in feminist theory and challenge the assumptions embedded in a feminist ethics of care whose maternalization of the concrete other repeats the problems of a nostalgic structure Irigaray exposes as the subsumption of difference into the logic of the Same. Staging the impasses that led to a stalemate between an antinormative antifoundationalism (Judith Butler) and a Habermasian feminism that remains committed to ethical norms (Seyla Benhabib), I called for a fuller articulation of the concept of the ethical other. Using Butler and Benhabib to expose, within this ethical impasse, an opposition between performative and narrative conceptions of subjectivity, I raised questions about the possibility of rethinking an ethics of alterity whose narrative-oriented critique of performativity remains suspicious of the rationalist assumptions about subjectivity and narrative coherence that undergird Benhabib's position. The current book extends those reflections on ethics by revisiting the performative/narrative opposition in the context of the queer/feminist split (chapter 2), by linking the feminist ethics of care to the more recent field of vulnerability studies (chapter 7), and by examining in detail how various narratives perform a different, erotic ethics that I link to a revitalized queer feminism (chapters 5 through 8).

More importantly, this book draws on the arguments I made in *Mad for Foucault*, where I approached sexual ethics through a Foucauldian lens that both historicizes sexuality within modern biopower and challenges the persistent violence of rationalist moralities. While sexuality studies scholars, and especially queer theorists, have focused overwhelmingly on Foucault's *History of Sexuality*, volume 1,[26] I argued that Foucault's sustained antifoundationalist critique of Western reason begins with his first major book, *History of Madness*, first published in French as *Folie et déraison: Histoire de la folie à l'âge classique* in 1961.[27] Although the story Foucault tells there is ostensibly about madness, it is also a story about modern sexuality. Focusing in *Madness* on the rise of rationalism over the course of the seventeenth and eighteenth centuries, Foucault describes the disappearance of unreason and the rationalist objectification of madness in the classical age. At the same time, he also narrates the gradual emergence of sexual subjectivity and the proliferating forms of sexual perversion that are the focus of *History of Sexuality*, volume 1. *History of Madness* thus has a crucial role to play in unraveling moral rationality and reframing the fraught question of sexual ethics.

In *Mad for Foucault* I reread queer theory through the lens of *History of Madness* in order to focus on the larger ethical stakes of sexuality in biopower, or what Foucault describes as the "life of the species," which biology invented in the nineteenth century as "life itself."[28] Contra some queer theorists, I argued that what is at stake in biopower is not the "liberation" of individual bodies into an orgiastic life of happiness and pleasure, but a life-ordering grid whose threat to "life itself" requires an erotic ethics of the other. Sidestepping the lure of "bodies and pleasures" proffered by Foucault at the end of *History of Sexuality,* volume 1, in *Mad for Foucault* I followed instead an erotic path through the sexual *dispositif* Foucault so painstakingly describes over the course of his oeuvre.[29]

Foucault's rethinking of eros begins in *History of Madness* and persists through the final volumes of *History of Sexuality* as part of his critical approach to the historical present. Rather than pinpointing eros as a distinctively Platonic term revisited by Foucault in his return to the ancient world, I redeployed eros as a concept to be refashioned from the perspective of our present age. I did so, specifically, by reframing Foucauldian eros within the structure of its modern Freudian borrowing. Classically conceived as a mad form of love, in *Civilization and Its Discontents* (1930) Freud transforms eros into another name for "life": the polar opposite of *thanatos* or death, eros is the life force or libidinal energy that lies at the origin of civilization itself.[30] Importantly, in theorizing eros through what John Rajchman calls "a fictive anthropology or prehistory of the 'primal,'"[31] Freud also recodes it in explicitly modern, scientific terms by placing "biological sexual instincts firmly at the root of erotic phenomena."[32] Not only life but the origin of life, Freud's primal eros paradoxically marks the culmination of the biological, developmental conception of life as bios that underpins modern biopower. He thereby also establishes, as Bartsch and Bartscherer put it, "the dominant analytical paradigm for approaching eros throughout much of the twentieth century" (2).

Freud's twentieth-century "erotic archaism" (Rajchman 108) both highlights and mystifies the scientific displacement of irrational, ecstatic, Platonic eros by the biological "life" of modern reason whose violence Foucault will challenge. Recoded in modernity as sexuality, eros-as-bios is the contemporary result of the great division between reason and unreason Foucault identifies in *History of Madness* with the Cartesian moment. In the post-Cartesian world, Foucault notes the loss of a premodern "homosexual lyricism" he links to an erotic "Platonic culture" (88). That erotic culture not only associates love with unreason—as "a blind madness of the body"—but also places unreason "in a position of knowledge" as "the great intoxication of the soul" (88). As a form of knowledge that includes madness, eros will be banished by the "I" of the modern Western cogito. Eventually swallowed up by *bio-logos* over the course of the nineteenth century, it reemerges in Freud as a mystification of modern, scientific life-as-bios through the tragic theme of the lost origin of civilization. From *History of Madness* to *History of Sexuality,* volume 1, eros appears, paradoxically, as a disappearance: a profile dissolving at the edge of the horizon, a shadow cast as it falls. Eros becomes the name for that which is lost in the moral rationalization of modern sexuality as the site of our intelligibility. In a movement that leaves eros behind as the unintelligible form of a fading unreason, it can only reemerge, in the historical present, as an atemporal rupture—as the lightning-quick flash of a "mad" mode of knowing—within the scientific specification of the sexual *dispositif*'s ever-proliferating list of perversions.

Beginning with the erotic murmur we hear in *History of Madness*, in *Mad for Foucault* I traced eros as an archaic name for modern life that contests the scientific objectification of life as bios. I argued that, in both *Madness* and *History of Sexuality,* volume 1, Foucault reverses Freud's prior reversal of ancient mad eros into modern rationalized life; in that re-reversal, eros emerges as a new name for an unreasonable, corporeal ethics of living in the biopolitical present. In making this argument, I did not conceive of Foucauldian eros as a timeless form of lyrical expression or as a transhistorical libidinal energy that persists as the force of life itself. Rather, if ethics begins with the Socratic question, how are we to live? eros is the name we can give to a mode of living both expressed and unexpressed, both appearing and not: an uncertain, embodied, disruptive encounter of subjects with others.[33] Consistent with my genealogical approach to queer feminism here, in *Mad for Foucault* eros named a Nietzschean practice of historical retraversal: a genealogical excavation of the land of sexual morality where the cogito lives.[34] This erotic retraversal is an ethical, self-transformative, self-undoing labor that exposes the Cartesian "I" to its own limits as a rational moral subject.

The theory of an erotic ethics I developed in *Mad for Foucault* opens a space in the present book for an erotic ethics of alterity and a restored queer feminism that picks up where *Maternal Pasts* left off. Specifically, this ethics of eros allows me to reframe the queer feminist split in terms of the self-fracturing structure of reason and unreason Foucault describes in *History of Madness* as a problem that also concerns the question of the subject in relation to others. From this perspective, the ethical tension between queers and feminists is also a tension between an antinormative, self-shattering queer flirtation with the irrational and feminism's seemingly more rationalist, normative, moralizing claims about sexuality in a gendered order. As mentioned earlier, that ethical tension is often expressed as an opposition between a feminist investment in narrative coherence and a queer embrace of performative disruption. Like Halley's convergentist/divergentist binarism, that opposition initially served a purpose, but is no longer useful. I genealogically excavate the contours of the binarism for the lens it brings to the problem of ethics in queer feminism. The feminist narrative versus queer performative opposition describes a corresponding difference between a feminist investment in narratively secured moral norms and a queer disavowal of normativity epitomized by performative rupture. Rather than choosing one side over the other in a falsely reductive opposition, I focus on a post-Levinasian ethics of alterity that Irigaray reframes through sexual difference as a function of narrative performance. In doing so, I rework the moral terms through which the ethics of sex have been debated.

Beyond queer and feminist theory specifically, my antifoundationalist approach to an erotic ethics also allows me to interrogate modernity itself by restoring to its ground the ungrounding cracks and instabilities that open up possibilities for transformed relations between subjects and others. This ungrounding restoration is not cause for alarm, but rather a reminder: there's nothing solid beneath our feet, and to persist in the illusion of solid ground is to perpetuate the epistemic and ethical violence that both Foucault and Irigaray repeatedly describe. In this sense, because the modern sexual subject is a function of Western rationalist morality, this book's inquiry into the ethical implications of the queer feminist split brings into relief what is at stake for us all as the inheritors of a tenacious but threatened Enlightenment sexuality.

Antifoundationalism, Difference, and Intersectionality

As these remarks make clear, my approach to ethics in feminist and queer theory is indebted to a primarily French antifoundationalist tradition of thinking that includes not only Foucault and Irigaray but other late twentieth-century thinkers as well. Importantly, this tradition of thinking has informed both queer and feminist thought. In some of its iterations in the 1970s and '80s, French antifoundationalism generated new ways of thinking about sex not only via Foucault on the "queer" side but also via the "feminist" work of Luce Irigaray, Hélène Cixous, and Julia Kristeva in particular. Problematically consolidated and institutionalized as "French feminism," these sometimes deconstructive, sometimes psychoanalytic approaches to "sexual difference" were eventually subsumed into a larger configuration that today is generally labeled as postmodern or poststructuralist.[35] At the same time, the seemingly more practical, empirically oriented sisters of this "difference" feminism have persisted in the trench work of a sociologically conceived "equality" feminism whose focus is not "sexual difference" but "gender."

In contemporary feminist thought, the terms of this now seemingly ancient opposition between a French-accented difference feminism and an Anglo-American equality feminism have shifted dramatically. As Robyn Wiegman has noted, with the rise of queer theory in the 1990s feminist antifoundationalism was, to a large extent, rechanneled as queer.[36] This is not to say that queer theory has drawn on any of the "French feminists" as among its primary sources; indeed, as I argue in chapter 1, it has not. But many of the most visible strands of queer theory spring from the same deconstructive and, especially, psychoanalytic modes of analysis that drove the work of the 1980s "difference" feminists. Together with the first volume of Michel Foucault's *History of Sexuality*, the writings of Lacan, Deleuze, and Derrida in particular are among the most important theoretical foundations for the antifoundationalist project we call queer theory.

At the same time, the project of feminist theory began redefining difference as a sociological term to nuance the one-dimensionality of feminist analysis focused only on gender. In doing so, it developed what has become a canonical story about difference and feminism. That oft-repeated story is usually this: in the beginning the seemingly unmarked (but actually white, middle-class, straight, Western) woman in whose name feminist thought often claimed to speak was quickly troubled by the emergence of other categories of difference: class, nationality, disability, and especially race and sexuality. A variation on this story is that in the beginning woman was always already disabled, nonwhite, poor, queer, and non-Western. In both versions, difference as the name for a feminist antifoundationalist claim about the instability of any ground in whose name a movement or mode of thinking might speak was gradually displaced. Difference became, increasingly, an empirically grounded theoretical claim about legible positions on a social grid that made identities more complex than previously conceived. And as the phenomenal rise of intersectional analysis over the past two decades attests, this well-known problem of difference produced shifts in feminist scholarship that were nothing short of paradigmatic.[37] As Robyn Wiegman puts it: "it is no exaggeration to say that intersectionality circulates today as *the* primary figure of political completion in U.S. identity knowledge domains."[38]

In that context, various strands of feminist thinking were institutionalized between the 1980s and the present: disability feminism, woman of color feminism, transnational feminism. Viewed from this perspective, the emergence of queer theory can be seen either as part of the larger intersectionality paradigm shift within feminism or, alternatively, as the birth of a discrete field separate from feminism. How one interprets the emergence of queer theory in relation to feminism depends on how one reads queer theory's relation to antifoundationalism and difference. How deep into the foundation's cracks does queer theory go? To what extent are those cracks still relevant to feminist theory? And what do the answers to these questions suggest for a restored queer feminism?

If conceived as one of many possible preexisting paths that meet at an intersection, queer sexuality can be and is attached by some to a subject with an identity: a fraught, contested, troubled, performative, unstable, shifting, marginalized identity, but a subject with an identity nonetheless. Indeed, Judith Butler's *Gender Trouble*, published just a year after the 1989 article by Kimberlé Crenshaw that put intersectionality on the map, frames identity in precisely these terms:

> If one "is" a woman, that is surely not all one is; the term fails to be exhaustive, not because a pregendered "person" transcends the specific paraphanelia of its gender, but because gender is not always constituted coherently or consistently in different historical contexts, and because gender *intersects* with racial, class, ethnic, sexual, and regional modalities of discursively constituted identities. As a result, it becomes impossible to separate out "gender" from the political and cultural *intersections* in which it is inevitably produced and maintained.[39]

In the big basket we've come to call postmodern feminism, the differences between this Butlerian conception of a fractured, intersectional identity and Foucauldian desubjectivation have gone unremarked.[40] Correspondingly, the queer performative ruptures made popular by Butler's work are seldom contestations of subjectivity itself; as Butler puts it in describing the performative subversion of a subject's identity through psycholinguistic reiteration and redirection: "a subject . . . remains."[41] This identity-rupturing sense of queer masks its investment in the solidity of the subject-making ground antifoundationalist philosophies expose as fissured and unstable. This Butlerian version of queer has generally been sympathetic to feminisms of various kinds, not just antifoundationalist ones. As Butler's use of the terms *intersect* and *intersection* suggest, "queer" in this sense could be categorized as part of a larger intersectionality paradigm shift within feminism.

Jasbir Puar points out that one of the developments to be traced from this conception of queer as an intersectional shift within feminism is the rise of queer of color critique.[42] Both José Muñoz and Roderick Ferguson, for example, place women of color feminisms at the heart of their influential queer of color critiques of canonical queer theory, *Disidentifications* (1999) and *Aberrations in Black* (2004), respectively.[43] And although Ferguson in particular draws extensively on Foucault, the standpoint epistemology undergirding a specifically queer of color claim gives epistemic and moral authority to the experiential truths of a coherent subject in ways that are in tension with Foucauldian desubjectivation. Queer of color critique begins with a recognition of historical marginalization as a desubjectivating experience to be remediated by critical resubjectivation. Rather than a disinvestment in subjectivity, queer of color critique tends to reclaim subjectivity, often in explicitly Butlerian ways, in order to interrogate the coherence of identity. Once again, the difference between Butlerian identity disruption and Foucauldian desubjectivation becomes crucial for recognizing this aspect of the field. As Juana María Rodríguez puts it: "Identity is about situatedness in motion: embodiment and spatiality. It is about *a self* that is constituted through and against *other selves*."[44]

If, on the other hand, one conceives of queer theory as following the cracks in subjectivity's foundations all the way down, queer theory's relation to intersectional feminism becomes more fraught. In this version of queer theory there are neither selves nor intersections, just an abyssal ungrounding that not only troubles identity but undoes subjectivity itself. This queer sexuality tends to name not only a split from foundationalist feminisms, intersectionality, and Butlerian identity trouble, but also an antifoundationalist repudiation of the very terms by which feminist intersectionality is comprehensible at all. The most prominent strand of this sexual thinking is the psychoanalytically driven antisocial thesis in queer theory and includes the work of Leo Bersani, Lee Edelman, Tim Dean, Janet Halley, and others. Edelman's work in particular has been the version of queer antisociality most often targeted by intersectional queer analyses critical of what Judith Halberstam calls "the excessively small, [gay male] archive that represents queer negativity."[45] As Halberstam's remark suggests, intersectionality's concern to bring "difference" into the unmarked white masculinity of canonical knowledge formations has made antisocial theory's antifoundationalism suspect in the eyes of many. As José Muñoz puts it: "It has been clear to many of us, for quite a while now, that the antirelational in queer studies was the gay white man's last stand."[46] While Halberstam's and Muñoz's concerns about racial privilege and canonical exclusions are important, I want to reiterate what Edelman points out in response to his critics: that the differences between the intersectional and antisocial strands of queer theory revolve more around differing investments in subjectivity than they do around success or failure in diagnosing an unjust present order. As Edelman puts it, in opposing "the engine of reproductive futurism, queer negativity *opposes the subject* of humanistic teaching as well."[47]

In a slightly different vein, Eve Kosofsky Sedgwick's work—from her early genealogical, literary writing on Western sexual epistemologies to her later reflections on desubjectivating forms of Buddhist ethics—also deploys conceptions of the queer that can be associated with an antifoundationalist strand of thinking. And although Sedgwick, like Edelman, has been criticized for drawing on an excessively narrow canon of (white male) texts, her work has also been used approvingly by some queer theorists of color, although not as extensively as Butler's.[48] Sedgwick's consistent critiques of the moralizing tendencies of contemporary theory are philosophically linked to an implicit critique of the uninterrogated epistemic authority of moralizing critical subjects.

In yet another desubjectivating vein, Jasbir Puar's Deleuzian frame of queer assemblage differentiates her work from the intersectional queer of color lens through which her work is often viewed. In *Terrorist Assemblages,* Puar explicitly shifts her focus away from intersectionality to queer assemblage. Importantly, she links that "move from intersectionality to assemblage" to a Deleuzian desubjectivation: "There is no entity, no identity, *no queer subject or subject to queer.*"[49] In doing so, she directly challenges the unquestioned stability of the subject implicit in feminist intersectionality theory.

These are broad brush strokes, and are meant to delineate trends rather than to articulate the nuances of particular writings. The brush strokes allow me to situate my own approach to queer feminism in the context of intersectionality. Obviously, my Foucauldian proclivities move me in the direction of desubjectivation, even as I take seriously the problems of canon formation, exclusion, and marginalization that foundationalist approaches tend to highlight. My antifoundationalist commitments should not be interpreted as a repudiation of the challenge to racism and other forms of exclusion intersectionality names. But I want to suggest that the institutionalization of intersectionality as the *only* approach to gender and sexuality that takes difference seriously masks intersectionality's investment in a subject-making form of power-knowledge that runs the risk of perpetuating precisely the problems intersectionality had hoped to alleviate.

More specifically, I believe a Foucauldian conception of subjectivity and its costs is basically incompatible with intersectionality.[50] As Wiegman and others have pointed out, intersectionality is defined through a "juridical imaginary."[51] From a Foucauldian perspective, the juridical imaginary at the heart of sovereign power is at odds with the actual workings of the disciplinary mechanisms of modern biopower.[52] As Foucault puts it in a 1976 lecture: "the discourse of discipline has nothing in common with that of law, rule, or sovereign will. . . . The code [the disciplines] come to define is not that of law but that of normalization."[53] This problem with the incommensurability between intersectionality's juridical imaginary and the "polymorphous disciplinary mechanism" that constitutes one of the axes of biopower exposes modern, disciplinary, subject-making power-knowledge as a problem for intersectionality.[54] If intersectional theory perceives itself as engaged in an agential, emancipatory knowledge project, that self-perception is at odds with a disciplinary conception of the techniques and discourses of knowledge—including those embraced by theorists of intersectionality—that contribute to procedures of normalization. As Roderick Ferguson puts it: "The dominant affirmation of intersectionality . . . works to facilitate the ideological presumptions of social scientific methodologies, particularly their claim to get at the truth of an unmediated reality."[55] I would add to Ferguson's remarks that the humanistic discourses Edelman critiques also contribute to the normalizing logic that Foucault associates with the human sciences broadly conceived. Intersectionality's investment in multifaceted, proliferating subjectivities elucidated by knowledges that prop up the subject risks turning a paradigm of liberation into a mechanism of normalization.

Symptomatically, the emancipatory political aims of intersectionality have come to be embedded in the kinds of human rights discourses Foucault spent his life critiquing. If racial and other forms of structural exclusion and inequality continue almost unabated, an array of institutions—from the United Nations to the National Women's Studies Association to identity-based academic departments of various kinds—have embraced the intersectional language of inclusion in ways that reflect the false promises of the Enlightenment exposed by antifoundationlist philosophies. Intersectional terminology has become pervasive, not only in academic and legal arenas but also in public policy discourse. As Nira Yuval-Davis points out in her analysis of international human rights discourse at the United Nations, both the language and concepts of intersectionality have become "part of gender mainstreaming."[56] This adoption of intersectionality discourse in the face of ongoing inequality points to the complexity of modern power-knowledge. As a knowledge formation, intersectionality serves more than a simple truth-telling function either as an empirically or interpretively based explanation of how complex subjectivities are lived in the world through processes of exclusion and marginalization. Intersectionality also articulates a political promise to eradicate the possibility of future exclusions. As Wiegman puts it, intersectionality "calls for scholars in identity studies to offer cogent and full accounts of identity's inherent multiplicity in ways that can exact specificity about human experience without reproducing exclusion."[57]

Most important for the ethical concerns that frame this book, the emancipatory political goals of intersectional knowledge have produced a critical ethos grounded in a *moral imperative* to exclude exclusion. Crucially for my analysis, especially in chapters 4 and 7, that moral imperative is often racially charged.[58] Repeatedly cited as the origin of intersectionality, Kimberlé Crenshaw's 1989 article situates the "accident" experienced by a black woman at the legal intersection of race and gender as paradigmatic for an entire field.[59] Jennifer Nash asserts in her analysis of intersectionality's institutionalization as theory that the concept "renders black women prototypical intersectional subjects."[60] Writing several years after Nash's trenchant critique, Nikol Alexander-Floyd contends, by contrast, that postblack conceptions of intersectionality in the social sciences have made black women disappear.[61] The fact that the place of black women in intersectionality theory has generated this kind of debate demonstrates the ongoing centrality of race as one of its terms.

In this context the white fear of complicity in the perpetuation of racial exclusion makes critiquing intersectionality tantamount to betraying an antiracist agenda, if not to undermining women and queers of color themselves. As Wendy Brown asserts in her critique of women's studies, "*guilt* emerges as the persistent social relation of women's studies to race."[62] This guilty fear of complicity, grounded in unspoken but powerful moral norms and reinforced by specific forms of institutionalization, has produced an intellectual environment of moral policing rather than political disagreement. That environment has rendered debates about intersectionality less robust and less honest than they might be.[63] "How did we become cops?" Wendy Brown asks.[64] The fact that the racism charge is often not political in Rancière's sense, but primarily *moral*—involved, as it is, in policing claims about good versus bad and about what one *ought* to believe and do—makes the problems of intersectionality, subjectivation, and the exclusion of exclusion especially relevant to the ethical terrain I explore in this book, particular with regard to interracial betrayal, a theme I explore in chapter 7.

With this context in mind, I want to examine, from an antifoundationalist perspective, the subject-making power-knowledge formations implicit in intersectional analysis. The kind of exploration I have in mind is neither psychoanalytically oriented, as antisocial queer theory is, nor is it Deleuzian, like the work of Puar. My queer feminist approach is genealogical, in the specifically Nietzschean, postmoral sense I've already described. As a critique of morality, genealogy helps to explain why we experience our inevitable failures to include some particular other in the anxious etceteras of our iterations of difference as not only inadequate on epistemic grounds but as moral failures. Importantly, such a genealogical approach does not mean we should give up on the critique of exclusion and marginalization that gave rise to intersectionality in the first place. But we might consider ceding the institutionalized moral language of intersectional policing to a less moralizing approach inspired by a conception of politics as contestation that remains suspicious of institutional straitjacketing.

Restoring Queer Feminism

Let me return to the problem of difference with which I began this inquiry into intersectionality and antifoundationalism. Again, in this book I reframe difference through a genealogical approach to sexual ethics as a function of modern subjectivity and I do so by drawing explicitly on an antifoundationalist heritage of thinking that is not only queer but explicitly feminist. In each of the chapters my perspective is rooted in an ungrounding queer feminist trajectory of thought that not only destabilizes or complicates sexual identities but also challenges the epistemological and moral foundations of subjectivity itself. Framed in this way as a restored *question* about the modern Western ethical subject, the old difference problem reappears as new.

Examining the queer feminist split by restoring to the question of sexual ethics its rifts, its instability, and its flaws, I thus interrogate an antifoundationalism many queer and feminist theorists share, but whose ethical stakes have yet to be examined. I develop my claim that sexual ethics lies at the heart of an internally fractured queer feminist nexus by carefully examining various political, institutional, and cultural sites where the queer feminist rift has been most salient. This book focuses in particular on queer feminist debates about sexual violence and the legal regulation of sexuality as well as underread literary and cinematic resources for rethinking erotic pleasure.

The divergent ethical perspectives revealed by this rift reflect different responses to the dual burden of ethics: first, the acknowledgment of harms and, second, the elaboration of alternatives to those harms. With its consistent attention to addressing and remediating sexuality as harm—sexual harassment, rape, incest, pornography, and other forms of sexual violence and objectification—foundationalist feminisms have not only developed strong moral claims about sexual subjectivity, but have pursued those claims through an institution-building politics. By contrast, antifoundationalist queer theorists have consistently targeted sexual morality itself as harmful and have tended to pursue the remediation of that harm through an antinormative, often anti-institutional discourse of negative freedom.

As an approach to ethics that combines critique with a rift-restoring transvaluation, *Are the Lips a Grave?* both confronts the moralistic tendencies of a foundationalist feminist tradition and addresses the normative force of queer antinormativity. The book's title, taken from the first chapter, highlights the shared antifoundationalism of a queer feminist heritage I embrace. In its allusion to two paradigm-shifting essays, one feminist and the other queer, the title harkens back to the feminist lips of Luce Irigaray's 1977 essay, "When Our Lips Speak Together," and to the abyssal figure of queer self-shattering theorized by Leo Bersani in his 1987 "Is the Rectum a Grave?"[65] With this title I hope to convey the book's aesthetic and philosophical ambitions: to offer a sustained, nuanced reflection on queer feminism that opens modern sexuality to a new erotic ethics.

I hope this book's most important contribution to contemporary scholarship will be its restorative claim to an ethical queer feminism and its transfiguration of ethics as erotic living. In philosophical terms, the book extends the post-Nietzschean project to rethink ethics "beyond good and evil" without underestimating, as some queer theorists have done, the persistence of a morality Foucault calls "catastrophic."[66] In elaborating a thinking-feeling ethics of the other, I challenge contemporary thinkers of sex and difference not to escape sexual morality but to reshape it from within.

In addition to this introduction and an afterword, the book includes eight chapters. Chapter 1, "Are the Lips a Grave?" articulates the frame for the literary, political, cinematic, and everyday scenes I engage in much of the remainder of the book. Rereading Irigaray through a Foucauldian lens, I make a case in this chapter for Irigaray as a feminist resource for queer thinking by exploring the philosophical antifoundationalism she and queer theorists share. Focusing specifically on the antisocial thesis of queer theory, and especially the work of Leo Bersani and Janet Halley, I examine in detail the contentious relation between feminist and queer conceptions of sexual ethics. I then move on to address new possibilities for a queer feminist ethics. Unraveling the aporetic knot of sexual ethics at the heart of queer feminist splits, the chapter pursues a philosophical understanding of sexual difference and erotic desubjectivation in modernity through the constructive elaboration of a queer feminist ethics.

Chapters 2 through 4 perform a genealogical retraversal of queer feminism by tracing some of the contours of the queer feminist split in literary, theoretical, and legal arenas. Specifically, these three chapters connect the seemingly abstract problem of alterity in narrative versus performative conceptions of subjectivity (chapter 2) to the concrete problem of sexual violence (chapters 3 and 4). Through an attention to narrative ethics I articulate a queer feminist conception of narrative as performance in order to bring out the political work that stories do. In chapter 2, "There Is No Gomorrah," I develop this concept of narrative as performance by interrogating the queer feminist split through an Irigarayan lens focused on the problem of the other. Defining ethics in deconstructive terms as the readable site of an inscriptional relation to an other, I develop an ethics of alterity here as one of the nodes of the erotic ethics theorized in chapter 1 and further developed over the course of the book. Focusing specifically on the question of the subject and the production of difference through acts of othering and erasure, my interrogation of ethics in "There Is No Gomorrah" addresses both a persistent feminist narrative concern about our ethical boundedness to others and, at the same time, a tenacious queer performative antimoralism that appears to privilege freedom at the expense of relationality and responsibility to others. Informed by Irigaray's theory of the "Other's Other" in *Speculum of the Other Woman*, my reading of the other across the queer feminist split highlights the problem of alterity as crucial for rethinking the ethics of sex through the lens of narrative performativity. Although not specifically Foucauldian in its approach, this chapter makes visible an ethics of the other that informs Foucault's ethical thinking as well.

Chapter 3, "Foucault's Fist," returns to Foucault by addressing the questions of sexual violence and pleasure in his work. Focusing on the figure of the fist in two well-known interviews with Foucault—one about French rape laws, the other about sex clubs—this chapter reads the ambiguity of that fist as not only violent but also erotic, thereby loosening the snag over which feminist readings of Foucault have stumbled. Arguing, with Foucault, for an ethics of the self in relation to others that is neither fully constrained nor completely free, in this chapter I pursue the strategic possibilities that might emerge from narrative performance and its retraversals of particular cultural spaces that are both thoroughly social (and therefore constrained) and radically new (and therefore free). This, I argue, constitutes one way of imagining what Foucault calls the "ethical work" of freedom: "to free thought from what it silently thinks, and so enable it to think differently."[67]

Chapter 4, "Queer Victory, Feminist Defeat? Sodomy and Rape in *Lawrence v. Texas*," examines the legal implications of the queer feminist split through a focus on storytelling in the law. Reworking the themes theorized in the book's first three chapters, this chapter explores the resonances of that theory in a queer feminist reading of the 2003 U.S. Supreme Court decision to decriminalize sodomy, *Lawrence v. Texas*. Bringing together chapter 2's focus on narrative performance and alterity with chapter 3's attention to sexual violence and pleasure, this chapter resituates those questions in the context of narrative legal theory. Tracing the deployment of Jean-François Lyotard's concept of the *differend* in critical legal theory and critical race theory, this chapter performs a genealogical reading of *Lawrence v. Texas* that uncovers beneath this story of freedom an earlier, archival story about forcible sex. In doing so, the chapter exposes a queer feminist split that is itself split by racial and sexual violence. Highlighting the fraught, irresolvable ambiguities of lived experiences of sexuality, the chapter asks specific questions about the violent ground of *Lawrence*'s widely celebrated "freedom."

In the following four chapters I retrieve an artistic queer lesbian feminism that lies outside the bounds of academic feminism and queer theory. With the institutionalization of queer theory over the course of the 1990s, the kinky, self-shattering lesbian feminist aesthetic tradition I uncover in this section has been all but occluded. Drawing on my reading of Irigaray in chapter 1, my purpose in these chapters is to ask about the stakes of a forgotten lesbian *jouissance* whose forgetting is itself forgotten. In doing so, I offer some snapshots of a landscape inhabited by figures who hover around the margins of the Anglo-American queer feminist canon. Focusing especially on underread texts, stretching from Colette in the 1940s to the iconoclastic French writer and filmmaker Virginie Despentes in 2006, I make a case in this section for the ongoing importance of literary and cinematic rewritings of classic themes and stories about sexual violence and pleasure.

Chapter 5, "One-Handed Readings," returns to the problem of "difference" in relation to lesbian sexuality and sexual pleasure by way of jouissance. The chapter focuses specifically on Violette Leduc's underread masterpiece, *The Bastard*, published in French in 1964, for the clues it offers in rethinking the ethical problem of alterity by narrating a lesbian erotic ethics and thereby theorizing an alternative conception of relational subjectivity and desubjectivation through jouissance. Chapter 6, "Queer Lesbian Silence: Colette Reads Proust," further pursues the problem of the other by examining in detail Colette's reading of Proust in her 1941 text *The Pure and the Impure*. Focusing on Albertine, Proust's controversial lesbian character in *Remembrance of Things Past*, I contrast Colette's reading of her with that of Levinas in order to conceive of Albertine as an opaque figure who opens new queer feminist spaces for rethinking the ethics of sex.

While chapters 5 and 6 focus primarily on eros as pleasure or jouissance, chapters 7 and 8 complicate erotic pleasure by weaving in the themes of sexual and racial violence and the ethical betrayal of women by each other. Chapter 7, "What If Hagar and Sarah Were Lovers?" weaves together an autobiographical account of an everyday moment of interracial tension with Sara Maitland's rewriting of the biblical story of Hagar's betrayal by Sarah and Abraham. Focusing specifically on the feminist ethics of care, the chapter performs an intertextual reading of Maitland and the Bible in the context of lived erotic experience. In doing so, the chapter reflects on the place of narrative performance for feminism's contemporary legacy of economic inequalities and racial betrayals that continue to divide queer women from each other even as we forge new ways of living.

Chapter 8, "After Sex," introduces Anglophone readers to the French fiction and cinematic work of the iconoclastic Virginie Despentes for another lens on a contemporary erotic queer feminism. Juxtaposing Despentes with the legendary American bad girl Valerie Solanas of *SCUM Manifesto* (1968) fame, the chapter returns to the problem of sexual violence and its relation to queer feminism. Exploring Despentes's conception of a "prostitute writing," the chapter ends with a focus on tenderness in the face of bodies that come undone after sex. Taken together, chapters 5 through 8 not only restore to queer feminism its rifts and its fissures but also reconstruct a variegated, underread queer lesbian archive that challenges both the received Anglo-American academic canon of queer feminist texts and the linear temporality of a story about queerness we have come to receive as a given: queerness as a self-shattering force that can only come *after* a more solid, schoolmarmish, heterosexual feminism.

Finally, in the afterword, "Queer Lives in the Balance," I bring the multilayered textures of the chapters back to the present and the everyday. Reflecting on the nexus between individual lives that are "out of balance" and biopolitical life, I conclude the book by raising questions about queer feminism as they relate to a present in which "life itself" is at stake. Framed as a question about biopower, the queer feminist ethics I call for in the book takes on a resonance that extends the erotic beyond the realm of individual sexual pleasure to a plurality of lives. If we ask, again, the Socratic question—how are we to live?—as a queer feminist question that contests biopower, an ethics of eros begins to emerge for new ways of living "in the present, that difficult tense."[68]

1   Are the Lips a Grave?

Are the lips a grave? It's a funny question, or maybe a scary one, but, funny or scary, it's a question I keep asking. With my feminist twist on Leo Bersani's queer title—"Is the Rectum a Grave?" (1987)—I want to begin my exploration of antifoundational queer feminism by opening a space for rethinking the place of Luce Irigaray in the world of queer theory.[1] For if queer theory has made a place for the rectum as a respectable topic of scholarly discussion (scarcely imaginable before the mid-1980s), such is not the case for the feminist lips made famous by Irigaray in her 1977 essay, "When Our Lips Speak Together."[2]

If the lips are feminist but not quite queer, to ask about the lips in queer theory is to ask, from the start, about new possibilities for a queer feminism. In that context, this opening chapter offers a theoretical frame for the explorations of sexual ethics that follow in the subsequent chapters. So doing, it contributes to a rich field of queer feminist inquiry that has much to offer, but has not yet adequately explored the philosophical foundations of a persistent queer feminist split. As I argued in the introduction, the divergence within sexual thinking that inaugurated queer theory in the late 1980s has since been repeated, again and again, in ever new queer feminist splits.[3] I have long been interested in how these splits occur despite a shared philosophical antifoundationalism that drives both queer theory and poststructuralist feminisms like Irigaray's.[4] As I argued in the introduction, I contend that sexual ethics lies at the heart of this internally fractured queer feminist nexus.[5]

Here in this chapter I want to characterize this problem of sexual ethics as a philosophical dissonance in queer feminism. Resisting the impulse to harmonize the discordant, I want to examine this dissonance by rethinking Irigaray through a Foucauldian ethical lens. Both Irigaray and Foucault offer powerful antifoundationalist perspectives on the question of sexual ethics: Irigaray by rethinking sexual difference, Foucault by rethinking sexual subject making. And if Foucault's aegis-creating role in relation to both poststructuralist feminism and queer theory seems incontestable, Irigaray's feminist-but-not-quite-queer place in relation to Foucault remains uncertain and virtually unexplored.[6] Reading Foucault and Irigaray together allows me to interrogate a shared antifoundationalism whose ethical stakes for feminist and queer theory and politics have yet to be examined in a sustained way. In opening a conversation between Irigaray and Foucault I hope to contribute to the work of building an ethical queer feminism that is not only capacious and erotic but also variegated, uneven, and shifting.

At the end of his life, Foucault asked: "why [have] we made sexuality into a moral experience?"[7] Explicitly conceptualizing sexual morality as a historical problem, Foucault's question opens possibilities for reconfiguring modern sexual ethics.[8] And although Foucault poses the question retrospectively, as a historical problem that sent him to the archives of the ancient world, he asks it here, in his final interview, from within modernity, as an entry point for understanding sexuality as a history of the present. Rethinking the implications of this later, ethical Foucault—his minute dissection of technologies of the self in the Greco-Roman and early Christian worlds as ethical practices of freedom—I reconceive his ethical project as spanning his entire oeuvre, from *History of Madness* (1961) to *The Order of Things* (1966), through the genealogical work on punishment and sexuality in the 1970s, and ending with the project on ethical subjectivation in the early 1980s.[9] In that context, I want to enlist Foucault's ethical approach to sexual subjectivity as a way to hear, if not to harmonize, the ethical dissonance that has split queers from feminists.

But what is this dissonance exactly? While feminists have developed a robust field of ethical thinking that ranges from virtue ethics to ethics of care to deontology to postmodern ethics of various kinds, queer theorists have been more reticent to engage with ethics. The relative thinness of ethical thinking in queer theory stems, in my view, from a number of factors; the most pervasive of these is an implicit queer distaste for a conception of ethics as morality that dominates everyday thinking, professional ethics, and many traditional moral philosophies.[10] Given the history of ethical systems that have condemned even the most benign forms of sexual deviation from the norm, the pervasive queer disengagement from ethics is not surprising.

Those queer theorists who do discuss ethics have implicitly adopted the approach of Continental ethicists who, following Nietzsche, distinguish between ethics and morality in a challenge to the exclusionary violence of moral norms. Importantly, some particularly influential antimoral queer complaints have specifically targeted *feminist* moral theory and politics. In *Split Decisions*, Janet Halley critiques the cultural feminist belief in "the pervasive *moral* character of patriarchy and feminism" (SD 61), repudiating feminism's view of a male-dominated world in which "female values have been depressed and male values elevated in a profound *moral* error that can be corrected by feminism" (SD 61, emphasis added). Along similar lines, Gayle Rubin's earlier critique of the "conservative sexual morality" of the feminist antipornography movement buttressed her call in the mid-1980s to split sexuality studies from feminism and the analysis of gender (28). And although neither Halley nor Rubin dismisses ethical thinking altogether—Rubin calls for a "true ethics" (15), while Halley calls for one that is "different" (SD 60)—their dismissals of feminist moralism do not include any clear articulation of exactly how their ethics is new. The same could be said of queer theorists Michael Warner and Tim Dean, who, implicitly rejecting morality and embracing ethics (although not explicitly against feminism), both argue for what appears to be a fairly traditional conception of ethics as moral autonomy.[11] At the radical end of the queer ethics spectrum, Leo Bersani and Lee Edelman (again, implicitly) reverse common conceptions of ethics as relational moral norms into a negative ethics that is nonrelational and antisocial.[12]

Let me resituate this problem of queer ethics within the genealogical frame that informs my approach to an ethical queer feminism. First, while the implicit ethics versus morality distinction we find in some queer theory may be heuristically and politically useful, it does not adequately respond to the Foucauldian problem of the historical link that binds sexuality to morality. Second, the distinction does not resolve what Judith Butler calls a "paradoxical condition for moral deliberation" that Foucault's lifelong work on subjectivity goes to great lengths to explore.[13]

That is, ethical subjects must negotiate their historically specific relation to morality even as their ethical practice both acknowledges and interrupts the force of morality in their own production as subjects. Thus, relating this paradox back to the problem of ethics in queer theory: if queer theory has attempted to do the latter—that is, acknowledge and interrupt morality in its violent production and repression of sexually deviant subjects by articulating either a new or a negative ethics—it has done so at the expense of a robust historical thinking about how subjects actually live and negotiate their relation to moralities. If we define ethics, in its broadest sense, as reflection that responds to the Socratic question how are we to live? queer theory must engage the ethical in ways that are more nuanced and varied than its now stock array of antinormativities allows.[14] Indeed, the fact that queer theory's antinormativities have acquired a normative moral force of their own dramatizes a crucial Nietzschean point: simply negating moral norms will not prevent the rebounding force of new moralities precisely at the site where morality has been contested.[15]

In this light, Foucault's historical question—why has sexuality become a moral experience?—opens a slightly different post-Nietzschean path through the queer feminist thicket that is sexual ethics. For, as Foucault well knew, if Nietzsche's challenge to morality is scathing, his solution to morality's violence is not a naysaying dismissal of moral norms in favor of a thinly articulated ethics. Rather, the development of what Foucault calls a desubjectivating ethics—an ethics of the self as a self-undoing practice of freedom—requires a retraversing, thinking-feeling transvaluation of the historical space that binds ethics to morality.[16]

That retraversal requires a return to the paradoxical position of the moral subject Butler describes, where even a resistant negotiation of ethics requires a recognition of one's production as a subject by and within morality. In recalling that paradox, we can also refine the broad Socratic question—how are we to live?—by remembering Foucault's definition of ethics as a historical interrogation of the relation between subjectivity and truth and to view that interrogation as simultaneously pursuing the question of a manner of living and jamming the machinery of moral subject production.[17] To ask about ethics in this genealogical sense is to ask about the historical constitution of a subject that is also unraveling: a non-self-identical form of desubjectivation.

More specifically, with regard to sexuality, this Foucauldian mode of accessing ethics begins with the assumption that the modern subject is, like it or not, both a moral subject and a sexual subject: indeed, it is within the *dispositif* of a morally inflected sexuality that we become intelligible to ourselves as subjects. Further, modern sexual subjectivity comes at the cost of what Foucault, following Deleuze, calls *assujettissement*: a subject-producing subjection that simultaneously creates and subjugates sexual subjects within an increasingly differentiated grid of deviance and normalization. Importantly, Foucault embeds this process of subjective sexualization in a genealogy that links the rise of rationalism to bourgeois morality: rationalism and morality go hand in hand in the modern system that both incites and imprisons us as sexual beings. Foucault teaches us, then, that we cannot leap free of sexual morality by ignoring it, denouncing it, or simply calling for a new ethics. Rather, the violent "land of morality" must be retraversed if we are to practice the freedom of a nonviolent ethics.[18]

Finally, in contrast to many of Foucault's interpreters, I conceive of Foucault's ethics as an ethics of the other. As we have seen, and as Foucault insists repeatedly in his later work, ethics involves an interrogation of the subject. Not a pregiven substance, that subject is a form that is "not primarily or always identical to itself" ("ECS" 290). As a non-self-identical process of emergence and disappearance, the ethical subject is historically linked to the emergence and disappearance of others. As the historian Elsa Barkley Brown reminds us, we live the lives we do because others live the lives they do.[19] And just as *assujettissement* produces and subjugates us within a grid that differentiates subjects in relation to others, so too ethical desubjectivation is a practice of freedom inextricably bound to the practices of others: "freedom," Foucault writes, "is the ontological condition of ethics" ("ECS" 284); and again, he says, "the freedom of the subject in relation to others . . . constitutes the very stuff of ethics" ("ECS" 300).

I use Foucault, then, to amplify the ethical resonance of my queer Irigarayan question: are the lips a grave? That resonance includes not only a critique of the sexual moralities undergirding *assujettissement* but also the opening of different ethical questions through a desubjectivating, other-oriented practice of freedom within the moralities of our historical present. Harnessing the Foucauldian genealogical critique of morality in the service of a possible queer feminism allows me to respond to what I identified in the introduction as the dual burden of ethics: first, the acknowledgment of harms and, second, the active elaboration of alternatives to those harms. Most important, as an approach that combines critique with transvaluation, this Foucauldian take on ethics forges powerful tools for both confronting the moralism of much feminist theory and addressing the thinness of ethics in queer theory. The ethics I offer is kinky and relational but attentive to harms: an erotic ethics of the other.

Although this kinky practice of freedom invokes orgiastic, even utopian images, this ethics refuses the consolations of utopianism.[20] Rather, I think of this ethical queer feminism as heterotopian: the articulation of a space that, as Foucault famously puts it, is both "utterly real . . . and utterly unreal."[21] Cobbled together out of bits and pieces, the shards of the queer and feminist work I engage here begin to form a shattered, troubled, but reorienting mirror of our age: a space in which to see, simultaneously, both the place where we are—the rational moralism of *assujettissement*—and the place where we are not—"that virtual point which is over there" ("DS" 179). In Irigarayan terms, it allows us to see and practice both a critique of the monosubjective, monosexual system of sameness she diagnoses in *Speculum of the Other Woman* (1974) and, at the same time, a different approach—as lips, perhaps—to the ethical question of the other.[22]

There is a long road to travel from my opening question—are the lips a grave?—to the queer feminist erotic ethics I've invoked. Moving across that distance is the work of this book. My argument in this chapter contributes to that effort by applying different lenses to the question of Irigaray's absence from queer theory. This approach allows me both to confront head-on the obstacles that make a queer feminist ethics so difficult, and to highlight the conceptual resources Irigaray has to bring to this endeavor. Because the ethics I'm after is a relational one, I focus especially on the explicitly nonrelational negativity of the antisocial queer theory initiated by Bersani. In addition to Bersani, I pay special attention to Janet Halley because her embrace of antisocial negativity so perfectly dramatizes the queer split from feminism I am trying to understand.

I develop my argument in this chapter in three distinct sections. First, I pursue the question of Irigaray's absence from queer theory by addressing the oft-noted problem of her putatively homophobic and heterosexist remarks about sexual difference. The first section, "Hommosexual (with a Double *m*)," asks specifically about the place of homosexuality or samesex relations in Irigaray's work and documents the exclusion of Irigaray from queer theory as the index of a certain kind of nonqueer feminist threat to the queer. I challenge this line of thinking by making a counterclaim to the charges of idealism that underlie the numerous critiques of her homophobia and heterosexism. Reading Irigaray with Bersani and Halley, the lips with the rectum, I show how both share what we might call a commitment to the queer undoing of modern subjectivity that distinguishes the antisocial thesis from other strands of queer theory.[23] Arguing for a queer heterosexuality in Irigaray, I demonstrate how Irigaray shares with Bersani a critique of the masculine monosubject and of redemptive sex.

The second section, "Lip Reading," uses the vehicle of the personal voice—a queer feminist mimesis of myself as a different subject in another time—to examine the lips as a figure for Irigaray's antifoundationalism. The return of the lips in this section dramatizes a spatiotemporal alterity as the rupture of the Same that characterizes Irigaray's thinking. Reengaging the question of Irigaray's absence from queer theory, I reflect on queer performativity as a methodology that harnesses the force of the negative in ways that include but go beyond antisocial queer theory. My parodic self-mimicry of an earlier instance of Irigarayan lip-reading serves, in this context, as a reminder that Irigarayan mimicry is a forgotten precursor of queer performativity. Understanding mimesis as camp, the athwart, the oblique, and the undecidable—all emblems of the queer—I show how the forgetting of Irigaray as an important feminist progenitor of queer performativity opens up the question of the other as a constitutive forgetting of sexual difference in queer theory that is itself forgotten. This raises, again, the question of ethics as a problem of alterity—a forgetting of the other—in relation to the negative ethics of antisocial queer theory. Returning once again to the lips, I show how their absence from queer theory demands an engagement with the problem of sexuality not simply as a force of negativity or rupture, but as a constitutive and forgotten relation to an other.

The third section, "Toward a Queer Feminist Ethics of Eros," reads Irigaray with Foucault to articulate a queer feminist ethics of the other. I flesh out the contours of this ethics by engaging the problems of alterity, transcendence, ethical subjectivity, and temporality, linking Foucault's genealogical method for writing histories of the present with Irigaray's assertion that sexual difference is a problem for our time. I thereby hold open a space in which a queer feminist ethics of alterity can be imagined. Together, Foucault and Irigaray articulate an ethical dissolution of the subject: this dissolution is also, oddly, that which binds us, each to the other, through the ethical force of relation.

Hommosexual (with a Double *m*)

Despite the centrality of Irigaray's work to contemporary thought about gender and sexuality, she remains either absent from queer theory or one of its negative foils.[24] This is somewhat surprising, at least at first glance. Like queer theorists, Irigaray attempts to rethink sex—that "fictitious unity" Foucault identifies as a "dense transfer point of power" which includes within its domain, at the very least, sex as organs, sex as biological reproduction, sex as individual gender roles, sex as gendered group affiliation, sex as erotic acts, and sex as lust.[25] Indeed, Irigaray's lifelong attempts to rethink this "sex" in the context of political, social, and epistemological structures of exclusion could be said to constitute the central theoretical concerns not just of feminism but of queer theory as well. But even a casual perusal of the theoretical sources for influential thinkers of the queer reveals Irigaray's glaring absence.

When Irigaray is mentioned, primarily in footnotes or brief asides, she usually indexes a feminist threat to the queer. In Eve Kosofsky Sedgwick's 1993 *Tendencies*, for example, Sedgwick cites Irigaray in a footnote to her chapter on Diderot as an example of the "respectable homophobic feminist-theory fantasy" that links male homosexuality to fascism.[26] Drawing on Craig Owens's dismissal of Irigaray as homophobic, Sedgwick describes the Irigarayan critique of the male homosocial bonds that structure patriarchal culture as a "potent polemical move" and a "dangerous and demogogic one."[27] In *Feminism Meets Queer Theory* (1997), Trevor Hope makes a similar argument about Irigaray's reading of a "necrographic" pact in *Totem and Taboo*'s founding "hommo-sexual" brotherhood, extending his critique to include "post-Irigarayan" feminists like Rosi Braidotti.[28]

A decade later, in *Split Decisions*, Halley aligns Irigaray with what she calls Robin West's "cultural feminism" and its "redemptive sexuality" (SD 65), distinctly situating Irigaray in a trajectory of thinking antithetical to Bersani's anal repudiation of redemptive sex. Irigaray's redemptive cultural feminism, Halley writes, "is a *lesbian* sensibility, and an entirely *feminine* sexual ethics" (SD 66). Writing not only on behalf of gay men but also, especially, on behalf of heterosexual women who desire masculine men, Halley asserts: "there seems to be no urgent need in [this redemptive cultural] feminism to understand women's version of what Leo Bersani . . . has called love of the cock'" (SD 65). Halley goes on to complain that in writing her book she has not found "*anyone* determined to produce a theory or politics of *women's heterosexual desire for masculinity in men*. It's just missing" (SD 65).

Halley's search for a queer woman's heterosexual love of the cock brings out the conceptual threads of the argument I develop in this section about a possible *queer heterosexuality* in Irigaray. To begin, it's not at all clear what Halley means by women's heterosexual desire, nor how this queer woman's desire for masculinity in men might be different than business as usual. Is the desire Halley seeks that which Bersani diagnoses as the result of a social imaginary that homophobically and misogynistically links both women and gay men with death? Promiscuous, insatiable, diseased, and infectious, this desire is deadly: both women and gay men, Bersani writes, "spread their legs with an unquenchable appetite for destruction" ("RG" 211).

Bersani twists this unsettling sexual negativity associated with women and gay men into what has become known as the antisocial thesis of a nonredemptive sexuality. Halley, for her part, splits from feminism by celebrating gay (and queer heterosexual) negativity in men, thereby appearing to blind herself to precisely what she seeks: a woman's queer, heterosexual desire for masculinity in men, figured by Bersani as the nineteenth-century female prostitute. Does the insatiable, promiscuous, antisocial figure of the female prostitute disappear from Halley's view because of her own insistence, via Irigaray, on women's sexuality as irrevocably redemptive? Why is the nonredemptive sexuality of Bersani's female prostitute occluded by Bersani's other queer figure: the "seductive and intolerable image of a grown man, legs high in the air, unable to refuse the suicidal ecstacy of being a woman" ("RG" 212)?

It may be that Halley misses this queer appearance of woman's love of the cock in Bersani's prostitute because, in its contemporary form, woman's desire for heterosex has been so seamlessly normalized: we find it in fairy tales, tax codes, romance novels, and hard-core porn. In contemporary life, women's desire for penetrative shattering looks very much like business as usual. As Bersani puts it, invoking Catharine MacKinnon (of all people), it's everywhere: "so-called normal sexuality is already pornographic" ("RG" 214), which is why we constantly want to tidy it up, make it bucolic, redeem it. Indeed, Bersani would probably agree with Valerie Solanas, that "Robespierre of feminism" (in Normal Mailer's words), who ranted in her 1968 SCUM manifesto: "The nicer she is, the more sexual she is. The nicest women in our 'society' are raving sex maniacs."[29]

I think Irigaray would agree with both Bersani and Solanas that nice girls are in fact pornographic. But she would also add that this sex maniacal desire for men—women's heterosexual desire for penetrative destruction—is not woman's desire at all, but rather the fantasmatic projection of woman as the Other of the Same, a desire that only functions as the complement to a masculine, phallic, macho model. This is the sexual economy of the Same as *homo* that Irigaray calls hommosexuality (with a double m), referring to the double *m* in the French word for man, *homme*.[30] This hommosexuality with a double *m*—this masculine economy of the Same that Irigaray rejects—is *not* the queer homosexuality we find in Bersani.[31] Rather, Irigaray rejects a *hommosexuality* as monosexuality that Bersani explicitly rejects as well, the sexuality Bersani calls gay men's identification with and desire for his oppressor, the straight macho man. Indeed, like Bersani, Irigaray wants to dismantle what Bersani calls a "commitment to machismo" that "is no longer permissible" ("RG" 201). And her morphology of the sexed body is not unlike Bersani's with its self-shattering rectum where, as he puts it, "the gay man demolishes his own otherwise uncontrollable identification with a murderous judgment against him" ("RG" 222).

Thus, when Bersani writes "the rectum is the grave in which the masculine ideal of proud subjectivity is buried" ("RG" 222), we can't help but see that he and Irigaray are going after the same phallogocentric, self-replicating target. To put it in philosophical terms, the force of the negative—figured by Bersani as a rectum—both exposes and shatters the false ideal of the other-destroying Western subject. It is the antifoundationalist, poststructuralist force that also powers the engine driving the antisocial thesis of queer theory, from Bersani through Edelman to Halley, in a nonredemptive, nonreproductive, anal-erotic sexuality.

If, as I'm arguing, Irigaray's antihommosexual (with a double *m*) antifoundationalism allies her with this queer self-shattering project, Halley's reading of Irigaray as a sex redeemer suddenly appears to be off target. Further, Halley's use of Irigaray to condemn cultural feminism more broadly not only inaccurately conflates the antifoundationalism of the one with the foundationalism of the other, but also obscures the later Irigaray who, ironically, might provide Halley with another, not-business-as-usual theory of women's "heterosexual desire" for men: one that Halley seeks but cannot find, even as she's staring right at Irigaray.

Anyone familiar with the later Irigaray knows that heterosex is precisely the problem she attempts to work through from within the trap of

ARE THE LIPS A GRAVE?

an economy of the Same. As Irigaray explains in a recent interview, over the course of her work she moves from a critique of the "monosubjective character of our Western tradition" to an attempt, in her middle period, "to define the necessary mediations to develop a culture in the feminine," to a third stage where she seeks "the means of making possible a co-existence between masculine and feminine subjects without subjection to one another."[32] From the 1992 publication in French of *I Love to You*, to her most recent book, *Sharing the World* (2008), Irigaray invokes the *heterosexual* not as the fake hetero-difference of an economy of the Same, but as the true hetero-difference of "the two."[33]

Irigaray's heterosex—not difference as the one, as the Other of the Same, but the different sexes of the two—is not business-as-usual hetero-sexuality. Might we call it a queer heterosexuality? Perhaps. Irigaray gives a powerful twist to what might otherwise appear to be the sex condemned by queer theorists as heteronormative. As Elizabeth Grosz, one of Iriga-ray's most consistent defenders, argues: "Irigaray's commitment to the project of speaking . . . sexual difference entails reexamining [the] reduc-tion of one sex to the terms of the other . . . [and] reasserting the necessity of *two positions* (not identities) in any relation."[34] This heterosex project, Grosz argues, requires "strategic, perhaps even therapeutic, relations [be-tween] women" as a precursor to "viable, ongoing relations between the two sexes" (344). Grosz asserts that "only when women take (up) a space and a time that are capable of mapping their unique morphologies, de-sires, and discourses can there be an encounter between, or touching of, the two sexes. Until then, we exist within a hom(m)osexuality that regards women only as objects, not partners" (346). According to Grosz, hommosexuality (with a double *m*) also persecutes those homosexuals (with one *m*), presumably like Bersani, who "subvert phallocentric sexual circuits" (346).

Although the aim of Grosz's argument and others like it has been to shield Irigaray from flat-footed charges of heterosexism, Irigaray's work on the heterosexual and the difference of the two has not been without its critics. Penelope Deutscher, in her book on the later Irigaray, admires the "conceptual instability" of Irigaray's early deconstructive writing, but ulti-mately bemoans Irigaray's later tendency to settle into a "paralyzed notion of sexual difference."[35] In *Lesbian Utopics*, Annamarie Jagose criticizes Irigaray's specularizing collapse of the distinction between homosexual (with one m) and hommosexual (with a double m) for "a new hetero-sexuality" that "walks free" (36). Shannon Winnubst similarly denounces

Irigaray's idealizing, dialectical construction of heterosexuality as the transcendent ahistorical site of difference.[36] Still others have argued that what Winnubst calls Irigaray's sexual "cannibalism of differences" (107) obliterates racial, national, religious, and economic differences.[37]

In addressing these concerns, I want to recall Grosz's comments about a different heterosex not only for a queer heterosexuality in Irigaray but also for an ethics of alterity. Importantly, Grosz links the difference of Irigaray's heterosex—what I want to call its queerness—to the place of sexual difference in her thought. In her more recent work on "life itself," Grosz goes so far as to call sexual difference "the first philosophy, the philosophy that founds all others, founds all knowledges."[38] But what, exactly, does sexual difference in Irigaray name? Although, as I noted, Deutscher bemoans the sometimes "paralyzed" state of Irigaray's "man" and "woman," she also mounts an important defense of sexual difference as a term for an impossible alterity at the heart of Irigaray's ethics. As a name for an alterity that both is and is not, sexual difference names more than the difference between "man" and "woman": it names more than heterosexuality as we know it, within the logic of the Same called hommosexuality (with a double *m*). Addressing concerns like those expressed above—that "alterity is hijacked in Irigaray's work and tethered to sexual difference"—Deutscher argues, echoing Grosz, that sexual difference is nothing less than "the rethinking of space, time, the interval, generation, culture, religion, race, love, nature, law, language, sex."[39] Deutscher calls this radical, heteronomous alterity the "far-flung elasticity" of a conceptual loop whose articulation as an "ethics of sexual difference" produces a "snap back" ("CEO" 250) to "man" and "woman" that appears to domesticate that alterity. This looping and snap back, Deutscher argues, is "peculiarly Irigarayan" ("CEO" 250): her way of naming alterity as a constitutive exclusion, as simultaneously *what is* and *what is not*.

These arguments about the queer alterity of heterosex that is sexual difference in Irigaray pose a challenge to the pervasive critiques of a heterosexism linked, by some, to her persistent idealizations. A comment from an interview with Elizabeth Grosz makes this challenge clear. Irigaray responds to a question from Grosz about same-sex relations: "Our culture is elaborated above all by one sex, but includes the two sexes as polarities of a presumed unique and neutral identity. It is thus never, at least today, a question of relations only with members of one and the same sex, unless at the imaginary level" (C 134).

To return to Deutscher's terms, the polarities of the two sexes Irigaray mentions in the interview are the "snap back" of "man" and "woman" that exists in tension with the far-flung alterity sexual difference both names and occludes. In the context of same- versus opposite-sex sexualities, it is the snap back of the polarities that gives us the illusion of a sexual difference between homosex and heterosex: extreme points at the far ends of what looks like a spectrum of differences, but is, in fact, the nondifference of "one sex." The organization of the sexual world into same- and opposite-sex relations feels real enough, but in Irigaray's view these sexual polarities exist only at the "imaginary level." There cannot be, "at least today," same- (or opposite-) sex relations because, as polarities, the concepts of same and opposite suggest a structure of difference, a mode of comparison, a field of alterity that would allow for something other than the "one." Like "the feminine," same-sex relations can only appear as what they are not, in a metaphysical language that hides them from view.[40]

This understanding of the imaginary polar "same" in same-sex relations—which is different than the "one" same of the masculine economy of the Same—not only complicates what many have viewed as simply homophobia or heterosexism, it also addresses the idealization charge that numerous critics have leveled against Irigaray. Irigaray's emphasis on the error of mistaking "the imaginary level" for a true sexual difference that both is and is not is consistent with her critiques, from *Speculum* onward, of the violence of idealizations and metaphysical reductions of various kinds. Like sexual difference, the concepts of same- or opposite-sex relations can only exist within a distorting hall of mirrors that is the specularizing economy of the Same: hommosexuality with a double *m*. The struggle for the difference of something other than hommosexuality—for something queer—*is* the struggle for what Deutscher calls the "far-flung elasticity" of sexual difference. As Irigaray puts it in *Sexes and Genealogies*: "we need above all our heterosexuality, our homosexuality."[41] We need, above all, the alterity of our sexual difference.

This line of argumentation in Irigaray suggests that she might be Halley's girl after all: someone who desires queer heterosexual relations that are not heterosexuality as we've known it. To be sure, the divergent repertoire of images used by each thinker makes their alliance seem unlikely. If Irigaray draws on the imagery of lips to describe what I'm calling a queer hetero-difference, Halley's search for a queer heterosexuality takes the form of the love of a cock she finds in Bersani's gay male rectum. Halley's obvious allies are nasty girls like Bersani: lustful, sex-positive, queer postmodernists who like to fuck. These nasty girls are her antidote to the feminist, redemptive "good sex" paradigm that she misdiagnoses in Irigaray's supposed cultural feminism. But as my Irigarayan glimpse into Bersani's rectum has shown, there's nothing "good" in sex for Irigaray either: this sex which is not one is her exposure of the same masculine ideal of proud subjectivity Bersani wants to explode with anal sex. And because Bersani builds his argument by analogizing the rectum of contemporary gay men with the promiscuous vaginas of Victorian prostitutes, we could even say without hesitation what our cultural imaginary already knows: if the rectum is a grave, so is the vagina.[42]

Lip Reading

Or is it? What is the relation between vagina and lips?

LUCE 2: Ah yes, the lips. They're still here, repeated, like a poem. But they're not just about pleasure, you know.

LUCE 1: Sounds pretty pleasurable to me. All those wonderful, funny combinations: mouth to mouth, mouth to labia, labia to mouth, labia to labia, inner labia to outer labia, outer labia to mouth, outer to outer, inner to inner, outer to inner, to mouth, to labia. . . . Doesn't that make you laugh?[43]

The lips made me laugh (and swoon) fifteen years ago when I wrote that passage. I had recently discovered labial pleasures myself and loved those lips and their funny combinations. They were so outrageous: sexy, queer, but also feminist. They both revealed something there I hadn't noticed before—sexual difference as what is—and held open an alternative space—sexual difference as what is not. In their singular plurality as "two lips kissing two lips" ("Lips" 210) they brought together, as a catachrestic relation, *what is* and *what is not*.

LUCE 1: Remember catachresis? Like the "face" of a mountain or a "head" of cabbage. That's what our lips are. Impossible. What those eggheads call "an abuse of trope." No way to say it, except as something it's not. Non-existent on his stage, except in his image, as his "face" or his 'head" ("Luce" 39).

In parroting myself here—staging myself as another self in another time—I now rediscover the catachrestic lips—metaphorical figures for which no literal terms exist—as Foucauldian heterotopias. Like an image in a mirror, the catachrestic "face" of a mountain seems real enough, and yet as a "face" it sends me spinning into an unreal, metaphorical abyss of infinitely reflected illusions, what Foucault calls "that virtual point which is over there" ("DS" 179). So too with the lips. As catachrestic heterotopias, the lips are both real and unreal, both what is and what is not. They cannot be pinned down as actual vaginas for the buttressing of cultural feminist projects: utterly unreal, they are neither here (on the mouth) nor there (between the legs). And yet, at the same time, in their movement between, they offer—both here and there—utterly real forms of erotic pleasure. "Two lips kissing two lips: openess is ours again. Our 'world'" ("Lips" 210).

If the lips did all this twisting, far-flinging, erotic work, why have they not been recognized as queer? Why did this most complex and most celebrated of Irigarayan images come to represent, in Halley's queer split from feminism, a redemptive, schoolmarmish, cultural feminist sexuality? Was it because queer theorists hadn't taken the time to really read Irigaray and, not knowing her well, failed to *know* the lips in the biblical sense?

Queer theory's failure to *know* Irigaray stems, in my view, from its failure to recognize her antifoundationalism. Casual references to Irigaray like Halley's tend to freeze the lips as a static figure that emerges most visibly and most dramatically in "When Our Lips Speak Together." But this is to reduce to a snapshot a long trajectory of lips that begins with *Speculum* and ends, most recently, in "The Return" (2010).[44] As the birth of the lips in the openly parodic, deconstructive *Speculum* makes clear, Irigaray is not an essentialist and the lips are anything but foundational. In *Speculum*, they are positioned as bookends to Irigaray's massive dismantling of Western philosophy, appearing both in the first chapter on Freud and in the last chapter on Plato. In Irigaray's sassy mockery of Freud, the lips are neither clitoris nor vagina, neither a little penis nor the concave space that will complement the penis in the morphology of sex as reproductive. In her deconstruction of Plato, they are neither transcendent phallus nor immanent womb-vagina. Not a repressed maternal origin taken as real by prisoner-children trapped in the shadows, they appear at the end of "Plato's *hystera*" as the figure of another path of knowledge-pleasure, in the sensible-transcendental space of the past conditional (*aurait pu*)—as a way *in and out* of Plato, the matrix, and Western thought as we know it.[45] That path emerges again, in "The Return," where the lips come back again as a figure for a "relation in two" that is, oddly, nondualistic (269).

Does this mimetic antifoundationalism make the lips queer, like the rectum? This question gets at the heart of the queer feminist difference I've been tracing. In the mimetic return of the lips in this section, they have begun to speak beyond the bounds I've laid out—the negative epistemology and ethics of the antisocial thesis—to engage the question of methodology. Specifically, in their return the lips speak to a quintessentially queer methodology that includes but goes beyond antisocial queer theory: the parodic, ironic, campy, disruptive repetition that has come to be known as performativity. Viewed from this angle, my opening question—are the lips a grave?—engages both the what (lips or grave) and the how of Irigaray's relation to queer theory.

Importantly, the stakes of that performativity include, as part of queer methodology, the feminist ethical question I've been tracking. If the far-flung snap back of sexual difference names the problem of the forgetting of the other, the mimetic return of sexual difference in the form of other lips from another time performs the drama of a forgotten feminist mimesis in queer theory. My earlier mimicry of my feminist self in another time exposes the forgetting of Irigarayan mimesis in the blinding glare of queer performativity. And although Irigaray is acknowledged and cited most obviously by Butler in *Gender Trouble* (1990) and *Bodies That Matter* (1993), Irigaray's subsequent absence from queer theory is evidence of a forgetting of her radical feminist practice as an always already queer method. Thus, if Irigaray tells the story of Western philosophy as a forgetting of sexual difference, Irigarayan mimesis stands in the place of sexual difference in queer theory's story about itself as performative, disruptive, and ironic.

This exposure of queer theory's forgetting of an Irigarayan feminist method is not an attempt to reclaim and restore her in a game of lost and found, nor is it a claim about a singular origin of queer performativity. Following Bersani, my approach to Irigaray (and feminism) is not redemptive. Rather, performativity's erasure of Irigarayan mimicry parallels what Irigaray shows in her Heideggerian readings of the forgetting of sexual difference: the forgetting of this feminist mimicry in queer theory is a constitutive forgetting of sexual difference—or what Deutscher calls, in Derridean terms, a constitutive exclusion—that "is itself forgotten."[46] In their mimetic return, Irigaray's lips show that Irigaray is doubly absent from queer theory: her forgetting has been forgotten. Importantly, when today I repractice that mimesis as a queer feminist performance, it is not simply to remember Irigaray by remembering myself in order to redeem her (and myself) in the fullness of the present. It is to mark the instability, the groundlessness, and the constitutive forgetting of any remembering that would claim to install a solid foundation—either epistemologically or methodologically—for thinking.

So are the lips a grave? As we have seen, the rectum as grave marks the force of the negative that drives the antisocial thesis of queer theory. Lee Edelman's "no future" notwithstanding, that negativity provides a seemingly inexhaustible depth from which antisocial queerness is extracted. The rectum may be a grave, but that hardly keeps it from speaking. The catachrestic lips, by contrast, can only speak as that which they are not. And yet, in doing so, they both mark the abyssal negativity the rectum names and, at the same time, dramatize the necessity of speaking otherwise. Simultaneously inscribing both a self-shattering undoing and a making—what Jane Gallop calls the lips as *poiesis*—the lips articulate an ethics of relation that differentiates them from the pure negativity of queer antisociality.[47] For it is in their catachrestic, heterotopian attempt to speak otherwise that the lips are simultaneously here and elsewhere, now and not now: not a pinned-down figure of the Other of the Same, but a hovering, catachrestic Other's Other. The lips name a heterotopian *ethopoiesis*, an ethical remaking of the erotic relation.

In this sense the lips both are and are not like the queer rectum. Like the rectum, the lips perform the work of the negative to expose and dismantle the violence of subjectivity as an ethical ideal. But, while Bersani's anal-erotic "practice of non-violence" ("RG" 222) shatters the ethics he attaches to a self, Irigaray's practice is *ethopoietic*: a dismantling of the self for a remaking of ethics. In this the feminist Irigaray is, once again, more Foucauldian than the queer Bersani. As I will elaborate in the final section of this chapter, Foucault's ethics is a practical art whose doing transforms the doer in the manner of what he calls, in *Hermeneutics of the Subject*, *ethopoiein*: "making ethos, producing ethos, changing, transforming ethos."[48] Like Foucault, Irigaray both engages negativity and redeploys it for the work of ethical remaking. Because, as I've argued, the

modern subject is a sexual moral subject, to simply shatter that subject—
and along with it, morality—is to ignore the first burden of a nonviolent
practice: the acknowledgment of harms, including, most importantly, the
constitutive exclusion or forgetting of the other.

Toward a Queer Feminist Ethics of Eros

Let me begin, in this final section, with a return to Foucault's
question about sexual ethics: why have we made sexuality into a moral
experience? Revisiting this question in light of the queer Irigarayan question are the lips a grave? I want to suggest that Irigaray and Foucault
offer an ethics of eros that can help us to listen more attentively to the
moral dissonance that has split feminists and queers. Such an ethics,
significantly, hinges on the idea of erotic transformation we can find in
both thinkers.

The notion of transformation begins to alter, from within, the mo-
rality-based ethics that simultaneously binds and produces us as sexual
subjects. Again, if code-based moralities are systems of normative values,
what Foucault calls "ethics-oriented moralities" (UP 30) open possibilities
for transformative desubjectivations from within. Thus, as Charles Scott
argues, to ask the question of ethics in this retraversing, post-Nietzschean
sense *must* mean to insist on "the noun"—*the question*—over and above
its "prepositional object"—*ethics*.[49] Such an insistence on the question
pries ethics open, ever so slightly, to produce what Scott calls "an interruption in an ethos" (4). To ask the question of ethics from this perspective is to ask "how questioning can occur in a manner that puts into
question the body of values that led to the questioning" (1).

Both Irigaray and Foucault work strategically, from inside the modern
episteme, to transform the conception of ethics as morality. As Irigaray
says in *Sharing the World*: "traditional morality will be of little use to us
here" (59). Foucault, even more strongly, calls morality "catastrophic."[50]
Further, that catastrophe springs, for both Irigaray and Foucault, from
the rational Western subject as morality's ground. Both Irigaray and
Foucault put into question the subject of truth: the ethical agent whose
moral judgments presume epistemic certainty about the world. From
this perspective, ethics in both Irigaray and Foucault can be explicitly
linked to the question of the rational moral subject whose undoing is not
only Bersani's self-shattering project, but that of at least two generations

of French postwar antihumanist thinkers. Just as Foucault's first major book, *History of Madness*, develops a critique of Cartesian rational morality through unreason's interrogation of the subject of truth, so too Irigaray's first major book, *Speculum*, begins with the ethical *question* of the rational moral subject.

As a question about the subject, this ethics is not unrelated to a certain thinking about alterity epitomized in the work of Emmanuel Levinas, a phenomenological thinker who is central to Irigaray's work and especially her conception of ethics.[51] For both Foucault and Irigaray, as for Levinas, subjectivity must be thought of as the interruption of the subject by an other; alterity precedes the subject and puts it into question through an always prior sociality. Further, as Tina Chanter demonstrates, Irigaray's Levinasian approach to alterity produces the powerful concept of the "sensible transcendental" as "that which confuses the opposition between immanence and transcendence."[52] As Chanter shows, Irigaray's sensible transcendental rethinks the Levinasian ethical system that subordinates what Levinas views as the less ethical alterity of eros—maternity, the du-ality of the couple, and fecundity—to the more ethical proximity of the face to face that Levinas links with universal morality. Because sexual difference consigns women to the subordinated immediacy of a world of immanence, with the sensible transcendental Irigaray seeks what Chanter calls an "intermediary middle ground" (EE 180) for ethics, the "path between heaven and earth" (Irigaray in EE 108). Chanter highlights Irigaray's description, in her reading of Levinas, of an erotic tradition that bestows divinity on the masculine lover (*l'amant*) and throws the femi-nine beloved (*l'aimée*) into the abyss: "Irigaray repeatedly appeals to the transcendence of the lover, which is dependent upon the submergence of the loved one in a world without ethics" (EE 215). With the sensible tran-scendental, Irigaray reworks this conception of eros that subordinates the beloved for the procreative transcendence of the divine lover. In doing so, as Chanter points out, Irigaray both poses a challenge to the heterosexual-ity implicit in Levinas and, at the same time, draws on eros to give "new life to lovers" (EE 220).[53]

This Irigarayan conception of alterity as a nonprocreative, sensible transcendental ethics of eros not only has much to offer queer theory but can also be closely aligned with a Foucauldian erotic ethics of the other that links the act of loving to knowing.[54] Importantly, like Irigaray and un-like Levinas, Foucault refuses a conception of alterity grounded solely in a transcendent principle of exteriority or divinity; Foucault's specifically archival philosophical practice demonstrates a conception of alterity that demands an attention to the immanent realm of the concrete historical world. Foucault practices his erotic ethics as an *ethopoietic* confrontation with the otherness of "infamous lives" trapped in the archival dust of the past.[55] In the space of the archive, Foucault practices an *ars erotica* where his position as the knowing subject—the lover (*l'amant*) or *erastes*—is transformed by the abyssal figure of the archival object—the beloved (*l'aimée*) or *eromenos*. In that encounter between knower and known, Foucault engages in an erotic, ethical listening that undoes the subject in his will to knowledge. As the site of that transformation, the archive becomes heterotopian: both there and not there, both real and not.

Although Foucault differs from Irigaray in his explicit attention to the archival relation, the erotic ethical resonances they share are difficult to ignore. Irigaray's reworking of the lover-beloved relation through the concept of the sensible transcendental is paralleled by a similar transformation in Foucault through an archival *ars erotica*. And if the figure of the beloved recalls a suicidal feminine, "legs high in the air," self-shattering gay man, both Irigaray and Foucault would implicitly reject antisocial queer theory's plunge into the abyss of a negative ethics. Foucault's explicitly genealogical approach to the other would disallow the psychic ahistoricity of such abyssal conceptions of self-undoing: in his heterotopian histories of the present, the spatio-temporal particularities of lives in relation to others matter more than the frozen negativity of an antisocial death drive. Like Grosz's description of the "strategic . . . relations [between] women" (344) that, in Irigaray, rework the space-time interval, Foucault's "tactical" genealogies bring into play an "insurrection" of "desubjugated knowledges" that alters space and time.[56] And while Irigaray is not, like Foucault, a thinker who finds her real-world material in the archives, she too refuses the paralyzing stasis of mythical beloveds trapped forever in the sexual underworld of the unconscious. As she puts it in *An Ethics of Sexual Difference* (1984), sexual difference is a question for our times.[57]

Within this frame for a historically situated, transcendent-immanent, insurrectional ethics of eros shared by Foucault and Irigaray, the possibility of a queer feminist ethics begins to come into view. In Irigaray's concept of the sensible transcendental, we find, once again, the far-flung elasticity and snap back of sexual difference, this time in terms of an erotic ethics poised in the space between a wide-looping "radical otherness" (*EE* 173) and the constricting immanence of an abyssal femininity. As the Foucauldian transformation of *erastes* and *eromenos* makes clear,

the relations of sexual difference Irigaray tends to describe as those between "man" and "woman" are also, in Foucault's hands, the asymmetrical relations between subject and object, knower and known, within a
modern episteme that defines subjectivity as both moral and sexual. In
this sense, both Irigaray and Foucault offer an ethical approach to sexuality that, unlike the antisocial theorists, takes seriously the historically specific relationality of the social world and, at the same time, acknowledges
the damage wrought by the normative codification of those relations.

Viewed through this lens, Irigaray's project appears not as a metaphysics, idealization, or essentialist ontology, as so many of her critics have
argued, but rather as a historically situated project of ethical desubjectivation within the modern episteme of "man" as a sexual moral subject.
The early critiques she and Foucault share of the rationalist morality on
which modern psyche-logos is built make them allies in the undoing
of modern subjectivity: just as Foucault narrates in *History of Madness*
a story about Freud as the apotheosis of an objectifying Cartesian gaze,
so too Irigaray in *Speculum* links Freud to Cartesian rationalism (S 27)
and denounces the "so-called scientific objectivity" (S 14) of a psychoanalytic project that puts woman "under the microscope" (S 14) in a "greedy
[quest] for scientific powers" (S 185), freezing the subject-object relation
between knower and known. Foucault's famous critique of the repressive hypothesis and the logic of the "closet" in the first volume of *History
of Sexuality* might similarly be compared with Irigaray's critique of the
specular logic in Freud, which, through a theory of repression, produces
femininity as a closetlike "black box" (S 20) to be opened and illuminated
by reason. Finally, throughout their work both Foucault and Irigaray are
driven by an antipathy to the Hegelian dialectic and its neat resolution of
ethical and political opposition through sublation. Irigaray presents the
feminine in her "function as the negative" (S 90) as "the power in reserve
for the dialectical operations to come" (S 90) and accuses the dialectic
of being "phallotropic" (S 52). Along similar lines, in the later interview
with Grosz, she emphasizes the difference between a Hegelian dialectical negativity and her own use of the negative as a way "to maintain [the]
irreducibility of the *you* with respect to the *I*" (C 127). Taken together, her
critiques of these Hegelian dialectical operations almost exactly repeat
Foucault's diagnosis of the dialectical logic that drives reason and unreason to produce the modern sexual subject endowed with an internalized,
unknowable negativity that Nietzsche calls conscience, or the soul, and
that Freud calls the unconscious.

To be sure, there are important differences between Irigaray and Foucault that remain to be explored. Not least of these is a deepening of the complex problem of subjectivity that forms the core of this book. Although, as I have argued, Irigaray's dismantling of a monosubjective economy of the Same can be fruitfully compared with Foucauldian desubjectivation, what happens for both thinkers beyond the undoing of the monosubject is open to question. While, for example, Kaja Silverman sees Irigaray as a thinker "quite willing to relinquish subjectivity" (EE 176), Chanter disagrees: "Irigaray," she argues, "is wary of the erosion of the subject" (EE 176). Nonetheless, if we take seriously Foucault's view that the modern subject is a sexual subject, it is not clear *which* subject's erosion Irigaray fears. If we agree that for both Foucault and Irigaray modern subjectivity means the sexed, asymmetrical subjection of *assujettissement*, surely Irigaray's recent call for a relationality "without subjection" (C 160) is not unlike Foucault's erotic testing of the self as a self-undoing that requires, paradoxically, both a return to the self and a self-release.[58]

As the ethical stakes of this book make clear, I believe not only that there is a place for Irigaray in queer theory but also, more broadly, that her alignment with Foucault opens up a place for an erotic queer feminist ethics. That place, no doubt, like the sensible transcendental, is paradoxical, discordant, and snagged: a nonexclusionary yet nonrelational, temporally unstable relation. It is not a utopian blueprint I offer, but a heterotopian willingness to be undone.

Coda: A Return

Having worked on Foucault for a number of years, I thought I'd left behind my earlier attachment to Irigaray. It has taken me a long time to find a way to return to writing about her. When I stopped working on Irigaray fifteen years ago, I left her trapped, in my mind, in *Speculum*: in the role of a queer Freudian patient who had never quite learned how to live in the world. I assumed that "*hysteria [was] all she [had] left*" (S 71). I kept teaching *Speculum*, in what felt like my own hysterical relation to that dazzling, breathtaking beginning and its hint of an opening through those luscious, pleasurable lips. But I also worried, each time I taught her, that the opening was already closed, from the start. That her deconstruction of Western philosophy left her with nowhere to go.

Perhaps my return to Irigaray here is still hysterical, but this time it has allowed me to pry open what had felt, for a long time, like an aporetic dead end. More than anyone, Irigaray has taught me that hysterical mimicry—language's performative force—"is not under [our] control, though sometimes it seems that way" (S 72). Time has a way of changing us, especially in relation to what we've written. That is how, in my return to Irigaray, I've experienced a self-othering, temporal force that, however disorienting, unlocks aporias. As Foucault puts it, we don't want to hear it, but "discourse is not life: its time is not your time."[59]

In writing and rewriting this chapter, I have come to value this strange, temporally syncopated, interrupted relation to Irigaray. It is this self-othering strangeness that allows me to return to her now, in writing, in the Foucauldian play of an erotic ethics. For, while I have repeatedly insisted, over the years, that the later Irigaray is less radical than the early one, and while I still must admit to an aesthetic preference for her parodic mockery of classic philosophers over her sober constructions of a shared world without subjection, when Irigaray tells me that across the three phases of her work her "position did not change"—"I know this is asserted," she says, "but it is a mistake" (C 124)—I have to hear, really hear, what she's saying. Here, in this return, the erotic ethics I've been pushing pushes back on me. It opens a space for a different Irigaray and a different thinking-feeling. In this self-altering transformation, my known object, a feminist Irigaray, not only dispossesses me of the Irigaray I thought I knew but also dispossesses me of myself. She becomes the *eromenos* whose erotic difference draws me up short: she puts me and my knowing into question. Given my difficult love for her, I can only describe this transformation of my *erastes* by her *eromenos* as self-shattering, nonredemptive, and deliciously queer.

2 There Is No Gomorrah
Narrative Ethics in Feminist and Queer Theory

Colette in Gomorrah

In her 1941 work *The Pure and the Impure,* the twentieth-century French writer Colette offers a series of oblique reflections on gender, sexuality, artistic creation, and the ethical questions that link individual expression to a social context of evaluation, judgment, history, and culture. She does this through an exploration of pleasure—the realm of the sexual and the aesthetic—in a kind of guided tour of the Parisian artistic underworld of the early twentieth century. Colette's portrayal of a French modernist version of Sodom and Gomorrah highlights the all-too-familiar tension that characterizes the queer feminist split, the opposition between rigid moral judgment, on the one hand, and, on the other, the seemingly infinite diversity of sexual expression.[1] Specifically, in a passage that reinvokes the biblical story of the cities of the plain, Colette confronts a narrative that, since the Middle Ages, has buttressed the edifice of moral purity against the purportedly impure dangers of sexual otherness. What she says is somewhat surprising: "There is no Gomorrah. . . . Intact, enormous, eternal, Sodom looks down from its heights upon its puny counterfeit."[2]

Admittedly, this passage is troubling, and in fact it has haunted me for over twenty-five years, despite the fact that I've chewed on it, written about it, and repeatedly discussed it with my colleagues and students.[3] To be sure, the mere mention of the names Sodom and Gomorrah is enough to haunt anyone, myself included, who falls outside the most rigid definition of sexual norms.[4] So when Colette reinvokes the paradigmatic biblical story about the righteous punishment of "sinners against the Lord," she reinscribes a narrative that has justified and sustained centuries of hatred, exclusion, and homophobic violence. Of course, that is not all there is to the story, especially for Colette. Obviously enough, it is not just the narrative from Genesis, but rather its *particular* form, in Colette's retelling of it, that produces the feeling of a haunting—of a text that, like a ghost, literally returns again and again. On one abstract, theoretical level, the retold story as *revenant* simply serves as a reminder of a general principle about the production of signification itself, namely the sedimentation of meaning that occurs as a result of repetition. But the ghost of Colette also points to a more important principle of language whose consequences are not at all abstract: namely, that repetition occurs, through time, *with a difference.*

In fact, there is more than one ghost here. For behind the *revenant* of Colette's text lie the spectres of a death of genocidal proportions. This genocidal death is the underside of biopower which, for Foucault, describes a modernity where "the life of the species is wagered on its own political strategies" (HS1 143). Indeed, with the perspective provided by historical hindsight, the immediate context of *The Pure and the Impure*—published in France during World War II—points both to the Holocaust and the bombings of Hiroshima and Nagasaki.[5] In that sense the biblical story of punishment by death serves to symbolize these and other historical acts of mass destruction. Here is the description from the nineteenth chapter of Genesis: "Then the Lord rained on Sodom and Gomorrah sulfur and fire from the Lord out of heaven; and he overthrew those cities, and all the Plain, and all the inhabitants of those cities, and what grew on the ground."[6]

The biblical imagery gives flesh and human form to the seemingly abstract principle of discursive effacement through repetition, metaphorically resurrecting the once living cities, their inhabitants, and all that grew within their borders. The violence of sulfur and fire from heaven allegorizes the moment, in language, of the snuffing out itself, the eradication of difference that both Irigaray and Foucault describe as the self-reflective, identitarian logic of Western thought. For Irigaray, that logic of the Same reduces difference or otherness to a repetition of sameness through the metaphorical operations of language. It is a logic whose effects can be quite literally murderous. In its most prominent manifestations, notably for Irigaray in the archetypical example of Plato's *Republic,* only a ghost of difference remains—the silent, invisible remainder of Truth. This is what Colette's reading allows us to see: "Intact, enormous, eternal, Sodom looks down from its heights upon its puny counterfeit" (PI 131–132). We are left with Truth—what Colette calls Sodom—and its symmetrical and therefore inauthentic copy, while true alterity remains inaccessible to us. There is no other: "There is no Gomorrah" (PI 131).

Colette's interpretation of the story of Sodom and Gomorrah not only highlights the problem of alterity but also allegorizes what Irigaray will theorize as mimesis by constructing Sodom's other as "counterfeit." Together, mimesis and alterity raise a crucial theoretical question: if a central principle of language is repetition, how can we distinguish between repetition *with a difference* and the murderous repetition of the *Same* theorized by Irigaray and allegorized by Colette as the mass destruction of the other? How do we know the difference?[7] The epistemological question—how do we know?—clearly has no definitive answer. Still, the crucial point is to ask the question, for to ask "what's the difference?" is to reopen the question of reading. This reopening of reading is especially important today, in an age where the literary itself is threatened by everything from budget cuts in the humanities to the ubiquity of visual technologies.

The practice of reading I have in mind revalorizes the increasingly rare method of close reading as an erotic approach to ethical questions. I follow Jane Gallop in her interest in an "ethics of close reading": an ethics that "has something to do with respecting what is alive, what is living in theory, trying to value theory's life, trying to resist all that deadens it."[8] In my reading of Colette, I engage in such a practice of close reading by interrogating the epistemological structures wherein difference and sameness emerge. Reading in this way allows me to focus on the concept of difference as an interdiscursive interpretive practice that opens an erotic space for the play of the other within the repetitive logic Derrida famously calls iterability.[9] It functions as a reminder about the ethics of reading: if language is infinitely iterable, our ability to hear the other—the *iter*—becomes a function of close reading. As Derrida puts it: the "iterable" is that which is "structurally readable" (7). This raises the explicitly ethical question: How do we read? How do we hear the one who has been effaced by the discursive violence of repetition *without* difference? In the sedimented, centuries-old text called "Sodom," how do we hear Gomorrah?

These incipient questions about repetition and reading form a point of entry into my more immediate concerns regarding feminism, queer theory, and narrative ethics. More specifically, my purpose here is to rethink the ideological and political issues raised by the feminist queer split by examining the role of ethics in narrative theory. In this sense my project differs significantly from other literary studies of the relationship between narrative and ethics,[10] as well as from the corpus of nonliterary, philosophical treatments of feminist and queer ethics.[11] To be sure, as I mentioned in the introduction, how to define ethics remains something of a problem, and queer theorists in particular have been loathe to clarify an implicit distinction between (good) ethics and (bad) morality. Especially for queer theorists, moral norms are unpleasantly loaded with the kind of conservative, puritanical, sex-phobic implications that link it to the biblical story of divine retribution against the sins of Sodom and Gomorrah.[12] For many poststructuralists, normative ethical thinking points to a heavy, deeply rationalist philosophical tradition of moral rule making whose meanings for modern day-to-day life seem irrelevant at best or, at worst, oppressive. Poststructuralists in particular have difficulty reconciling a normative project that addresses moral considerations with the radical epistemological and ontological doubt that is the hallmark of postmodernity.[13] Even those who have tried to soften ethics by critiquing and relativizing some of its most rigid, universalist underpinnings have done so by short-circuiting political questions about power.[14] As a result, many progressive intellectuals, especially those who identify as queer, believe that ethical thinking leads to inherently conservative political positions.[15]

Given the baggage that has accumulated around the term, it would seem counterproductive to offer yet another definition of ethics without taking seriously its particular contexts. Remembering the Socratic question that frames this book—how to live?—I engage the specific problem of narrative ethics in this chapter by approaching it obliquely, through the back door, entering its complexities by asking questions about the relationships between literature, gender, sexuality, and the normative claims that connect the problems of reading and knowing with the possibility of political action. Rather than offering the Archimedean "view from nowhere,"[16] which, most often, forms the backdrop for ethical thinking, I propose to talk about ethics within the context of the postmodern critique of the subject and, specifically, the conceptual frameworks offered by contemporary feminist and queer theory.

In that context, let me briefly return to the problem of intersectionality I discussed in the introduction. There I highlighted how intersectionality contributes to a critical environment where the moral imperative to exclude exclusion produces the repeated failure to live up to that ideal. I also argued that intersectionality's juridical conception of subjectivity is incompatible with an antifoundationalist Foucauldian approach to subjectivity as the effect of disciplinary power-knowledge in biopower. It is worth noting here, in the context of this chapter's focus on narrative ethics, that intersectionality epitomizes feminism's investment in narrative. Kimberlé Crenshaw's 1989 article, which put intersectionality on the map, begins by questioning "how courts frame and interpret the *stories* of Black women plaintiffs."[17] In her return to intersectionality two years later, Crenshaw objects to the either/or logic that turns "woman of color" into an identity "that resists telling."[18] Crenshaw's remedy is a narrative one: "to advance the telling of that location."[19] Subsequent work that draws on the intersectional paradigm has picked up on that narrative strand. As Alice Ludvig puts it in her analysis of intersectionality through personal narrative: "It is through narration that the axes of identity and subjectivity become explicit. When we acknowledge that subjectivity is the way people make sense of their relation to the world, it becomes the modality of identity."[20] The importance of narrative to intersectional conceptions of subjectivity cannot simply be dismissed in the name of performative shattering. Rather, the relation of narrative to the recognition of historical absence and marginalization—the nonplace of the category "woman of color," for example—must be approached as an ethical question to be retraversed.

As a point of entry into the narrative ethics I articulate in this chapter, I will begin with a phrase that Butler uses in a different context in order to theorize ethics as a "site of inscriptional space."[21] Returning to Sodom and Gomorrah, if we follow Colette across the devastated biblical plain of Genesis, we can define this site as the place where something once was: the empty inscriptional space of the other who has been x-ed out by repetition—a place called Gomorrah—with all of the sedimentation of violence marked by that name. Thinking Butler with Colette (the philosophical with the literary), the ethical question then becomes: how can the other reappear at the site of her inscriptional effacement?

The answer to that question is a function of the interdiscursive practice of close reading that I have already articulated. In my own allegorical
reading of Sodom and Gomorrah, to read for the other means to read
for her return, which I dramatize by reading Colette *revenant*.[22] As an
inhabitant of Gomorrah who, upon her return, can speak her own erasure, Colette draws attention to the other effaced in death.[23] Thus, just as
Irigaray haunts the ancient philosopher-king of Plato's *Republic*, so too
Colette is the ghost who haunts Gomorrah.[24] In this sense, ethics as a site
of inscriptional space becomes an empty place haunted by moral, genealogical questions about the processes that produced the haunting. And if
we rethink the notion of ethics as a site of inscription within the ghostly
frame of a haunting absence-as-presence that Levinas calls the question
of the other, narrative ethics can provisionally be defined as *the readable
site of an inscriptional relation to an other*.[25]

If Gomorrah marks the ethical place of the other here, some might,
quite appropriately, ask: but what about the violent effacement of Sodom?
For Sodom and Gomorrah were destroyed together. Importantly, as those
familiar with Colette's work may know, there is a mediating intertextual
reference to consider here, and in fact the passage from *The Pure and the
Impure* that I cited at the beginning of the chapter is introduced by the
phrase: "Ever since *Proust* shed light on Sodom . . . " (PI 131, emphasis
added). Indeed, Colette's immediate intertext is not the Bible, but rather
its rewriting in another queer French text, *Remembrance of Things Past*.
And, as any reader of *Remembrance* will immediately recall, the theme of
the sodomite is central to Proust's work. My interest in Colette's reading
of Proust is not the sodomite per se, but rather the gendering of the Sodom and Gomorrah pair. For, in fact, Proust renders the two destroyed cities of the biblical plain as an opposition between men and women.[26] Most
explicitly, the fourth volume of *Remembrance* begins with an epigraph
from Alfred de Vigny: "Woman will have Gomorrah and man will have
Sodom." Now even a cursory glance at Colette's intervention reveals, from
the start, the asymmetry of Proust's neat, binaristic gendering of the biblical source. And, not surprisingly, it is the women of Gomorrah—Mlle
Vinteuil, Albertine, the *jeunes filles en fleurs*, Léa, and so forth—who, for
Colette, do not exist, except as Sodom's puny counterfeit, his inauthentic,
apocryphal copy. In the shadow of what Colette calls "the dazzling light
of truth that guides us through Sodom" (PI 131), indeed, "there is no Gomorrah" (PI 131).

Out of this densely intertextual slice of literature there emerges, for me, an allegorical conflict that points to the uneasiness of a contemporary set of conceptual and political issues, all of which are caught up in the problem of repetition I mentioned earlier. In that allegory, Colette is the feminist taking Proust to task for his blindness to the asymmetries and exclusions of gender, even in a context that is arguably queer. To be sure, Colette hardly identified as feminist any more than Proust identified as queer, but I'm treating them as allegorical figures here, both to suit my conceptual purposes as well as to reflect a plethora of recent feminist and queer-oriented work on the two authors. In that context, Colette the feminist and Proust the queer function as ciphers for the ongoing theoretical project that interrogates the links between the study of gender and the study of sexuality.[27]

Let me place this allegory inside the frame of repetition with which I began, for it is in the frame that I hope to engage the fields of narrative, feminist, and queer ethics. My agenda here is driven, as it is throughout the book, by my Foucauldian fascination with desubjectivation and what self-undoing might mean. More specifically, it is driven by my desire to reengage the question of the subject in feminist and queer theory. In that context, I engage the problem of reading in this chapter to reopen the question of the readability of the modern subject as a narrative, ethical question. In the context of queer and feminist theories, the ethical question becomes a question of reading the subject in her relation to an other within the conflicting frameworks of feminist and queer: narrative coherence and performative disruption, respectively. At stake in these conflicting readings of the subject is the answer to the question how do we know, read, and hear the other? If ethics is the site of an inscriptional relation to an other within the genocidal logic of biopower, how we answer that question will determine what we find at that site of inscription: the possibility of difference or the devastated plain of the Same.

Queer Performances and Feminist Narratives

One of the hallmarks of queer theory is its rejection of traditional narratives in favor of the more liberatory performativity discussed in chapter 1. D. A. Miller, for example, argues that "queer" stories are embodied by what he calls the "discontents" of narrative, discursive threads that cannot be neatly bound by closure.[28] Similarly, in her well-known work on gender performativity, Judith Butler insists on the importance of performance over narrative, asserting that "performance may preempt narrative as the scene of gender production."[29] In another piece, Butler goes on to highlight narrative's inherent incapacity to express the excess that is sexuality itself: "sexuality," she writes, "may be said to exceed any definitive narrativization."[30] In yet another example, Michael Warner and Lauren Berlant contrast the "generational narrative" (554) or "love plots" (556) of heteronormativity with a public performative spectacle of erotic vomiting where, as they put it, "sex appears *more sublime than narration itself*, neither redemptive nor transgressive, moral nor immoral, hetero nor homo, nor sutured to any axis of social legitimation" (565, emphasis added).[31]

To be sure, many queer theorists recognize, perhaps better than anyone, the problems with binarisms, and thus would be the first to challenge a dialectical opposition in which one term is rejected in favor of a second, more "liberated" term. Indeed, to claim that queer theory categorically posits a static opposition between "old" narratives and "new" performances would be to simplify a complex discursive field fraught with ambiguities and internal contradictions. In fact, some of queer theory's paradigm-shaping work is also, arguably, the least categorical and the most complex. Butler's arguments, for example, when viewed across the entirety of her corpus, reveal a conceptual pattern in which performativity and narrative are implicitly linked.[32] Butler's later work moves, in fact, in a decidedly narrative direction.[33] In a similar vein, Eve Kosofsky Sedgwick articulates a complex model of queer performativity in connection with narrative through a series of close and subtle readings of literary texts. Along the same lines, Cindy Patton argues that identity and its disruption are interdependent and thereby describes performativity as a strategic tool to be used within the "rhetorical closures" of the narrative "grammar of identity construction."[34] Nonetheless, despite the complexity and ambiguity of these exemplars of the queer, queer theory has solidified into a legitimate discursive and academic field over the course of the last two decades and has therefore become more fixed (as all legitimated discourses do) in its claims to self-definition. Thus a metanarrative has developed in which the fluid, destabilizing queer performance stakes out its difference from that which came before by setting up a stable, fixed feminist narrative as its nonqueer identitarian other.

As I argued in chapter 1, in that metanarrative about feminists and queers, ethical problems have emerged as a highly contested terrain over which theorists of sexuality and gender struggle. Again, in some versions of the story, this struggle solidifies into a battle between warring camps where sexuality, queerness, performativity, and aesthetic play line up on one side of the divide against, on the other side, gender, feminism, narrative, and moral norms. Both feminist and queer theorists have contributed to the contentious and oppositional nature of this struggle, where ethics becomes the prize to be won in a broader battle over the meanings and values of postmodernism. And while particular players often become the targets of particular critiques, in my view these players are mere markers of a deeper ontological and epistemological crisis that lies at the heart of a conception of postmodernism as a narrative problem.[35]

Butler has commented on this phenomenon of a queer feminist opposition in an attempt to dislodge it, noting "how quickly a critical encounter becomes misconstrued as a war" ("Against Proper Objects" 1). No one has taken more hits in this war than Butler herself, precisely because her work, along with Rubin's and Sedgwick's, dramatically brought the two sides into contact with each other. It is worth noting that Butler has repeatedly resisted the queer feminist opposition, situating her work "in the interstices of the relation between queer theory and feminism" ("Against Proper Objects" 1). Nonetheless, Butler's concept of "gender trouble" has been claimed as a model by feminist and queer theorists alike. Despite her own careful interstitial self-positioning, Butler's critique of rigid gender norms—the heteronormative model of girl versus boy—has often been transformed and institutionalized into a new binarism: the paradigmatic feminist versus queer opposition. In the new paradigm the queer performative presents itself as correcting and surpassing a heteronormative feminist narrative about gender; at the same time, feminist narrative becomes the unsexy guardian of a moral order threatened by the libidinal excesses of the queer.

My purpose here is not to rehash the important arguments made by a range of theorists who find themselves uncomfortably straddling this queer feminist divide. It is useful to remember that both sides have legitimate complaints: feminism often masks its own heterosexist underpinnings; at the same time, the queer position often masks an equally entrenched misogyny.[36] My approach builds on the insights of these interstitial theorists by asking about what is at stake in the queer feminist debate. And while I agree that it is crucial to continue to name the inevitable blindspots of both feminist and queer theory, I want to relay my

questions about ethics through the epistemological and ontological questions at the heart of the debate and, so doing, attempt to break through
the rigid lines across which the queer feminist opposition is constructed.
This return to the philosophical questions of being and knowing opens
up, once again, the question of the subject.

I say "once again" because, clearly, the question of the subject constitutes the humanist ground upon which the entire project of the antihumanist critique of the Enlightenment has been built. To return to
the specific antifoundationalist scenario I've been describing, feminist
narratives bump up against queer performatives, producing a collision
from which a variety of points of contention emerge: the problem of identity, the nature of desire, the role of sexuality in relation to gender, the
importance of language, the concept of community, and the connection
between representation and politics. But behind this plethora of complex
issues hovers that ghostly other—the ethical subject—who both marks
and occludes the epistemological and ontological unraveling that characterizes antifoundationalist thinking. To be more specific, when Butler
famously critiques the heteronormative pairing of boy with girl, she is not
merely demonstrating the inextricable relation between gender norms
and compulsory heterosexuality. Rather, her critique of gender is also
a critique of the coherent subject whose emergence depends on "story
lines . . . which effect a narrative closure on gender experience" ("Gender
Trouble, Feminist Theory," 329). In this view, gender norms and compulsory heterosexuality are symptomatic of a more fundamental humanistic
illusion: namely, that a stable subject exists, sui generis, prior to its narrative construction.[37] In fact, the revelation of this illusion of a prenarrative
subject explains the common conflation of coherent subjectivity, ethical
norms, and traditional narrative forms.

Queer performativity, on the other hand, openly acknowledges both
its own constructed status and, in a Foucauldian vein, subjectivity as a
function of productive disciplinary power-knowledge. In its specifically
linguistic performative conception, the emergence of the speaking subject coincides with the moment of utterance of the speech act itself. Thus,
while both narratives and performatives produce subjects, narrative depends on a retroactive legitimation of the subject position through the
temporality of narrative grammar, while performativity admits that the
subject it speaks in the present moment of the utterance is the only subject there is. The performative subject, therefore, is always under erasure;

correspondingly, queer performativity appears to occupy the privileged site of antifoundationalist disruption, moving beyond the categories of gender altogether to subvert identity.[38]

To be sure, the opposition I've just described is completely untenable, as are all oppositions subjected to analytic scrutiny. Most famously, in his oft-cited proclamation that postmodernism disallows any recourse to the "grand narratives" of the past, Lyotard also suggests that even postmodern forms of knowledge (which he groups together under the term *paralogisms*) are shored up through the continual "return of narrative" in the discourses that legitimate that knowledge. From a more specifically narratological perspective, a number of theorists have convincingly demonstrated that narrative is more accurately conceptualized *not* as performativity's oppositional other, but rather as a speech act with a particular kind of performative force.[39] Even more to the point, recent work in narrative ethics argues that narrative's "performative dynamic" lies in its dialogic structure, where a subject addresses an other; in this view narrative performs a structure of intersubjectivity through the relations between characters in a story, between narrator and narratee, or between author and reader.[40] As a performative structure that stages a dialogue between a subject and an other, this relational narrative performance puts the autonomous status of the sovereign humanist subject into question without shattering subjectivity altogether. Thus narrative performance opens possibilities for rethinking the antifoundationalist claims of postmodernism together with the ethical dimensions of intersubjectivity.[41]

The early articulations of performativity in queer theory, on the other hand, tended to divorce the performative subject from its discursive others. This move explains, at least in part, a tendency in some queer theory to abjure narrative; as Lyotard explains, narrative transmits the pragmatic rules that constitute social bonds. Thus the loss of narrative that for Lyotard characterizes the postmodern age corresponds with the destabilization of the subject as a being constituted through those narratively established social bonds. This also explains why, rather than articulating an intersubjective relation, queer performativity often describes itself as explicitly *self-referential* and *asocial*. As Eve Kosofsky Sedgwick puts it:

> Part of [queer's] experimental force as a speech act is the way in which it dramatizes locutionary position itself. Anyone's use of "queer" about themselves means differently from their use of it about someone else. . . . "Queer" seems to hinge much more radi-

cally and explicitly [than "gay" and "lesbian"] on a person's under-
taking particular, performative acts of experimental self-perception
and filiation. A hypothesis worth making explicit: that there are
important senses in which "queer" can signify only *when attached
to the first person*. One possible corollary: that what it takes—all it
takes—to make the description "queer" a true one is the impulsion
to use it in the first person.[42]

In this description, Sedgwick links performativity and queerness to an
experimental first-person utterance. Two important points emerge from
this passage. First, Sedgwick introduces queerness as an experiment: as
an explicitly self-referential structure of address, where the most important other is the one who resides *within* the speaking subject. In this
early iteration of the queer, a self-referential, specular structure locates
alterity within the subject; it is *this* other within the self that constitutes
the key ingredient of the subject's queer *difference*. Butler picks up on this
in *Bodies That Matter*: "speaking is always in some ways the speaking of
a stranger *through and as oneself*" (242, emphasis added); along similar
lines, in *Homos* Leo Bersani describes gay desire as a "desire for the same
from the perspective of a self already identified as different from itself."[43]

Second, the Sedgwick passage implicitly brackets intersubjectivity as a
framework for this experimental queer performativity. This is not to suggest that intersubjectivity is not important in Sedgwick's work, especially
in her later writings on Buddhism, affect theory, and Melanie Klein. These
remarks apply specifically to her earliest articulations of queer performative experimentation, remarks that have been taken up and generalized
beyond the experimental by a subsequent generation of queer theorists.
But this early queer performative bracketing of the intersubjective relation resonates with the radical rupture of sociality and community that
characterizes not only the antisocial thesis but also less radical queer de-
ployments of negativity. Thus Berlant and Warner describe their project
of "queer world-making" as "by definition *unrealizable* as community or
identity" ("Sex in Public" 558). Along the same lines, Bersani suggests in
Homos that "we should be questioning the value of community and . . .
the notion of relationality itself" (52), embracing instead "a potentially
revolutionary inaptitude—perhaps inherent in gay desire—for sociality
as it is known" (76).[44] Even José Muñoz, whose most recent book argues
against the antisocial thesis in favor of a queer utopianism, argues in his
first book, *Disidentifications* (1999), for a queer politics whose performing

subjects demonstrate "a desire to escape the claustrophobic confines of 'community.'"[45] As these examples demonstrate, the two premises of self-referentiality and asociality articulated in Sedgwick's early queer experiment lead subsequent queer theorists to posit a performative speaking subject and, in the same gesture, to disavow any sustained investment in intersubjectivity and community. Thus the queer performative subject emerges as fractured, unstable, and permanently dislodged not only from its humanist foundations in the "grand narratives" of History, Truth, and Man but also, and more significantly, from any sense of the interdependency and connectedness with others that lie at the root of the social realm.

Let me briefly retrace the lines of my argument in this section. Behind the untenable opposition between feminist narratives and queer performatives lies the question of the status of the subject. To claim, as I have, that the opposition is untenable, is therefore to claim that there is more to the question of the subject than either feminist or queer theorists have admitted. If feminists seem overinvested in coherent narrative female subjects, many queer theorists appear disingenuous in their embrace of the queer subject's radical instability. Further, to insist, as I have, that we think narrative *with* performativity, is also to intervene in a philosophical debate about the epistemological and ontological stakes of ethical subjectivity.

The shift toward a primarily performative conception of the subject that is a hallmark of early queer theory and a continuing trait of antisocial queer theory marks a philosophical move away from the other as constitutive of the queer subject. This atomistic notion of the subject dislodged from sociality corresponds to the loss of narrative that for Lyotard emblematizes the condition of the postmodern subject. Put somewhat differently, in embracing performativity as both self-referential and radically antisocial, this strand of queer theory has denied a crucial aspect of subjectivity, namely, the subject's ethical enmeshment in its relations with others, particularly insofar as others embody "an 'unlimited' responsibility that exceeds and precedes" the subject's freedom.[46] This relational concept of subjectivity is precisely what narrative as performance both dramatizes and enacts, while queer performativity alone occludes the problem of otherness, and therefore ethics, understood as *the readable site of an inscriptional relation to an other.*

However, this queer occlusion of the other is a ruse that allows the antisocial queer to define itself as radically open to multiple forms of deviance and, at the same time, to ignore the self-reflective, self-reproducing logic on which queer theory is founded. The flip side of queer theory's definitional capaciousness (we're all queer) is the unacknowledged condition of possibility of queerness: the exclusion of some others in their delineation as the nonqueer. As the last section of this chapter will demonstrate, queer theory often masks its own investment in subjectivity and, in so doing, performs its own operations of othering and erasing through that disavowal. In that process, queer theory's performative first person— the radically unstable queer "I" or "we"—simultaneously assumes and denies its own claim to discursive authority. This unmarked assumption of the right to speak is founded precisely in a particular kind of narrative coherence that, like the subject, remains unacknowledged in some queer theory. The coherence I have in mind here is a self-legitimizing narrative of authority that confers recognition on some speaking subjects and, at the same time, excludes others from those implicit contracts of recognition. Queer theory's claim of radical inclusivity—what Bersani calls "bringing out, celebrating, 'the homo' in all of us" (10)—makes sameness a precondition of recognition, thereby revealing radical queer inclusivity as a falsely universalizing claim. For that claim of universality brings us right back to where we've been: the question of the subject and the problem of ethics. Put another way, behind queer theory's seemingly infinite possibilities of unconstrained local performances lurks the age-old trap of universalism: its subsumption of difference into the sameness of a seamless "we."

A Queer Universalism: The Rights of Man

When Bersani states, in the prologue to *Homos*, "I have become an ambiguous 'we'" (7), what is at stake, in ethical terms, in the universalizing gesture through which that "we" comes into being? More specifically, what happens when an "I" speaks as a "we" and, simultaneously, disavows the subject position that allows the speaking to occur? In asking these questions about the subject who, through repetition, transforms the singular "I" into the plural, unspecified "we," I want to return to the problem of linguistic repetition with which I began the chapter. At first glance it would seem that the performative, poststructuralist "I" stands in the place of repetition *with a difference*, since queer performativity explicitly rejects the repetition of sameness at the heart of identity politics.

In rejecting any notion of fixed identity, queer theory would appear to be rejecting the logic of analogy through which meaning coheres as a repetition of the *same*. However, I want to argue that this appearance of repetition *with a difference* in antisocial queer theory is often deceptive and that the repetitions of the "I" as the "we" of this queer theory foreclose the possibilities of difference precisely because queerness often remains impervious to the interventions of the other who would hear the queer, put her into question, and ask: how do we know the difference between the sameness of the "we" and the difference of the other?

To put the argument somewhat polemically: there is a consistently universalist logic at work in the deployment of the seemingly anti-universalist category of "queer." Further, that logic works through analogy to construct categories of inclusion and exclusion that look a lot like the asymmetrical relationships of power between Sodom and Gomorrah foregrounded by Colette. But what does this mean, precisely, within the context of this critique of queer universalism? To begin, although Sodom and Gomorrah are explicitly gendered in Proust, my critique of the queer here is not simply about a misogynist exclusion of women in some queer theory (to which a number of feminist theorists have pointed). Rather, when Colette writes "there is no Gomorrah," she is pointing to something more subtle and more pernicious than its specific symptom as "Gomorrah" or the invisibility and ontological impossibility of lesbian existence.[47] That something more subtle and more pernicious is best described not as a noun but as a complex verb, as a combined action of othering and erasing, an epistemological and ontological operation through which alterity is eradicated. In the case of the instantiation of the queer, this act of othering and erasing occurs through the queer subject's disavowal of its own investment in subjectivity. Within this context, then, Colette's phrase—"there is no Gomorrah"—marks the limits of the epistemological framework and political strategy of queer theory, whose unspecified, self-referential, and asocial "we" x-es out the particularity of the other in her difference.

Indeed, the forms of alterity produced by history's acts of othering and erasure are staggering in their particularity: the specific and different cruelties of racialization under American slavery, in twentieth-century Rwanda, or in medieval Iberia; the details around which class solidifies in a nineteenth-century European textile mill, a twentieth-century electronics plant in an export processing zone, or the toilets and offices of a North American university; the referential specificity of sexuality for the medieval "sodomite," the New England "witch," or the modern-day "faggot" left hanging on a fence in Wyoming. I mention these random examples in order to make a point about particularity. When Sedgwick introduces the queer as self-referential, she does so as a particular "I" performing an experiment. However, when this experiment is universalized as queer theory, the particularity it names is rendered invisible in the face of a general claim about the queer. This is less an argument against Sedgwick, who is explicitly experimenting here, than it is with how she has been taken up in explicitly antisocial strands of queer theory.

In its denial of its own investment in subjectivity as the place from which to speak and be heard, antisocial queer theory fails to acknowledge its own narrative enmeshment in the historical and institutional particularities of power that allow some to speak at the expense of others. The logic of this exclusionary move replicates the logic of analogy that Irigaray finds in Plato's *Republic* and that Colette finds in Proust's rendering of the cities of the plain. In each case what is left behind is what Irigaray calls the "Other's Other," a voiceless and invisible alterity which, by definition, is both produced and obliterated by the "shining light" of a self-recognizing, self-legitimating standard, the pillar-like truth of Sodom—intact, enormous, eternal.

All of this, I know, is counterintuitive for many of those who have immersed themselves in queer theory these last two decades. Again, Warner and Berlant's formulations are exemplary here, this time in their guest column written for the *PMLA*, "What Does Queer Theory Say About X?"[48] If universalism is a belief that there exist meaningful general statements about the world that are universally and permanently true, Berlant and Warner's "anti-encyclopedia entry" (344) would seem to constitute just its opposite. Here is their antidefinition of queer theory: "Queer theory is not the theory *of* anything in particular, and has no precise bibliographic shape" (344). They go on to say that "the danger of the label *queer theory* is that it makes its queer and nonqueer audiences forget . . . differences [of context] and imagine a context (theory) in which *queer* has a stable referential content and pragmatic force" (344).

On one level, Warner and Berlant are pointing to the dangers of *any* theory about anything, where there is a loss of specificity, contingency, and particularity through the generalizing move involved in the production of what we call theory. But what endangers *queer* theory is not, as Berlant and Warner suggest, the possibility of its reduction to a "stable referential content" (344), but, rather, quite the contrary. For what queer theory claims, specifically, as constitutive of queer theory itself, is the instability and undecidability of the term *queer,* to the point where being "queer" and being "undecidable" have become virtually synonymous. Indeed, I would suggest that this is a *specifically queer theoretical* claim that, for the most part, is *not* borne out in the lives of people who, whether they identify as queer or not, are continually interpellated as subjects.

Let me make a link here to the question of the subject raised in the previous section of this chapter. Queer theory's embrace of undecidability is consistent with poststructuralism's embrace of performativity and the concomitant undoing of narrative. In other words, the undecidability problem of queer theory is linked to a problem it shares with a performative conception of language as utterance, where the problem of iterability intersects with the problem of reference. As J. L. Austin already taught us long before deconstruction, truth itself—language's ability to refer in a stable, eternal, and permanent way—is radically put into question in the recognition that all utterances are performative. When I make a constative statement—a statement of truth about the world—I'm hiding the conditions of enunciation that allow me to make that statement. Thus, behind the constative statement "all men have XY chromosomes" lies the performative force of something like "I assert that, I contend that, I promise that all men have XY chromosomes." The same could be said for universal ethical claims like "all men are created equal." Thus any referential utterance that language makes about the world—an empirical referent outside itself like "all men"—is also an utterance language is making about itself. The performative behind the universal claim (I contend that "all men were created equal") is the self-referential, self-legitimating authority of the truth-wielding speaking subject.

How might we express this question of performativity more precisely as a problem of reference? In her analysis of the paradoxes of French feminism and the Rights of Man, Joan Scott makes a point about universalism in the context of the French Revolution that is instructive for our understanding of reference in relation to contemporary queer theory. "If citizenship," Scott asks, "was an attribute of abstract individuals, could it also represent people in their concrete existences?"[49] We could ask a similar question about citizenship in the "queer nation."[50] Does the term *queer,* when generalized and abstracted, represent people in their concrete existences? Scott suggests that these questions about political representation are also questions about representation itself, "the nature of the relationship between sign and referent" (20). Again, Scott asks: "To what real entities, after all, could the patently abstract notions of 'nation' or 'people' or 'rights-bearing individual' or 'citizen' . . . actually refer?" (20–21). To what real entities might the abstract notion of "queer" refer?

Although the universal subject of Scott's analysis is the decidedly non-queer, stable, Enlightenment subject, the unstable subject of the modern queer "we" is produced through the same logic of repetition and abstraction of the "I" into "we" as Scott's eighteenth-century universal man. Let me be more specific. When Warner and Berlant affirm that "what brings 'us' together is sexual culture" ("Sex in Public" 563), who is the queer but nonetheless universal "we" to which they refer? Does their invocation of the "we" differentiate their queer "we" from the repetition as sameness of the universal Enlightenment "we"? If this "we" is, like Naomi Schor's contemporary French feminist version, a "postparticularistic, differentiated universal," how do we know?[51] To be sure, as Schor's work on feminist universalism demonstrates, this question of the "we," the masked but ever present authority behind every utterance, is hardly new, especially to feminist theorists. But I want to argue that queer theory, more than any other oppositional theoretical discourse, lays claim to a "we" that is more radically unstable, pluralizable, and therefore more universalizable than even the most universalizing French feminist "we," because the promise of a potentially infinite pluralization of that "we" is constitutive of the meaning of queer itself. But because queerness privileges performativity, the universalizing position of the queer "we" is masked by the seeming instability of the performative subject. That instability occludes the structure of discursive power, which, like the structure that articulated the universal Rights of Man, upholds the term *queer* through the universalizing narratives of legitimation that allow the queer subject to speak.

The result of this unacknowledged universalization of the queer speaking position is the denial of specificity to the queer "we." In that queer refusal of specificity, the subject of queer theory perpetuates an analogical structure—reinforced by performativity's self-referential specularity—where repetition leads to the infinite production of sameness. Further, this specular sameness underscores antisocial queer disavowals of community, shutting out the possibilities of reading and otherness. Because "queer theory is not the theory of anything *in particular*,"[52] it ends up referring to everything and nothing, thereby repeating its own invisible but hegemonic subject position ad infinitum. In rhetorical terms, this undecidable, infinitely pluralizable "we" can only speak about itself in the atemporal and asocial structure of a performative utterance that *refuses to be read by an other*.

What are the political implications of queer theory's asocial, self-referential structure? For some time now there has been a recognition of the conflicts—between Sodom and Gomorrah, queer theory and feminism—that are symptoms of this rhetorical and philosophical truth about the hidden, self-authorizing conditions of enunciation of universalist discourses. Again, this is less about a conflict between nouns—men versus women, queers versus feminists, sexuality versus gender—than it is about processes of othering and erasure. Cathy Cohen's oft-cited argument about heteronormativity clearly demonstrates this point. Cohen argues that "queer theory" consistently defines itself in opposition to the category of heteronormativity, but fails to examine the ways in which processes of exclusion consign certain *heterosexuals* to a place outside the heteronormative center. Cohen points specifically to the historical prohibition against marriage between African Americans during slavery, the pathologizing of the black family in the 1965 Moynihan report, and the late twentieth-century demonization of poor women as "welfare queens" as examples of heteronormativity at work against those whom it would be presumptuous if not downright imperialist to call "queer."[53]

I'm not suggesting that queer theory claims to refer specifically to poor single women on welfare when it invokes the category of the "queer." But that is precisely my point: according to the logic of queer theory, if "welfare queens" aren't "queer," that means they must be "nonqueer." This reveals the internal contradiction of queer theory's logic, because if queer theory, in all its multiplicity, is *not* referring to heterosexual single women with children who are on welfare when it invokes the "we" of "all queers," this is *not* because "welfare queens" aren't marginalized by heteronormativity. Rather, it is because "welfare queens" generally lack the structural discursive authority through which queer theory disseminates itself *as* theory. And these reasons are not unlike those that historically excluded all women and nonwhite men from the "we" of the Enlightenment subject.

Does this mean that queer theory is obligated to speak for all those who are marginalized, no matter what those categories of marginalization might be? Not necessarily, although attention to the operations of othering and erasure can at least open up the problem of otherness in a more complex way than the unspoken postulation of the other fixed forever as the heteronormative nonqueer. More important, I want to suggest that any theory—including queer theory—has an obligation to examine the conditions of possibility of its own speaking position *as theory*, where theory is defined as a set of truth claims that, by virtue of their utterance as theory, move away from particularity toward generality. In fact, this examination of one's own speaking position is *an ethical obligation of theory*, because this is what allows theory to remain open to the possibility of hearing and reading the particularity of the other. Thus, in demonstrating that queer theory is more invested in subjectivity than it would like to admit, I am challenging queer theory to rethink the question of ethics in the context of the communities that constitute its own conditions of possibility.

Toward an Ethics of Narrative Performance

Where do we go from here? How do we open up the ethical, narrative, and performative space of alterity that is repetition *with a difference*? To begin, we need to think about the performative force of narrative in the context of a sociality that has been anathema to so many antifoundationalist thinkers, especially to antisocial queer theorists. This rethinking of narrative performance as socially embedded may help us to bridge the gap between those whose praxis is determined by a view of subjectivity and the world as an unstable linguistic construction and those whose praxis revolves around "real life" situations with stable subjects—"real" women and "real"men—who think this notion of linguistic construction masks a refusal to deal with the empirical world. It may also help us to deal with the ever present problem of reference by linking it up with the notion of narrative as action in ways that would bring queer theory into conversation with Arendtian feminist political theory.[54] And finally, it will help us to think through iterability in the Derridean sense, as a "logic that ties repetition to alterity."[55] If structuralism and poststructuralism tell us that we only have access to the world through a grid of language, as a linguistic construction, this notion of narrative performance tells us: that may be true, but that's not the only point, because we're interested in more than epistemological questions. We're also interested in the ethical questions that determine and constrain our politics. In other words, our goal is not simply cognition or gaining understanding but also, and importantly, acting in the world. This narrative dimension of performativity offers a more promising philosophical view of interaction than is offered by queer performativity alone, because the structure of narrative breaks open the self-referential, asocial structure of the universalizing performative utterance. In other words, narrative performance opens the speaking subject to the otherness of reading; in that process it offers a way of thinking about a relational world where signs *do* refer, although contingently, through their use among a community of users. As Austin famously put it: "*Our word is our bond.*"[56] And those words refer not transcendentally, or in the infinite specularity of self-repetition, but because they occur in a context of evaluation and judgment by others. In this sense narrative performance reminds us that meaning is more than a matter of a self-enclosed system of linguistic convention, but also one of history and culture.

To be sure, this call for an attention to history and culture is nothing new; however, the particularities of sexual histories and cultures are often *not* considered in the abstract formulations of antisocial queer theory. An attention to specificity will allow the alterity of histories and cultures to emerge—not as reproductions of ourselves, nor as the nonqueer Others of our Same. Medievalists like Carolyn Dinshaw and Karma Lochrie, among others, have critiqued postmodern theory's use of an often reductive historiographic narrative to assert the "queer difference" of the present moment. Similarly, anthropologists like Kath Weston have pointed to a reductive homogenization of cultural specificities into static familiar categories like the "third sex" that correspond to features of our own society. Narrative performance would replace the question "is it queer?" with a more interesting question: "what's the difference?" What allows the "differences" of history and the continually shifting contexts of our present to emerge without becoming a reflection of ourselves or the symmetrical other of our sameness?

Some of the answers to these questions will emerge in the chapters that follow. These answers draw on and extend the growing corpus of queer work on difference, especially as a specifically constructive project that, as Elspeth Probyn puts it, takes seriously the desire for belonging.[57] One way to connect difference with alternative forms of belonging is to rethink the concept of narrative performance in conjunction with the familiar notion of intertextuality, developing that link in order to theorize a socially embedded model of reading. This model can provide an understanding of close reading as a process of alternating identification and disidentification between subject and other, narrator and narratee, text and world. Such a process puts the knowing subject into question and, in so doing, allows the alterity of the other in its difference to emerge.[58] If, as Muñoz puts it, "the promises made by disidentification's performances are deep,"[59] we need to articulate more fully the intersubjective relations through which those promises can be realized. Further, if "our charge . . . is to continue disidentifying with this world until we achieve new ones,"[60] we might be helped in our task by asking more insistently about how to inhabit—right now—those present moments of disidentification. Such an insistence on the present not only takes seriously Lee Edelman's antisocial critique of reproductive futurism but also heeds Sedgwick's complaints about a tendency in critical theory to invoke a "beyond" that we never quite reach, but proclaim incessantly.[61]

One way to approach this difficult habitation of a present we also resist is to put theoretical pressure on our understanding of *reading* within the frame of a narrative performance that constantly negotiates between identification and disidentification. This focus on reading insists on the narrative dimension of subjectivity and belonging. Further, this insistance on narrative and close reading can put queer theory in dialogue with some of the ethical claims about the importance of reciprocity, mutuality, and difference articulated in contemporary feminist theory. In particular, this model of reading displays the features of *asymmetrical reciprocity* theorized by Iris Marion Young. Taking traditional moral theory to task for its assumption that moral respect assumes "taking the place of the other," Young asserts that this ideal of identification as a necessary ingredient for ethical relation in fact upholds "a conceptual projection of sameness among people and perspectives, at the expense of their differences."[62] Young's theory of asymmetrical reciprocity, on the other hand, suggests that "we acknowledge the difference, interval, that others drag behind them shadows and histories, scars and traces, that do not become present in our communication" (53). Those shadows and histories, scars and traces, mark the places of asymmetry in our relation to the other, the place both of damage and the possibility of transformation that we can never fully grasp, articulate, or understand. As a theory of reading, however, this is not just another version of the linguistic sublime—the "beyond" of some versions of French antifoundationalism. Rather, the acknowledgment of the gap between the subject and the other becomes an honoring of that alterity in its specific, genealogical, ethicopolitical dimensions.

Thus the principle of the performative force of intertextual repetition becomes not just a static mosaic of texts written in stone, but the intertextual repetition of our lives as actors and interpreters of the world. Our readings of texts, people, ourselves, and others engage in what Ross

Chambers calls the "'presencing' of otherness"; however, that "presenc-ing" is never static or temporally fixed. Rather, as an intersubjective model that, paradoxically, undoes the subject, intertextual narrative per-formance enlarges the transformative potential of interpretation, where speaking subject, reader, and discursive traces themselves remain linked but porous, interdependent, and open to change. As an interactive model enmeshed in the realm of the social, this ethics of narrative performance can rightly be called an ethics of bounded alterity. It suggests that we are, in fact, literally "bound" by the threads of the narrative performances that constitute our pasts and our shifting presents. And yet, both our pasts and our presents are open to transformation. Intertextuality speaks to that binding ethical openness. Thus, in this reading of queerness, Sedgwick's experimental first-person "queer" cannot continue to float free; rather, it becomes "bound" (like it or not) by others. In that sense the ethics of narrative performance can never be anchored in a discourse of freedom alone, for its grounding assumption is that we are never completely free from the other who binds us. In that binding, we drag behind us those who are present and those who have been lost to us, even as we work to transform the unfreedom that constitutes those relations. Therein lies the ethics of narrative performance: the possibility of reading the site of an inscriptional relation to an other *as* other, *as* Gomorrah, as the "shadows and histories, scars and traces" of the place that is her difference.

3   Foucault's Fist

Fisting for Beginners

Much has been made of Foucault's promise, in the penultimate sentence of *The History of Sexuality*, volume 1, that "one day, perhaps," we will find ourselves "in a different economy of bodies and pleasures."[1] Queer theorists in particular have hailed Foucault as a prophet of corporeal and subjective freedom, the harbinger of a postsexual utopian future brought into being through strategic acts involving "strange parts of [our] bodies."[2] As Annamarie Jagose points out, the "bodies and pleasures" passage in *History of Sexuality*, volume 1 has been received by scholars as an "oracular invocation . . . at once momentous and momentary, not only of great consequence but also fleeting, a temporal placeholder, the rhetorical structure of invocation gesturing towards without securing a future possibility."[3] And although the new economy of bodies and pleasures is only glimpsed, queer theory has tended to celebrate sadomasochism, leather, or BDSM[4]—and fisting[5] in particular—as the kind of practice Foucault had in mind when he spoke of strange body parts and different pleasures.[6] Fisting has held special appeal for queer theory because of its empirical status in the history of sexuality as a truly "new" practice. As David Halperin writes in *Saint Foucault*, "fist-fucking . . . *is*, historically

speaking, a new pleasure" (92), invented, he claims, in the twentieth century.[7] Along similar lines, Michael Warner writes that "a public sex culture
changes the nature of sex" and offers Foucault's remarks on gay male
fist fucking to support his claim.[8] More than any other particular practice, fisting seems to promise a future of bodily pleasure freed from the
normalizing constrictions of sexuality and desire.[9] According to Halperin
and other queer theorists, fisting is among those acts that contribute to
the creation of "a gay praxis" (SF 93) or even, as Foucault puts it, a "way
of life [that] can yield a culture and an ethics."[10]

What are the implications of the queer claim that strategic acts like
fisting contribute to a gay praxis and a new way of life? To be sure, sexual
practices change historically, and gay praxis is no exception. To a certain extent, queer claims about fisting communities from the 1980s and
'90s are no longer relevant to contemporary BDSM communal practices.
As Margot Weiss points out, the "new guard" BDSM community in San
Francisco is "very different from both the men's 'old guard' leather scene
known as Folsom and the representation of SM in the public imaginary."[11]
Importantly, queer theorists have supported their utopian claims about
bodies and pleasures by referring primarily to Foucault's comments in
interviews about his participation in San Francisco BDSM in the 1970s
and early '80s. But those communities no longer exist. What was once a
queer utopian longing looks more and more like nostalgia.

Nonetheless, I want to ask about fisting as a figure for the lens it brings
to the queer feminist split and the ethics of sex this book explores. If fisting did offer the promise of a culture and an ethics, what is the status of
that promise for theory? I argue that fisting points to the paradoxical position of queer theory itself in relation to the repressive hypothesis Foucault
critiques and the very idea of the invention of new pleasures. I want to
argue, more incisively, that fisting is a figure that registers the paradox of
sexual repression and expression at the heart of the queer.

To begin, fisting participates in queer theory as a linguistic act with
particular performative force. In its self-invention as theory through the
discursive shock effect of words like *fist fucking,* queer discourse created
avenues of expression that hadn't existed before, especially in an academic context. At the same time, this shock effect of early queer theory
(Bersani's *rectum* is a classic example) created the unspoken assumption
that those who will be shocked by all this anal imagery are the hetero-,
genito-normative: the nonqueer. Indeed, to be shocked is to be nonqueer.
This unspoken assumption of queer discourse unwittingly perpetuates

the linguistic production of perversions through an incitement to talk dirty in theory. This queer incitement to speak is precisely the target of Foucault's critique in *History of Sexuality*, volume 1 as one of the central mechanisms of the normalizing apparatus of sexuality. As Foucault memorably puts it: "It may well be that we talk about sex more than anything else; we set our minds to the task; we convince ourselves that we have never said enough on the subject, that through inertia or submissiveness, we conceal from ourselves the blinding evidence, and that what is essential always eludes us, so that we must always start out once again in search of it. It is possible that where sex is concerned, the most long-winded, the most impatient of societies is our own" (HS1 33). Seen in this way, the queer evocation of fisting and other "perverse" pleasures participates in an intellectual project that runs the danger of becoming the very thing it sets out to dismantle.

This paradoxical condition of sexual discourse reveals a foundational contradiction within queer theory that has, with very few exceptions (most notably Sedgwick), remained unacknowledged. Significantly, this contradiction's most immediate source can be found in queer theory's Foucauldian foundations. As Sedgwick puts it: Foucault's "analysis of the pseudodichotomy between repression and liberation has led, in many cases, to its conceptual reimposition in the even more abstractly reified form of the hegemonic and the subversive."[12] Specifically, like the other strategic utterances of queer theory,[13] the evocation of fisting is invested in a structure that Foucault describes in *Sexuality One* as a "fable" (HS1 35) of repression that *scientia sexualis* articulates as the "repressive hypothesis." Through the revelatory surprise of its own utterances, queer theory risks buying into the scientific fable of repression so thoroughly interrogated by Foucault in that work, as it discursively both reinforces an apparatus that links sex to power and, at the same time, rebels against it, reproducing repression's utopian promise: "tomorrow sex will be good again" (HS1 7). Indeed, Foucault's description of the gratification derived from imagining ourselves through a Marcusian theory of sexual repression and liberation could easily be applied to some of the bad boys and girls of queer theory: "We are conscious of defying established power, our tone of voice shows that we know we are being subversive, and we ardently conjure away the present and appeal to the future, whose day will be hastened by the contribution we believe we are making. Something that smacks of revolt, of promised freedom, of the coming age of a different law, slips easily into this discourse on sexual oppression" (HS1 6–7).[14]

Further, following the logic of the repressive hypothesis, queer theory not only aligns sex with power but also runs the risk of reproducing disciplinary sexuality within a system of power-knowledge. In this sense one could justifiably argue that queer utterances, far from disrupting the regime of sexuality, in fact reinforce it; indeed, the queer speaking of previously unspoken acts perpetuates the repressive myth of sex as a secret to be confessed. Thus fisting becomes yet another example of sex as confession in a system of power-knowledge. Indeed, how *do* nonfisters—queer or not—*know* about the "new pleasure" of fisting? The answer, of course, is clear: we *know* fisting because of the confessional acts of fisters themselves—confessions that emerge from the darkest of the body's shadowed places.[15] These acts of confession transposed as theory inevitably consign fisting—like the missionary position, voyeurism, blow jobs, or barebacking—to the disciplinary apparatus Foucault describes as "sexuality, and the power that sustains its organization" (HS1 159). Talking dirty might feel transgressive, but, if we believe Foucault, once we speak those inventive acts they become "sexuality" as "power-knowledge-pleasure" and thereby reinforce its disciplinary grip.

Ironically, then, as sexuality is shored up in its production *as* queer theory—as an apparatus bound up with a system of power-knowledge-pleasure—queer theory comes close to contradicting its own explicit investment in the undoing of sexuality. This is queer theory's constitutive contradiction. The moment queer theory talks about strategic pleasures and strange body parts, those parts and pleasures become assimilated into a web of power-knowledge that traps us all, queer and nonqueer alike. Foucault himself knew this, long before queer theory's emergence in the early 1990s. Nowhere is the paradoxical position I've described more clear than in the final sentence of *History of Sexuality*, volume 1. Referring back to sexuality's current "economy" as "the endless task of forcing its secret," Foucault concludes the volume: "The irony of this deployment is in having us believe that our 'liberation' is in the balance" (HS1 159). Talking about the titillating things we do in the dark—"confessions from a shadow" (HS1 159) as Foucault puts it—can feel edgy, especially in an academic space bent on erasing pleasure, but that rebellious feeling hardly undoes the ironic knot of sexuality's disciplinary power.[16]

To be fair, queer theory is vast, and different theorists have worked hard to distinguish between different forms of sexuality as they appear across a spectrum of time and place. In this sense they have complicated any simple notion of sexuality as the confession of sex acts. Nonetheless, much queer-inspired work inevitably becomes theorized within a teleological framework that hopes to replace the familiar, normalizing economy of sexuality, desire, and liberation with a "different economy" of bodies, pleasures, and resistance that, in the present moment, can only be glimpsed. As José Muñoz puts it in his defense of queer utopianism: "Queerness is ideality."[17] Some queer theorists, attentive to the ruses of the repressive hypothesis, have seized explicitly on Foucault's call, at the end of *History of Sexuality*, volume 1, that we replace sex-desire with a new economy of bodies and pleasures. Rather than "liberating" ourselves from the repressive prison of conventional sexuality and desire, the argument goes, we should follow Foucault's lead and pursue instead "a body- and pleasure-centered strategy of resistance to the apparatus of sexuality."[18] As Ladelle McWhorter puts it in her genealogy of bodies and pleasures: "If we are going to engage in queer practices and enjoy queer pleasures yet also be free of heterosexist oppression, we cannot start with our desire; we have to start elsewhere. If elsewhere is going to be bodies and pleasures, the first order of business is to be very sure that we are not thinking bodies in ways that subordinate them once again to the domination of sex-desire."[19]

However, even here, in McWhorter's sophisticated genealogy of a normalizing versus resistant economy of bodies, Foucault's paradox returns with a vengeance: the minute we speak of "a body- and pleasure-centered strategy of resistance" we become, in that speaking, part of the mechanism we're trying to resist. The only way out of this familiar conundrum is to go on inventing new pleasures with strange parts of the body, never speaking of them at all. And whether or not such silent maneuvers actually produce sustainable forms of ethical belonging is open to question.[20] Gayle Rubin's ethnographic histories of the demise of urban queer cultures in the contemporary age are especially sobering in this regard. As John Waters puts it in the 2000s: fisting and chaps have become "mortifyingly out of fashion."[21]

From a feminist perspective, yet another paradox inhabits queer theory's founding investment in Foucault's thought, and that is the paradox of identity. Given queer theory's positioning as the nonidentitarian response to feminism and identity politics more generally, the role of gender has been especially vexed, as numerous feminist critiques of Foucault and queer theory attest. Indeed, queer theory's foil—the blushing "imperial prude," Queen Victoria, that opens *History of Sexuality*, volume 1—is clearly a feminine figure, the emblem not only of sexuality as repression but also of a long-standing tension between moralistic feminists and libidinous gay men. And, although this tension has been extensively

analyzed by a number of scholars, the question of how the conflicts between feminists and queers are connected to Foucault's call for a new
culture and a new ethics invites sustained consideration.[22] Can women,
like men, forge a queer praxis and a new way of life? Which body parts
are required to get the job done? Can women do it too?

This evocation of body parts brings me back to the apparently gender-
neutral body part with which I started: the fist. I focus on the fist in this
chapter in order to unravel this paradox of identity and speaking at the
heart of queer antifoundationalism. My approach to reading the fist is
explicitly narrative, as is my approach to the object of knowledge we call
Foucault. Further, my conception of narrative *as performance* is antifoundationalist, as elaborated in the previous chapter. I insist on narrative
performance here in order to focus on the fist's temporality. Just as "Foucault" is a story in time that can be traced along a temporal continuum
from early to late to the "final" Foucault, so too the fist is an object with
a temporal dimension. As such, like Foucault, the fist can be read as a
performative narrative movement. And, queer or not, we all know that
the fist is also a hand, its shape determined by its temporal unfolding:
folding, unfolding, and folding again. The fist as hand is like a narrative
performance: never fully open or closed. A narrative performance has a
shape we call the arc of the story—beginning, middle, end—and yet a
story is never fully read. Like a fist, a narrative performance contracts to
become the container that gives it a specific form as fable, epic, epistolary
novel. But the process of reading allows the fist to expand: becoming a
hand, it opens to the new, becomes something other than itself, then
closes again for another reading.

What's in a Fist?

In *The Queen of America Goes to Washington City*, Lauren Berlant
suggests that "live sex acts" offer possibilities for a counterideology to
the "dead citizenship" of a heteronormative culture.[23] As a well-known
queer theorist who articulates the relationship between sexual alterity
and the cultural processes of normalization that link sexuality to national
identity, Berlant emblematizes a specifically queer American reception of
Foucault's work. Fortuitously, Berlant uses the image of the fist to punc-
tuate her reflections on the "live sex acts" claimed by queer theorists as
models of transgressive political practice, the new forms of life evoked by

Foucault. As Berlant sees it, the live acts of sex radicals constitute strate-gies to "countercorporealize at every moment" and, in so doing, "de-elect the state and other social formations that have patriarchalized and paren-talized national culture" (QA 80). Unmasking the fantasy of the private realm to which all "good" straight "national" sex is consigned, Berlant compares this process of demystification to the removal of a Band-Aid from an unhealed wound. If the wound is national heteronormativity, tearing away the fantasy of privacy itself "in order to open the wound to air" (QA 81) is a necessary step toward what remains to be "taken, seen, and critiqued, *though not rated* with an X, a PG, or a thumbs-up—unless the thumb is related to something else, *like a fist*" (QA 81).

I ponder this fist, and wonder about its meaning. Although I am not concerned with Berlant's focus on national culture here, her evocation of public sex is paradigmatically queer. So what's with the fist? Is this a per-formative feminist redeployment of the weapon of patriarchal violence so often wielded in the same space of the private demystified by Berlant? Is it a more general collectively rebellious fist raised in anger and protest in an act of resistance to the powers that be? Or is this perhaps the erotic fist that symbolizes the diverse sexual practices of what Foucault calls "a non-disciplinary eroticism: an eroticism of the body in its volatile and diffuse potentialities, its chance encounters and uncalculated pleasures?" Whose fist is it, and what is it doing?

Indeed, whose fist is it, and what *is* it doing? For the moment, at least, I'll allow this fist to be a cipher, a queer proxy, perhaps, for that old femi-nist whipping boy, the phallus.

In that vein, it seems pertinent to recall that Foucault's work on sexu-ality has been both celebrated and derided by his Anglo-American read-ers and that this divergence of opinion has been especially pronounced in feminist and queer interpretations. Indeed, this disagreement about Foucault's value has been surprisingly longstanding. In 1982, for exam-ple, Biddy Martin wrote of the "danger" posed to feminists by Foucault's thought, "that Foucault's challenges to traditional categories . . . could," problematically for feminists, "make the question of women's oppres-sion obsolete."[24] Writing fifteen years later in the volume *Feminism Meets Queer Theory*, Martin makes a similar argument about Foucault's danger to feminism: "*queer* uses of Foucault," she writes, "are responsible, in part, for an overly sociological and negative view of gender, identity, even interiority as traps and prisons."[25] In a footnote she identifies Judith But-ler as one of the culprits. Leo Bersani, for his part, is critical of Catharine

MacKinnon and others who, unlike Foucault, see new "technologies of the self" like sadomasochism as mere repetitions and reinforcements of the relations of dominance and subordination that characterize sexual relations between men and women.[26]

Bersani, Butler, MacKinnon, and Martin function as signposts here for the divergent feminist and queer interpretations of Foucault that have proliferated since Foucault's death in 1984. My interest is *not* to detail all the permutations of these debates, nor is it to take sides in that divergence. Rather, I want to suggest that the queer-feminist divergence articulates a split between "two" Foucaults that are often seen as being incommensurable with each other. The first is the Foucault of disciplinary power who appears most obviously in *Discipline and Punish*. The second, more capacious Foucault emerges out of the last pages of *History of Sexuality*, volume 1 into volumes 2 and 3 and Foucault's ethical work on self-transformation as a practice of freedom. Precisely because the feminist-queer divergence emerges at the point, right at the end of volume 1, where Foucault seems to suggest a way out of sexual subjectivity as we know it, a quick sketch of that divergence is useful for thinking about gender in relation to the question of a gay praxis and new way of life.

The first Foucault is, obviously enough, the Foucault of what Martin calls "traps and prisons" (110), the genealogist of the regulatory, disciplinary regimes through which sexuality is constructed in the nineteenth century. This first Foucault constructs sexuality as the product of "techniques, 'sciences' . . . that permit the fabrication of the disciplinary individual" within a normalizing regime of power and knowledge.[27] The well-known result is "that great subjugation " (HS1 21) wherein the subject can be sexual only as the product of subjection and subjugation and where acts of the body become "the object not only of collective intolerance but of a judicial action, a medical intervention, a careful clinical examination, and an entire theoretical elaboration" (HS1 31). Sexuality, in this view, remains firmly enclosed in the panoptical grip of discursive relations of power, the iron fist not of a central law, but of the more diffuse and effective regimes that, in Foucault's description, are able to incorporate and contain even the fist raised in protest against it.

This is the Foucault who has often been critiqued by an early generation of feminist readers. More specifically, because sexuality in *Sexuality One* is conceived as part of a larger regime of what Foucault calls a "carceral archipelago" (DP 298), feminists have focused on Foucault's views on sexual violence as a neutralization of sexuality itself. For example, in response to questions initially posed by the French Commission for the Reform of the Penal Code about rape law in 1977, Foucault made comments that soon became a lightning rod for feminist critique. In response to the question "What should be said about rape?" Foucault argued: "One can always maintain a theoretical discourse that consists in saying: in any event, sexuality can never be the object of punishment. And when rape is punished, it should be exclusively physical violence that is punished. And you can also say that it is aggression, and nothing more: there is no difference between punching someone in the face and putting a penis in someone's vagina. . . . But first: I'm not sure that women would agree."[28]

Not surprisingly, many women in fact did not agree, although some, notably MacKinnon, have described sexual violence in exactly the same terms.[29] For most feminists, however, the female specificity of body parts involved in sexual violence did (and does) matter. Monique Plaza's critique of Foucault on the issue of rape is typical of the early feminist response to Foucault, where he is taken to task for his refusal to acknowledge the asymmetrical disciplining and victimization of women's bodies in a regime that punishes some bodies more violently than others. Just as Angela Davis has criticized Foucault's *Discipline and Punish* for its blindness to the role played by race in the development of the prison system, so too feminists have taken Foucault to task for his blindness to gender.[30]

It is important to note here, for the sake of accuracy, that Foucault's views on rape are complex. In a later interview he revised his earlier statement: "there are sexual acts like rape which should not be permitted whether they involve a man and a woman or two men. I don't think we should have as our objective some sort of absolute freedom or total liberty of sexual action."[31] I draw attention to the interview with David Cooper in order to focus on a moment of genealogical rupture in the queer feminist story, emerging here as a Foucault-feminist split around the issue of rape. In this lightning rod interview about sexuality and the penal system, Foucault invokes an image of ostensibly sexual violence, the penis, but only after desexualizing it and the violence it inflicts through a relationship of analogy: "there is no difference between punching someone in the face and putting a penis in someone's vagina." Fist or penis, face or vagina: no difference.

The feminist critique of this desexualizing move argues that Foucault effaces the differential relations of power through which sexuality is constructed for men and for women. As Plaza puts it: "Rape is an oppressive act exercised by a (social) man against a (social) woman. . . . It is sexual in the sense that it . . . opposes men and women: it is social sexing which underlies rape."[32] The rape example serves, then, to illustrate a more general feminist critique of Foucault's concept of power. In Kate Soper's words: "Foucault presents power as an essentially neutral rather than gendered force, and nowhere shows much interest in relating his account of the power/knowledge axis to the feminist critique of phallocracy."[33] Foucault's collapsing of fist in face and penis in genitalia is, on this view, symptomatic of his refusal to acknowledge the differential meanings of body parts in hierarchical social contexts.

Early queer theorists, by contrast, wanted to move away from that moment to focus on the escape hatch out of sexual normativity Foucault seemed to hold open at the end of *History of Sexuality*, volume 1. Once out of that volume, some queer theorists followed the escape hatch into a second Foucault, one who emerges in *The Use of Pleasure*, *The Care of the Self*, and a handful of interviews as a self-transforming practitioner of pleasure. This other Foucault, and this other fist, is the one that promises new practices of pleasure, previously unimagined corporeal experiences that create new modes of belonging and new forms of being. Foucault describes these new practices of the self as "the elaboration and stylization of an activity in the exercise of its power and the practice of its liberty" that constitutes "the ethical work that one performs on oneself."[34] This, then, is Foucault's other fist, an instrument of pleasure for forging a new ethics of the self as well as new modes of relation between men. As Foucault puts it in "The Gay Science":

> These uses of the body could be defined as desexualized, as devirilized, like fist fucking or other extraordinary fabrications of pleasures, which Americans reach with the help of certain drugs or instruments. . . . The relations between these men in everyday life, who are sometimes equally involved in the practices of a communal sexual life, are tender and affectionate. . . . They use the signs of masculinity but not at all to return to something that would be of the order of phallocratism or machismo, but rather to invent themselves, to allow themselves to make their masculine body a place for the production of extraordinarily polymorphous pleasures, detached from the valorizations of sex and particularly the male sex.
>
> (396–397)

I want to focus for a moment on Foucault's invocation of fisting as a privileged means of inventing these new forms of relation, because the fortuitous parallel between the queer fist of sexual pleasure and the phallic fist critiqued by feminists provides insights not only into the divergent interpretations of Foucault I've been mapping here but also into the broader philosophical and political issues that are at stake in that divergence.

David Halperin's well known "gay hagiography," *Saint Foucault*, serves as an exemplum of the queer celebration of Foucault and is, in true queer style, unabashedly excessive: "I do worship him," Halperin writes. "As far as I'm concerned, the guy was a fucking saint" (SF 6). It seems, in fact, that not only was Foucault a "fucking saint," but he was even more precisely a "fist-fucking" saint. Central to Halperin's celebration of fisting and S/M practices more generally as creative and transformative queer sex is the concept of the "desexualization" of pleasure, which, as Halperin explains, might be more precisely translated as "degenitalization," the proliferation of sites of pleasure through the eroticization of nongenital parts of the body. Halperin goes on to explain that, for Foucault, fisting may be one modern version of the "arts of the self" described in *The Use of Pleasure* as the Greek practice of ascesis.[35] This new, modern "art" of fisting might then be viewed as a "physical practice" where "intensity and duration of feeling, not climax, are the key values . . . [in the practice of] a kind of anal yoga" (SF 91), as Halperin puts it. In other words, if the normalizing fist of disciplinary sexuality threatens to hold us all in the grip of discursive regimes of power that construct even what we think of as our innermost desires, the fist of fisting promises to "undo" that normalizing construction of desire through the shattering of nongenital bodily pleasure, what Foucault calls "the decentralization, the regionalization of all pleasures" (SF 91).

Given this context for understanding the fist of pleasure, Foucault's remarks on fisting quoted earlier are worth repeating: "These uses of the body could be defined as desexualized, as devirilized, like fist fucking or other extraordinary fabrications of pleasures." Significantly, Foucault's comments on fisting occur in the context of a neutralization of masculinity itself and the fabrication of new selves beyond gender. "They use the signs of masculinity," Foucault asserts, "but not at all to return to something that would be of the order of phallocratism or machismo, but rather to invent themselves, to allow themselves to make their masculine body a place for the production of extraordinarily polymorphous pleasures, detached from the valorizations of sex and particularly the male sex."

Halperin, for his part, makes much of the idea that, in this devirilizing gesture, Foucault was making a case for fisting and BDSM generally as the basis for a possible alliance between gay men and lesbians (perhaps even feminists?), because these practices dephallicize the male body and inscribe that body within what he calls "communitarian practices of life and sexuality" (SF 99). Recalling Foucault's description of the gay leather scene as "masculine theatrical display" (SF 89), Halperin argues that gay fisting makes possible "the creation of a masculine sexual identity that need no longer be centered in the penis" (SF 90). As a result, masculinity is "reconstituted in a devirilized form: that is, it can be constituted not phallocentrically but symbolically, or *performatively*" (SF 90, original emphasis). This, it seems, is the quintessential celebratory queer reading of Foucault.

Given the trajectory I've briefly traced through the figure of the fist, what are we to make of this divergence between the very different readings of pissed-off feminists and queers who claim to be pulverized by pleasure? It's not just that feminists and queers are constructing different Foucaults. Rather, the divergence points to radically different political and philosophical orientations. Foucault's interest, especially in the later volumes, is to find a way to undo *assujettissement* as disciplinary subjugation, and the way to do that is to transform subjectivity as we know it, to rethink and transform subjectivity as a technology or practice and thereby to "get free of oneself" (UP 8). Following Foucault, queer theorists have described modern bodily practices like fisting as practices that accomplish this getting free of oneself through the disaggregating experience in which subjectivity dissolves into the "sensorial continuum of the body" (SF 95).

Feminists, for the most part, have not taken up this aspect of Foucault's thought, although there has been increasing feminist interest in Foucault's technologies of the self as applied to contemporary practices.[36] Rather, they have criticized the Foucauldian effect through which disciplinary regimes and *assujettissement* are flattened and despecified and where the particularity of violence against women, for example, becomes illegible. They have critiqued Foucault not only for his earlier political refusal to argue for rape laws that recognize the asymmetries of gendered domination and violence but also for his understanding of power itself, which, as Lynn Hunt argues, "is surprisingly genderless."[37] So if, for Foucault, sexual freedom ultimately occurs through the transformative experiences in which familiar identities are reconfigured, feminists claim, as does Hunt, that "such self-transformation is inconceivable without a notion of self-possession, of a self that owns itself and its own body" (85).

This unacknowledged assumption of individual self-possession in Foucault's thought carries over into some of the uses made of Foucault in queer theory. As I've argued, queer theorists have been especially drawn to Foucault's rejection of sex-desire in favor of polymorphous pleasures at the end of *History of Sexuality*, volume 1. There Foucault writes that "the rallying point for the counterattack against the deployment of sexuality ought not to be sex-desire, but bodies and pleasures" (HS1 157). In later interviews, Foucault develops this link between bodies and pleasures to include a rethinking of relationality: "Another thing to distrust is the tendency to relate the question of homosexuality to the problem of 'Who am I?' and 'What is the secret of my desire?' Perhaps it would be better to ask oneself, 'What relations, through homosexuality, can be established, invented, multiplied, and modulated?'"[38]

Some queer theorists, most notably Halperin, have reworked these ideas from Foucault to construct nothing less than a political program for attaining a future of sexual freedom. At the same time, this program often takes the shape of an ineffable promise. Berlant and Warner's queer world-making project is exemplary here: "world making, as much in the mode of dirty talk as of print-mediated representation, is dispersed through incommensurate registers, by definition *unrealizable* as community or identity."[39] Ultimately unrealizable as either an individual or collective entity, the "queer" may in this way free itself from the disciplinary grip of heteronormative power, but only by bracketing its enmeshment in the social world.

Nonetheless, in queer theory's world-making reading of Foucault, the fist that represents the grip of power can be transformed into the fist that operates a political and sensorial transformation of both the body and the body politic. As Bersani puts it in *Homos*, this transformation involves not "a struggle against prohibition, but rather a kind of counterproductivity. It is . . . a question of . . . consciously, deliberately playing on the surfaces of our bodies with forms and intensities of pleasure not covered, so to speak, by the disciplinary classifications that have until now taught us what sex is" (81). Berlant and Warner, for their part, argue for the "counterintimacies" (562) of a "queer counterpublic" (560). For queer theorists generally, this counterdisciplinary potential of queer practices of pleasure not only "opens up the possibility for the cultivation of a more impersonal self, a self that can function as the substance of ongoing ethical elaboration" (SF 97), but also reveals the political efficacy of queer culture. As Halperin puts it: "The transformative potential of the queer sexual practices that gay men have invented" creates "a queer praxis that ultimately dispenses with 'sexuality' and destabilizes the very constitution of identity itself" (SF 96–97).

As someone who consciously occupies both the feminist and queer positions in this story, I can't help but stumble over Halperin's slippage here, the subtle slide where those degenitalized, radically genderless "queer sexual practices" suddenly become practices "that gay *men* have invented." If the undoing of identity is also the undoing of gender, as Foucault and Halperin have claimed, then what is the construct "gay men" doing here? Strangely, the feminist and queer positions on identity and subjectivity have suddenly been reversed. If Lynn Hunt bemoans Foucault's "surprisingly genderless" view of history,[40] here the queer ruse of that genderlessness is unmasked in the slippage where "queer" means "gay men." This is not just a matter of semantics, but, rather, demonstrates what I identified in the previous chapter as a masculinist universalism at work in the deployment of the seemingly inclusive category of "queer." In Halperin's queer disavowal of his own investment in masculine subjectivity, the act of erasure through which the genderless "queer" becomes gendered as "gay men" is rendered invisible.[41] In turn, it puts into question the extent to which queer political practices like fisting really do, as Halperin claims, undo gender and "disrupt normative sexual identities" (SF 97).

Dénouement/Unknotting

Given the multiple meanings that *fisting* takes on in the trajectory I've traced over the course of this chapter's reading of the figure of the fist, let me close by repeating my opening question. Does fisting create a new culture and a new ethics? In answering that question, the knot of contention between queers and feminists turns out to be an investment in "self-naughting,"[42] on the one hand, and, on the other, an insistence on a persistent and pervasive "social sexing."[43] Given this contention, one might want to draw on Foucault himself, who insists in *The Care of the Self* on the importance of sociality: "work of oneself on oneself . . . constitutes, not an exercise in solitude, but a true social practice."[44] However, often in Foucault as well as in some queer theory, the realm of the social is limited to men.[45] The specificity of Foucault's ancient experiment, like Sedgwick's experimental queer "I" discussed in the previous chapter, is subsequently generalized and abstracted, thereby repeating the asymmetrical logic of gender first articulated by Simone de Beauvoir, where "man" occupies both the positive and the neutral and "woman" disappears as the Other.[46] Queer theory's claims for new forms of sociality does not relieve it, or any of us, of a certain burden: the ethical burden to examine the conditions of possibility of the discursive structures through which our own inscription in a social practice can even be thought at all. This self-critical "ethical work" constitutes an obligation of thought, because this is what allows thought to remain open to diffuse "otherness," that sense of newness, invention, and difference so dear to Foucault.

In the case of queer theory, one of those conditions of possibility is masculine self-possession and the authority to speak. Most feminist critics of Foucault and his followers continue to argue that this basic point remains lost on many queer theorists. Queer theorists, for their part, continue to complain, as Janet Halley does, about the sex phobia and moralism of feminist thought. And so the debate goes on. As for me, I want to interrupt the shouting match by clearing the way for a different conversation between queers and feminists. That conversation would acknowledge the legitimacy of both positions, without degenerating into what James Faubion identifies as the age-old "dilemmas of decisionism and determinism."[47] Such a conversation would open a new theoretical space for thinking about gender and sexuality; it would embrace, together, both the feminist insistence on social sexing and the queer challenge to normative sexuality as immutable truth. Most important, the expanded thinking that would inevitably result from such an expanded conversation would foster more robust thinking about gender and sexuality in relation to the ethical field.

My desire to expand the limits of our current speaking and thinking about these issues brings me back, once again, to Foucault's philosophical effort in *The Use of Pleasure* and *The Care of the Self* to rethink the self as a technology or practice and thereby to "get free of oneself" (UP 8).[48] In a shift of focus from his earlier work on disciplinary norms, Foucault suggests that these technologies might be conceived as practices of freedom. Indeed, for Foucault these technologies contribute to an "aesthetics of existence" (UP 12) that produces a subject neither fully constrained nor completely free. For Foucault this aesthetic conception of the subject constitutes an ethics of freedom: "the freedom of the subject and its relationship to others . . . constitutes the very stuff [*matière*] of ethics."[49]

I want to linger for a moment on the suggestive connection between the "stuff of ethics" and a conception of the self neither fully constrained nor completely free. It seems, however elliptically, that here Foucault offers a way to rethink the classic dilemma identified by Faubion between determinism and freedom, the very same impasse that has lined up feminists on one side and queers on the other. If for Halperin and other queer theorists new forms of pleasure such as fisting serve—like the ancient arts of existence—the "etho-poetic" function of enabling individuals "to shape themselves as ethical subjects" (UP 13), that etho-poetic practice is constrained by rules that govern the way subjects relate to others.[50] Just as ancient ascesis represented, for Foucault, an ethical model linked to the erotic through the regulation of pleasure, so too this concept of regulation can govern the positions we take and the way we hear (or refuse to hear) each other.

What would a regulated ethical relation between the female feminist critic and her queer male counterpart look like? Or the relation of that same critic to other queer women or to her own queer ways of being? Where, indeed, do these questions leave her? In all these relations—to others and to herself—she is neither constrained nor completely free—curiously enough, a bit like BDSM relationship as Foucault describes it: "what interests the practitioners of BDSM is that the relationship is at the same time regulated and open."[51] If "women" have long perceived ourselves as the victims of our male (albeit sometimes queer) masters, those regulated practices teach us that the positions are fungible, reversible—part of a structure of relations that "resembles a chess game" (151) in which, surprisingly, "the master can lose" (152).

In a sudden move, the Hegelian game between master and slave shifts dramatically to reveal the aesthetic logic of the game itself. As in fisting, so in writing; indeed, as Bersani suggests, Foucault himself was "seeking a new, desexualized austerity in the very act of writing."[52] And so, in a move aligned with an ethics of the subject in relation to others that is neither fully constrained nor completely free, let me invoke one more bodily displacement through the act of writing, one that draws the hand, opening and closing, toward other horizons of transformation. Thank you, Pat Califia,[53] for giving us "Handmade":

Give it up

Arch
Your back,
Beat the mattress with your arms
Like wings,
Grab handfuls of
The sheet

And spread
Till you feel the pull
In the sockets of
Your thighs—

Spread for me

Let it feel good—
The last finger,
The thumb tucked in,
My hand sliding in
The length of another knuckle

Until the idea that
This time it might really happen
Closes your cunt up
Tighter than a valve in the aorta
Sealing itself against
The heart's great thrust of blood

I don't mind
We can wait here,
You and I,
Until you decide
How much of me you want.[54]

This is another scene, another fist, another gendered configuration of body parts. But if, as Amber Hollibaugh puts it, "fisting is a pleasure . . . not defined by gender,"[55] our efforts to think otherwise must nonetheless remain attentive to the distances we all travel from gendered subjectivity to its polymorphous shattering and back again to what feminists insist we acknowledge as the reality of "social sexing." After all is said and done, I still don't know if fisting is a form of cultural invention or not, any more than I know if aesthetic transformation, including writing, is really enough to move us toward an ethics of freedom. It all depends on who is doing it, in what context, and with whom. Such practices of cultural invention are never given a priori; they are only created in historically specific ways. As part of an ethical field, those practices of cultural invention constitute something different than political utopias that hover in the realm of the ineffable. As Margot Weiss points out, the changes in BDSM culture in San Francisco over the past four decades can only be understood "in concert with the neoliberal turn of the 1970s, when the first two BSDS organizations in the United States were founded."[56] Neither utopian nor dystopian, sexual practices are embedded in social relations rather than a radical break from them.[57] And yet they also open up the strategic possibility for careful traversals of particular cultural spaces that are both thoroughly social (and therefore constrained) and radically new (and therefore free). Only in that complex process of invention can the disaggregation of the body into the dispersed pleasures of its parts acquire cultural meaning—not as the reinscription of homophobic or misogynist violence but as the "ethical work" of freedom: "to free thought from what it silently thinks, and so enable it to think differently" (UP 9).

Thinking differently, Foucault remarked not long before he died that "sex is boring," at least as an object of thought.[58] Ultimately, it seems, his three-volume history of sexuality is less about sex than it is about the subject in its relation with others. And if we agree that, in the end, sex is not what really matters, we might also agree that what does matter is the desubjectivating *matière*—the stuff—of an ethics that erotically undoes us.

4 Queer Victory, Feminist Defeat?
Sodomy and Rape in Lawrence v. Texas

Prologue: Two Stories

2003

In Houston, Texas, officers of the Harris County Police Department were dispatched to a private residence in response to a reported weapons disturbance. They entered an apartment where one of the petitioners, John Geddes Lawrence, resided. The right of the police to enter does not seem to have been questioned. The officers observed Lawrence and another man, Tyrone Garner, engaging in a sexual act. The two petitioners were arrested, held in custody overnight, and charged and convicted before a Justice of the Peace.[1]

1998

Anthony San Juan Powell was charged in an indictment with rape and aggravated sodomy in connection with sexual conduct involving him and his wife's 17-year-old niece in Powell's apartment. The niece testified that [Powell] had sexual intercourse with her and engaged in an act of cunnilingus without her consent and against her will. Powell testified and admitted he performed the acts with the consent of the complainant. In light of Powell's testimony, the trial court included in its jury charge instructions on the law of sodomy. The jury acquitted Powell of the rape and aggravated sodomy charges and found him guilty of sodomy, thereby establishing that the State did not prove beyond a reasonable doubt that the act was committed "with force and against the will" of the niece.[2]

Narrative, Retelling, and the *Differend*

Upon a first reading, there is little to connect these fragments of a legal mosaic, two very different stories about what Foucault described as that "fictitious unity" called "sex."[3] In the first fragment, "sex" is queer; in the second, it is heterosexual. In the first, "sex" is consensual; in the second, seemingly not. However, within the discourse of the law these two different stories are deeply connected as fragments of sodomy: sodomy stories that, through their telling and retelling in legal decisions, produce "sex" as something to be regulated by the law. As singular descriptions of events, the stories are incommensurable. And yet, through their reiterative appearance within the law, they end up telling the same story.

The first story, narrated by Supreme Court Justice Anthony Kennedy, is for many a familiar one; indeed, it has attained the status of legend as the narrative upon which the Supreme Court's landmark 2003 decision, *Lawrence v. Texas*, is built. The second story, narrated by Chief Justice Robert Benham of the Supreme Court of Georgia, is less familiar. Those in the know—mostly lawyers, judges, and some law professors—will recognize it as the back story for *Powell v. State*, the 1998 appellate decision that overturned the infamous Georgia sodomy statute that the U.S. Supreme Court had upheld in *Bowers v. Hardwick* twelve years earlier.[4] Along with many other queer legal cases, the story of *Powell* has become a citation used in amici briefs for *Lawrence* and in Kennedy's opinion to buttress the argument that sodomites, like straights, have a right to sexual intimacy.[5] Although charged with heterosexual rape and aggravated sodomy, Powell became a figure, among others, for the sexual autonomy of consenting adults in a larger emancipatory narrative about queer freedom.

As a legal narrative, *Powell* both comes before and is a part of *Lawrence*. However, in its status as citation there is much in the story of *Powell* that disappears and becomes incoherent in the context of *Lawrence*. On a basic level, then, my retelling of *Powell* narrates that which is suppressed in the official, celebratory political story that claims *Lawrence* as a victory for individual freedom. Retelling thus makes explicit an ethical and political claim: the story of *Powell* retold, unlike its reduction as legal citation, breaks with legal discourse as a tangible configuration to open a space for what Rancière calls "the part of those who have no part."[6] Specifically, *Powell* produces fractures in the "original" stories told by Justices Kennedy and Benham along lines of race, sexuality, and gender. Those fractures unsettle both *Lawrence* and *Powell* as the coherent foundation of truths about "sex" upon which the law is erected. Further, those unsettled truths expose similar fractures in the conceptual underpinnings of certain feminist and queer political projects.

My purpose in this chapter is to retell *Powell* as part of the celebratory story of *Lawrence* in order to acknowledge and interrogate that which has been rendered silent by the law. If the law reduces *Powell* and *Lawrence* to the same story, the performative narrative redeployment of the two can bring out, once again, the differences between them. Thus retelling requires an approach to reading that looks not for conceptual sameness but for narrative singularity. This narrative singularity names difference as the *differend*: the term Jean-François Lyotard gives in *The Differend* (1983) for the unacknowledged harms and unheard voices whose claims are incommensurable with the idiom of the law through which disputes are negotiated and resolved: "I would like to call a *differend* [*différend*] the case where the plaintiff is divested of the means to argue and becomes for that reason a victim. If the addressor, the addressee, and the sense of the testimony are neutralized, everything takes place as if there were no damages. . . . A case of *differend* between two parties takes place when the 'regulation' of the conflict that opposes them is done in the idiom of one of the parties while the wrong suffered by the other is not signified in that idiom."[7]

Lyotard's elaboration of the differend within the performative narrative frame that I developed serves to clarify my use of the terms *narrative* and *story* in this chapter. Specifically, the differend emerges from two different conceptions of narrative famously developed in Lyotard's earlier book, *The Postmodern Condition* (1984). The first, the "grand narrative," describes a narrative form—such as History or the Law—that claims to explain all other narratives and to incorporate them into its own logic.

By contrast, the second conception, the "little narrative," describes a particularistic, singular story that resists incorporation into generalizing concepts. As Bill Readings explains, while grand narratives, or metanarratives, "claim to totalize the field of narrative" and thereby "suppress all *differends*," little narratives allow for the appearance of inconsistencies, contradictions, multiplicity, and conflict.[8] Drawing on my conception of narrative as performance in chapter 2, my use of the terms *narrative* and *story* in this chapter extends this concept by following Lyotard in his understanding of the little narrative: a singular story "that opens culture as a site of transformation and dispute" and reengages politics as what Rancière calls disagreement.[9]

With this in mind, my project in this chapter can best be understood as a performative narrative retelling carried out at that site of transformation and conflict: the place of the differend. Specifically, I retell the story of the plaintiff in the original trial against Powell as a particular instance of the emergence and suppression of the differend. So doing, I ask how her claims might be heard and how the harm of the erasure might be redressed. Implicit in this asking is a demand, an ethical call for new forms of narration that challenge the limits of juridical litigation: "To give the *differend* its due ("Faire droit au différend"), is to institute new addressees, new addressors, new significations, and new referents."[10] Importantly, this ethical demand has political implications and, therefore, requires an analysis of power. In the second half of the chapter I engage Foucault's conception of productive power in order to shed light on long-standing conflicts between feminist and queer approaches to sex, the role of the state, and the problem of regulation. Ultimately, by retelling the differend as a performative story about power, I offer a queer feminist challenge to the increasingly homologizing, legalistic shape of contemporary identity-based sexual politics.

Here, then, is the singular story as the place of the differend, in the words of the plaintiff during the original trial that describe the moment of sodomy with Powell. The questioner in this dialogue is Assistant District Attorney Pamela South during her direct examination of the plaintiff:

Q. What did he do with your legs?
A. He pulled them apart.
Q. Now, this is before he put his mouth on you?

A. Yes, ma'am.

Q. Now, how was your body lying there? Were you stiff? Were you relaxed? How was your body?

A. I was tense. I wasn't relaxed at all.

Q. After he pushed your legs apart, what did he then do?

A. He started licking me.

Q. And by licking you, what part of your body was he licking?

A. My vagina.

Q. Do you know how long this lasted?

A. No, I don't

Q. Now, while he was licking your vaginal area, what were you doing?

A. I was crying.[11]

Available only in unpublished form as part of the transcript of the original case against Powell in August 1997, these words have been all but forgotten in the years that have passed since the event in question. Read in light of the role of *Powell* in arguments for *Lawrence*, the story is a jarring reminder of the gap that separates raw testimony from the elegant if unreal formulations of legal decisions. And although its apparent meaning—nonconsent—contradicts its eventual interpretation by the jury as consensual sex, the passage is ambiguous enough to provoke questions. Indeed, at first glance, what is meant by the phrase "I was crying?"

To begin, the phrase names a moment of nonarticulation in the event itself: the plaintiff's inability at the time of the encounter to say the word "no." This moment of nonarticulation is highlighted by the prosecutor's next question—"were you making a sound?"—and the plaintiff's answer: "I was making a sound, but it wasn't a loud cry. It wasn't an outcry." "I was crying" as a nonoutcry thus points to a kind of negative cry, what Lyotard calls the "negative phrase" of the plaintiff's inability to speak. That "negative phrase" signals a feeling, an "affect phrase" that destabilizes the legal meaning of the encounter within the context of the law.[12] Given this instability, it might be easy to disregard the nonoutcry: to fail to hear the affect phrase. As Lyotard puts it in his critique of the law's inability to hear silence as anything but consent: "To say nothing is to consent."[13] This inability to hear describes, precisely, the law's intepretation—the production of the differend—not only in this trial, but in all the subsequent renderings of *Powell*. Indeed, with each succeeding citation the plaintiff's silence becomes more deafening.

I want to offer a different reading of the plaintiff's testimony and of the event she fails to name in terms the law will register. To do so requires not only a close reading of the testimony through the lens of the differend but also a contextualization of that reading within a larger frame. This frame includes the four sections that follow: 1) the role of storytelling in the law and the place of the emotions in legal judgment, 2) feminist versus queer conceptions of the ethics of sex in the context of juridical conceptions of power, 3) the political implications of narrative retelling, and 4) the role of power in feminist versus queer understandings of the relation between the law and politics. I then conclude the chapter with 5) a return to the testimony as a place of opening toward different narratives that can 6) serve as resources for new political forms of engagement around the question of sexuality and state regulation.

Narrative and Its Contexts: Injustice and Feeling

Like the other readings in this book, my reading of *Powell* here draws on the resources of narrative analysis and antifoundationalist approaches to language and culture. There are a number of reasons for this approach in the specific context of legal analysis. First, I resist a conception of the law as only a normative system of rationalizing abstractions, one that reduces *Lawrence* and *Powell* to the same story. If the work of rationalist philosophies and legal argumentation is the transformation of multiplicity into a generalizing grid of concepts, the work of narrative as performance is precisely the opposite: to bring out multiplicity and difference. This is particularly true if one understands narrative performance as dialogic and context bound, the discursive articulation and transformation of intersubjectivity within a temporally shifting social frame.

In addition to the formal dimensions of narrative that situate my approach to *Lawrence* and *Powell*, the reasons for my resistance to conceptions of the law as a system of rationalizing abstractions are ethical and political as well. If the differend marks the dangers of injustice within the legal justice system, it can also serve a cautionary function for both a feminist politics focused primarily on combating sexual violence and a queer politics centered on achieving sexual freedom. Both these political projects rely on unifying idioms that draw on and repeat the silencing mechanisms of legal discourse. The unifying idiom that produces the differend in the legal system and in law-oriented feminist and queer political projects relies on an epistemological structure that, as I showed in the first two chapters, Luce Irigaray has identified as the subsumption of differences into a logic of the Same.[14] That unifying logic of the law not only reduces *Lawrence* and *Powell* to the same story within the formal legal system but also reinscribes *Lawrence* within a larger American progress narrative. Most obvious in the majority of what Jasbir Puar calls the mainstream, celebratory "homonormative" reception of *Lawrence*— the official gay citizen's rights narrative—is a trajectory whose final aim is expressed as freedom.[15] In that story of progress the sexual freedom represented by *Lawrence* constitutes a signal victory in a struggle for civil rights that began with *Brown v. Board of Education*. As E. J. Graff writes in a 2003 *Boston Globe* editorial hailing the decision: "*Bowers* was the lesbian and gay community's *Plessy v. Ferguson*, that 19th-century Supreme Court opinion that gave a thumbs-up to racial segregation and shoved blacks to the back of the bus. *Lawrence* is our *Brown v. Board of Education*, declaring us full citizens, entitled to all the rights and freedoms held by our siblings, colleagues, and friends."[16]

This story of progress both effaces the differences between feminist, LGBT, and nonidentitarian queer political struggles and denies the possibility for articulating *Lawrence* in a less than celebratory mode. In this way, the legal system works together with dominant lgbt political actors to produce the erasure of racial, sexual, and gendered differences: the process of silencing and exclusion that is the differend.

In its focus on the performative narrative dimensions of *Powell* and *Lawrence*, my analysis is thematically and methodologically linked to a well-established and growing field of work on narrative and rhetoric in the law, a field that reflects both a public and scholarly interest in the ways law, as Paul Gewirtz puts it, "brings together story, form, and power."[17] My analysis here is particularly indebted to the work of feminist critical race theorists for whom stories represent an oppositional stance to the purported neutrality of legal concepts and rules. Originating with the work of Mari Matsuda, Patricia Williams, Derek Bell, Richard Delgado, and others in the late 1980s and early 1990s, critical race theory has continued to emphasize what Matsuda calls "outsider jurisprudence"— "jurisprudence derived from considering stories from the bottom"[18]—as a way both to expose the biases of legal rationalism and to bring to the fore previously excluded perspectives. Critical race theory's commitment to stories represents not only an intersectional call to make the unheard heard but also to challenge legal modes of thinking where particularity and context are suppressed in the formation of principles and rules. As Sherene Razack explains: "The rule of law is 'the consistent application of prior stated rules,' a process theoretically uninformed by politics or ethics. Storytelling in law, then, is an intellectual movement that is 'a rebellion against abstractions.' Its purpose is to interrogate the space between the knower and the thing known; its function is one of putting the context back into law."[19]

Significantly, Lyotard's concept of the differend has been deployed by some critical race theorists as an important analytical tool for explaining the value of outsider narratives. For example, in their introduction to critical race theory, Richard Delgado and Jean Stefanic describe narratives as a form of language that can "bridge the gaps in imagination and conception that give rise to the *differend*."[20] These narratives thus serve as a corrective to the silencing effects of traditional litigation: "They reduce alienation for members of excluded groups, while offering opportunities for members of the majority group to meet them halfway."[21]

Delgado and Stefanic's attention to the differend highlights a crucial link between critical race theory and poststructuralism that, departing from more traditional approaches, flourished with the rise of the legal storytelling movement in the 1980s but has since waned. Since the mid-1990s the storytelling movement has come to be dominated by "law and literature" perspectives: legal hermeneutic, narratological, rhetorical, and thematic approaches that tend to view the role of narrative in the law as one of either application or exemplification.[22] Against this trend, I want to return to what I view as the more radical strand of the legal storytelling movement's promise in a critique that links a crisis in knowledge (philosophical antifoundationalism) to an ethical and political intervention (feminist, queer, and critical race theory). In this context I focus here on Lyotard's articulation in *The Postmodern Condition* of the late modern crisis in knowledge as a narrative crisis that resonates with the underlying premises of critical race theory. While more mainstream law and literature practitioners continue to engage in long-standing debates about "law in literature" versus "law as literature" (following Weisberg), antifoundationalist critical race theory challenges the very separation of law versus literature upon which those categorizations depend. Like Lyotard and other antifoundationalist thinkers, critical race theorists expose the unstable foundations upon which the legal system is built, raising philosophical and political questions about justice, narrative, and power.

As an oppositional discourse aimed at the legal establishment, story-telling in the law has triggered numerous critiques. Not surprisingly, some of the movement's most vocal critics have decried in particular story-telling's reliance on a rhetoric of persuasion that privileges the emotions over reason and objective analysis. Daniel Farber and Suzanna Sherry complain, for example, that legal storytellers privilege "the emotive force of the stories" and, so doing, impede further dialogue by shutting out rea-son and objectivity.[23] Along similar lines, Richard Posner criticizes legal storytellers for privileging the emotions at the expense of truth, creating an "uneasy relation between storytelling and truthtelling."[24] Posner is par-ticularly critical of legal scholars like Patricia Williams who, he argues, "have had difficulty specifying the appropriate role of emotion in the legal process. Those who think it fine that a criminal defendant at his sentenc-ing hearing should use the story of his life to awaken the jury's sense of pity are appalled when the prosecutor uses the story of the plaintiff's life to awaken the jury's retributive sense, although the prosecutor is merely restoring the emotional balance.[25] Like Martha Nussbaum in her consid-erations of the emotions in the law, Posner welcomes the emotions only to the extent that they serve reason.[26]

In response to these critics, law and literature supporters have de-fended the place of the emotions in a number of ways, either by claiming that the emotions have value within the context of the law or by insist-ing that the challenge of the emotions will remain separate from the law as a formal structure. Arguing for the first position, Razack asserts that "stories, in the context of law, bring feeling back into jurisprudence, and they tend to work from experiential understanding" (38). Defending the second position about the separateness of the law, Yoshino reassures law and literature critics that in the context of legal scholarship, literature and its dangers (including feelings) occupy a separate realm from the core state functions of legal institutions: "Legal scholarship can be seen as a venue in which reflection and experimentation can occur without threat to the consistency of the law" (60).

Both these responses, while courageous for their inclusion of the emo-tions in the law, nonetheless remain open to challenge. Despite her de-fense of the emotions, Razack still assumes narrative to be a transparent vehicle of expression rather than a complex patterning of the said and the unsaid, speech and silence, where a feeling might appear as something that remains unspoken. Yoshino, for his part, does not allow literature or the emotions to fundamentally challenge the conceptual underpinnings of the law itself; while defending the value of literature and feeling, he continues to affirm the consistency, coherence, and efficacy of the law as a separate, authoritative domain. Finally, none of these defenses of the emotions in the legal arena address the problem of a biopolitical intensification and regulation of intimacy and affect that, for Puar, lie at the center of *Lawrence*.[27]

Against the denunciations of Posner and others, I want to assert the importance of a conceptual and practical consideration of the nonrational dimensions of the law (such as feelings) associated with storytelling and narrative theory. Like many of storytelling's defenders, including Razack and Yoshino, I view stories as valuable forms of knowledge. At the same time, I want to argue that narrative as performance functions to mark the limits of knowledge as well as the limits of justice. Following Foucault's critique of the repressive hypothesis, I do not view stories as modes of expression that allow for the articulation of feelings that would otherwise remain repressed. Rather, as patterns that include the said and the unsaid, stories are valuable for their capacity to render silence as gaps or narrative breaks that fulfill important aesthetic functions and disrupt cognitive regimes of thinking. These narrative silences signal something— Lyotard calls it feeling—that remains unexpressed. Following Lyotard, I view that signaling function as belonging to a different order of meaning than those that are legible within the increasingly minute, penetrating calculations of a biopolitical grid.[28]

Importantly, I frame this signaling function of narrative silence as one of the ethical dimensions of the differend. As Lyotard puts it in *The Differend*: if "every wrong ought to be able to be put into phrases," justice is limited by the fact of the differend as "the unstable state and instant of language wherein something which must be able to be put into phrases cannot yet be" (13). And although the differend's silence is "a negative phrase," it also calls forth other possibilities of articulation: "it also calls upon phrases which are in principle possible" (13). This unstable, silent state of possibility is signaled, for Lyotard, by "what one ordinarily calls a feeling" (13). Thus storytelling becomes, paradoxically, both a source of knowledge and knowledge's limit, a form of expression and a rendering of that which, as nonexpression, eludes both legal conceptualization and biopolitical forms of legibility.

In this context, feeling operates as a narrative signal that, while resisting expression, nonetheless has the capacity to signify as a call for politics, however indeterminate the shape of that politics might be. This call for politics is not simply a command to replace silence with voice, however; rather, the differend's call is a demand for a different kind of reading. This aesthetic, nonrational reading calls forth the silence for what it signals, opening up what Rancière calls "the part of those who have no part."[29] Rationalist models of interpretation, on the other hand, are incapable of reading the aesthetic signal and, therefore, cannot "hear" the differend's political call. The differend's silence, signaled as feeling, thus uncovers both the epistemological and ethical impoverishment of a rationalist discourse whose exclusions mark a political failure.

Narrative and the Ethics of Sex

This attention to the differend and the ethical dimension of narrative situates my analysis of *Lawrence* and *Powell* within a larger series of reflections on the ethics of sex in feminist and queer political projects. In these reflections I once again take as my point of departure the Foucauldian question I invoked in chapter 1: "why [have] we made sexuality into a moral experience?"[30] And although, here in this chapter, I am less interested than Foucault was in turning toward the ancient historical dimensions of that question, I want to further explore that genealogical question by examining its implications in a contemporary setting. Specifically, I want to pursue here, in relation to *Lawrence*, this book's framing question about the sometimes conflicting ways in which feminist versus queer theories and practices play themselves out in relation to the ethics of sex and the politics of sexuality more broadly. My reading of *Lawrence* highlights how these queer feminist ethical divisions sometimes mark divergent political perspectives with regard to a number of present-day issues, including sex law and, more broadly, the role of the state and other forms of governmentality in the regulation of sexuality.

From this perspective, it is important to note that not all progressives have celebrated *Lawrence*. There has been some contention among both feminist and queer theorists about both the legal reasoning and the political implications of the Supreme Court decision. These challenges can be grouped into two camps: 1) antinormative queer critiques of the Court's normative assumptions about domesticity, respectability, and intimacy and 2) feminist equality arguments that challenge the Court's assumptions about sexuality and consent in the private sphere. For example, in their queer rhetorical readings of the *Lawrence* decision, Katherine Franke and Teemu Ruskola both object to the heteronormative assumptions that undergird the Court's opinion. Franke argues that in *Lawrence* "the Court relies on a narrow version of liberty that is both geographized and do-mesticated,"[31] a "privatized liberty" (1404) that, while decriminalizing sodomy, "does not necessarily mobilize any particular ethical projects, or for that matter, any ethics at all" (1411). Extending her critique to in-clude extralegal political questions, Franke also criticizes a mainstream LGBT political movement that "places too much emphasis on state-based recognition and legal legitimization" (1424) and whose goals mirror the "domesticated liberty" of the *Lawrence* decision. Along similar lines, Rus-kola asserts that, while no one can deny the desirability of the sexual freedom granted by the *Lawrence* decision, the price of that freedom is gay respectability: "The Court, and the Constitution, will respect our sex lives, but on condition that our sex lives be respectable."[32] Also with an eye to its lesson for politics, Ruskola objects to the political implications of this limiting conception of sexual freedom. If *Lawrence* is "ultimately grounded in the principle of privacy" but sex is "ultimately political and public," then *Lawrence* "forecloses important avenues for political engage-ment" that would question the legal fiction which continues to consign "good" sex to the private sphere.[33]

Drawing on the queer critiques of Franke and others, Puar criticizes the *Lawrence* decision not only for its heteronormativity but also for the racialized homonormativity implicit in its celebratory reception among gays and lesbians. Situating *Lawrence* in the racially charged, anti-Muslim atmosphere of the post-9/11 war on terror, Puar examines the role played by *Lawrence* in "the actualization of an American national queer liberal subject before the law" (120) whose legitimation reracializes the sodomitic acts of alien others. Puar also challenges assumptions about intimacy embedded in the decision and its mainstream liberal reception, arguing for a reorientation of our public-private paradigms to the domain of inti-macy as a site of intensification in the biopolitical ordering of life. Along similar lines (although without citing Puar), queer theorist David Eng argues in *The Feeling of Kinship* (2010) that our interpretation of *Lawrence* must include an intersectional analysis "attentive not only to questions of neoliberalism and globalization but also to issues of empire, sovereignty, and terrorism."[34]

If queer theorists tend to situate their critiques of *Lawrence* within an antinormative frame, many feminist legal theorists have tended to found their concerns in a reiteration of the equality norm in the context of sexual violence. Like Franke, Ruskola, Puar, and Eng, Catharine MacKinnon objects to the "privatized liberty" on which *Lawrence* is founded, but she does so from a feminist sexual equality perspective that views the Texas sodomy statute as a law that institutionalized male dominance through "the 'gender caste' system of sex."[35] If queer theorists are concerned about the domestication and respectability of the normative gay sex promoted in *Lawrence*, MacKinnon challenges the sexual norms it hides for a different reason: the inclusion of homosexuality into what she calls "heterosexuality's closet, where truly unspeakable acts—sexual abuse—are hidden."[36] MacKinnon asserts that by arguing as it did "the Court effectively extended heterosexuality's right to sexual privacy and sexual autonomy to gay men and lesbian women," thereby expanding "the tacit norms of male dominance from heterosexual sex to homosexual sex."[37] Like MacKinnon, Marc Spindelman argues from a feminist sexual equality perspective, asserting that the "like-straights" logic of the *Lawrence* decision is implicitly based on a "presumption of consent" that refuses to critique the patriarchal underpinnings of heteronormativity, thereby denying the ongoing sexual violence, straight and queer, that continues to occur, often unpunished, in the private sphere.[38]

These feminist and queer challenges to a legal or political position that simply celebrates *Lawrence* are multilayered and complex and are presented here not for their detail but for their relevance to this book's larger argument about queer and feminist tensions regarding the ethics of sex and their implications for sexual politics. As I've argued in the preceding chapters, that argument traces the divergent approaches to ethical thinking that stem from competing conceptions of subjectivity.

A Mosaic of Citations

This context sets the stage for reading *Lawrence* as a case where storytelling and the differend instantiate new possibilities for thinking about feminist and queer politics. To be sure, the pre-*Lawrence* criminalization of consensual sodomy was unjust; overturning *Bowers* in *Lawrence* can therefore be read, from a certain liberal perspective, as the just outcome of a long struggle for sexual freedom. But, despite that legal achievement, as a decision *Lawrence* also papers over other stories about sex that are, in fact, part of the narrative material from which *Lawrence* is pieced together. In this sense, then, storytelling is both part of the law and its rejected other, the dialectical remainder of the law's sublation as concept. Legal decisions are the consequence of particular narrative decisions, choices about which parts of stories should be retained and which parts should be discarded. Those narrative choices produce a prevailing image of the law as a discourse that transcends the singularity of stories: a complex grid of general, objective rules that cohere to a rational set of norms. That image of the legal decision as a rule with a binding force produces what I have been calling narrative's performative dimension. We can extend this here to encompass what Robert Cover calls, in an explicitly legal context, the performative force of the law.[39] That performative saying as doing denies its own narrative beginnings to abstract itself as explicitly nonnarrative: the law of the land is no longer a story but a universal principle to be applied to all.

The appearance of the differend exposes the ruse of the law's dialectical logic and its concomitant rejection of the singularity of stories in the non-narrative performative gesture of judicial decision. This exposure of the differend, although not new, does open up new questions about legal storytelling in the context of queer versus feminist sexual debates. What precisely is the role of stories in the construction of legal precedent? Further, what are the ethical and political meanings of the explicitly narrative choices that produce legal decisions such as *Lawrence*? Specifically in *Powell* as a citation in the *Lawrence* decision, the narrative process of fragmentation and recombination transforms a story about sexual violence into a story about consensual sodomy. This raises specifically ethical and political questions about sex and stories. How could retelling *Powell* as a story about *non*consensual sex alter the way we read *Lawrence*? Specifically, how does *Powell* as story open up a space in which the differend in *Lawrence* can be read? What new phrases or possibilities of articulation are brought forth by that reading? And finally, how do these new articulations interface with the discursive apparatus of state power that produces and reproduces the "fiction" of "sex"?[40]

In broaching these questions I pair Lyotard's concept of the differend with an *intertextual* conception of law as story, thereby bringing into focus the "mosaic of citations," to use Julia Kristeva's famous term, out of which the law is constructed.[41] I use this conception of narrative performance as the citational repetition of prior stories in order to highlight the ethical and ultimately political dimensions of the law as a process of intertextual retelling. So doing, I theorize retelling as both a critical and a constructive process that simultaneously unmasks and remakes the law's stories. In the simultaneity of its critical and constructive dimensions, performative retelling thus does two things: first, it exposes the differend by unburying the hidden antagonisms and stories of violence perpetrated and effaced by the law; and, second, it calls forth the possibility of a non-policing politics.

In that double capacity of unmasking and remaking, retelling for the differend thus engages ethics as a double imperative: first, to name harms and, second, to think and feel differently in a process of imaginative transformation. Again, Foucault's commitment to thinking differently is relevant here. As Foucault, following Nietzsche, puts it: "The object [is] to learn to what extent the effort to think one's own history can free thought from what it silently thinks, and so enable it to think differently."[42] Within this particular ethical frame, intertextuality can thus be conceived as a contestational *political* practice that both brings out the violences effaced by the law and, through narrative performance, enacts alternative visions of the social order. As a project of unmasking and remaking, retelling en-larges the ethical potential of interpretation as a relational process among narrative actors who, while equally enmeshed in the law, use different idioms and have differing capacities to be heard. Ethical intervention in this sense requires more than an attentive reading of that which had been previously expressed but was discounted or ignored by the legal system. It requires, rather, a mode of reading for affect or feeling as the signal of *that which remains unexpressed*. In other words, this is not just a matter of reading, for the purpose of reforming the law, the pieces of the inter-textual mosaic—discarded testimonies and buried stories—that the law once read but forgot. Rather, ethical rereading means reading the cracks between the pieces—the illegible narrative silences signaled as feeling— that the law in its rationalist dimension is incapable of reading.

Significantly, this ethical task of reading the law as a "mosaic of cita-tions" has implications for an analysis of a discursive and political field that extends far beyond the law as a formal structure. Again, my interest here is to read *Lawrence* as part of the larger project of this book about the ethical questions that divide feminists and queers regarding the politics of sex and sexuality. As I've repeatedly argued, a major source of division between feminists and queers is the differing conception of subjectivity that ground each of them. Specifically, in chapter 2, I demonstrated that while feminist theory has tended to build on strictly narrative models for thinking about the self in relation to others, from its inception queer theory has embraced the performative rupture of constrictive (hetero)narratives, including those narratives that would bind the queer subject in any static or definitive way. I also argued that an intertextual model of reading and retelling both acknowledges and challenges this impasse between feminists and queers. Moving beyond the narrative versus performative opposition that has divided us, this new model articulates instead an intertextual conception of political intervention that takes seriously both the narrative and performative, feminist and queer, dimensions of subjectivity. This means, ethically and politically, that we take seriously both our (narrative) boundedness and our (performative) capacity to engage in practices of freedom that unravel that which binds us. It is precisely this kind of intertextual model of narrative performance that I hope to develop in my reading of *Lawrence* here.

Further, this conception of intertextual retelling within a theory of narrative performance links narrative to action in ways that resonate with political theory: an understanding of narrative not as (constative) description, but as a series of utterances (or linked phrases, to use Lyotard's terms) with a performative force. It is precisely in its performative narrative dimension that retelling becomes a political intervention (this is why critical race theory is important), a contestation of other performative utterances, be they those of queer and feminist theorists, members of the legal profession, or Supreme Court justices. Importantly, that political narrative performance is always checked by ethics, not as a set of norms, but as an erotic, desubjectivating practice of freedom in relation to others. If we understand intertextuality as a relational process that uses storytelling to reengage subjects in relation to others, we who are rereading and retelling the law are bound by others, even, and especially, when those others cannot speak or be heard. Bound as we are by the other's silence, the real question then becomes, as Lyotard reminds us: after the silence, what are we to say?

A Sexual Mosaic

Answering the question of what to say—in theory, in the law, or in politics—requires a rethinking of the narrative considerations articulated thus far with a more concrete examination of the workings of power in the specific context of *Powell* and *Lawrence*. Here, the Kristevan conception of intertextuality as a "mosaic of citations" can serve as a rubric for reengaging the question of power as Foucault presents it in *Discipline and Punish* and *History of Sexuality,* volume 1. This consideration of intertextual retelling in a Foucauldian genealogical context returns us to the question raised earlier about how performative storytelling and the differend interface with the discursive apparatus of state power that produces and reproduces the "fiction" of "sex."

Viewed from the perspective of Foucauldian genealogy, the intertextual mosaic of the law can be analyzed, through *Powell* and *Lawrence,* as a refracting mechanism that splinters the "fictitious unity" of "sex" into what Foucault calls the "sexual mosaic" of modern perversions (HS1 47). Elaborating on his concept of productive power introduced in *Discipline and Punish,* Foucault demonstrates, in *History of Sexuality,* volume 1, how power acted in bourgeois society "by multiplication of singular sexualities" and thereby "produced and determined the sexual mosaic" (HS1 47). This Foucauldian understanding of productive power plays itself out in *Powell* and *Lawrence* with regard to the larger question of the role of the state in the regulation of sexuality. Specifically, Foucault's "sexual mosaic" returns us to the queer feminist tension implicit in MacKinnon's and Spindelman's critique of the "presumption of consent" underlying the *Lawrence* decision. To recap: if lawyers for *Lawrence* basically argued that, "like straights," queers deserve the sanctity of a private space free from state intrusion, feminist law reform projects have been arguing for decades that the space of the private is precisely the realm where gendered violence is most likely to occur and is, therefore, in need of regulation.[43]

From a theoretical perspective, this queer feminist conflict plays out a conflict between two different conceptions of power that Foucault has famously described as disciplinary versus juridical, where the juridical names power as levy, a taking away through which the state can not only wound (by fining, locking up, or even executing innocent people, for example) but can also protect (by fining, locking up, or executing "true criminals"—sexual harassers, pornographers, rapists, wife beaters, murderers). Feminist legal reform has tended to use the state in its juridical, "repressive" dimension, drawing on power as levy and thereby making it easier to harness the power of the state to prosecute sexual harassers, pornographers, rapists, wife beaters, and murderers. Queers, on the other hand, because of their historical criminalization through the law, are more attentive to the disciplinary, subject-making function of the law, the way in which the law produces the deviant, the delinquent, the criminal, and the sodomite.

As I argued in the introduction, this distinction between juridical and disciplinary conceptions of subjectivity has implications for intersectional analysis. In *Powell* and *Lawrence*, racial difference and racialization play a crucial role and point, again, to the existence of the differend. As Carpenter, Puar, and Eng point out, race is central to the *Lawrence* case. The fact that the case involves an interracial pairing between Lawrence, a white man, and Garner, an African American man, is viewed by Puar as part of a symbolic economy that perceives sodomy as a racialized act and exposes a fraught history of interracial tensions that includes not only black and whites but also relations between blacks and nonwhite immigrants.[44] Puar reads the annexing of the discourse of civilization in the *Lawrence* decision to a "black-white sodomy duo" as either "the ascendency of whiteness achieved through the sexual and racial hybrid couple" or "as a surrogate citizenship to black subjects who remain economically disenfranchised" (137). In both interpretations, the black-white duo at the center of *Lawrence* displaces the reality of anti-Muslim exclusion, vilification, and racial profiling in the wake of 9/11. Along similar lines, Eng highlights the racial underpinnings of the *Lawrence* case to ask about the emergence of queer liberalism through the "racialization of intimacy" and the "constitutive forgetting of race" (36). Drawing on *Lawrence*, Eng argues that intimacy should be regarded as a "racialized property right" (45) that exposes a history of inclusion and exclusion in the liberal polity.

I want to reframe the race question in *Lawrence* in the context of critical race theory, storytelling, and the queer feminist rift. If it is true that feminist legal reform has tended to draw on juridical power to lock up those who would hurt women, that project of reform has been challenged by the recognition among critical race legal theorists that the disciplinary production of deviance is often racialized. Thus Angela Harris, for example, has expanded Catherine MacKinnon's theory of sexual violence to include the history of the criminalization of African American men through the myth of the black rapist and the complex position of African American women in the history of the law, both in their relation to the criminalized black male body and as unacknowledged plaintiffs deserving of legal redress.[45]

All of these dimensions of power are played out through the story of *Powell* in *Lawrence*. As sodomy stories, *Lawrence* and *Powell* replay deep historical and ethical conflicts, simultaneously telling and effacing multiple stories of violence with multiple perpetrators. As performative stories about "sex," they are particularly fraught with the tensions embedded in a nineteenth-century conceptual creation that is, paradoxically, at the same time a "fictitious unity" and a mere fragment of an ever expanding "sexual mosaic."

This complex nexus of race, gender, sex, and power brings me back to the original trial in *Powell* as the place to read for the differend: that which has been erased both by the law and by political movements for sexual freedom. In *Powell* a scene unfolds around a figure whose story was rendered silent by the discursive machinery of the law and politics working together. To rediscover her name—Quashana—and her testimony—forty-four photocopied pages from the August 1997 jury trial proceedings in Lawrenceville, Georgia—is hardly to right the wrong of an originary injustice. When I first read through the transcript of the original trial, I increasingly understood why this African American teenager failed to convince the jury that sex had occurred against her will. As a black teenage girl who knew her assailant and never said the word "no," her chances of getting a conviction for forcible rape and aggravated sodomy were not good, and this is borne out by the jury's verdict. There are holes in her testimony; she is frequently incoherent. At the very opening of her testimony, she cannot remember her age. Powell, on the other hand, comes across as believable and coherent. His defense is simple: he thought she wanted it. As Powell puts it during direct examination: "I felt like she wasn't stopping me, and so I continued. If she had stopped me or said anything, then I would have stopped, but she wasn't saying anything."[46]

Despite the seeming clarity of Powell's believability versus the doubts raised by the plaintiff's incoherence, the verdict was not a simple acquittal but rather a conviction for sodomy that, at the time, carried a stiff penalty of fifteen years with five to be served in confinement. In other words, the (consensual) sodomy verdict points to the jury's desire to find some form of sexual guilt by using another weapon in the state's arsenal to convict Powell. In that move the state's power to repress sex as rape is transformed into a more pervasive, diffused, productive form. In convicting Powell, the state literally creates a sodomite. At the same time, in its creation of Powell as the (iconically white) sodomite, the state also masks its ongoing production of black men as criminals.

In his brief discussion of the *Powell* case, William Eskridge points out that this story about a rape charge producing a consensual sodomy conviction is hardly unique. Indeed, Eskridge specifies that in the decade following the 1986 Supreme Court decision in *Bowers*, which upheld sodomy

statutes like Georgia's, there were more than nine hundred reported sodomy convictions. Of those convictions, 86 percent involved opposite-sex
sodomy, usually where a man was brought before the court for assaulting
an adult or minor woman.[47] In other words, buried within the story of
sodomy is a story about the law's failure to deal with sexual violence and
the use of sodomy as a fallback measure for punishing perpetrators in
cases where juries are not willing to believe that the act was committed
"with force and against the will" of the plaintiff. Indeed, this story has
nineteenth-century roots in American jurisprudence, as Kennedy himself
admits in the *Lawrence* opinion: "A substantial number of sodomy pros-
ecutions and convictions for which there are surviving records were for
predatory acts against those who could not or did not consent, as in the
case of a minor or the plaintiff of an assault."[48] Here Kennedy could, in
fact, be describing *Powell*, as one of those cases involving "predatory acts,"
and yet, when eight pages later he cites *Powell*, it serves as part of the
"chain of law" upon which is founded the privatized liberty guaranteed
by the due process clause of the Fourteenth Amendment.

   Given this context, what then is the purpose of rereading the trial transcript and retelling Quashana's story? Clearly it is not to bring Powell to
justice and to right the wrong of Quashana's violation. Frankly, I do not
know what "really" happened in Powell's apartment that night in 1996.
My feminist inclination is to believe Quashana. But even assuming, as
I do, that Powell had sex with Quashana against her will, retelling her
story here hardly constitutes, in practical terms, an intervention that can
somehow lead to a just outcome. Neither is my purpose to locate the
aporetic appearance of injustice in an abstract game whose aim is simply
to spot the differend. Rather, I want to draw on this particular story about
sex and the differend to change our thinking about sexual violence and
the ethics of sex by focusing on the historical, mutual imbrication of rape
and sodomy as part of a larger sexual, intertextual mosaic of perversions
that plays out conflicting discourses of power. The logic of my retelling
of *Lawrence* through *Powell*, and specifically through Quashana's story, repeats both a historical and conceptual logic that works through the law to
divide feminists and queers around issues of gender, sexuality, and race.
Specifically, *Powell* is part of *Lawrence* just as rape is part of sodomy law,
and this relationship of identity is inextricably linked to a history of racialization that is part of the social construction of rape. Even more specifically, Powell is a black man accused of rape, inscribed within a history of
productive power; as Angela Davis points out in her classic essay, "Rape,

Racism, and the Myth of the Black Racist," the mythical construction of black men as rapists served historically to justify lynching following the American Civil War.[49] That legacy continues today through the pervasive criminalization of African American men, a full third of whom will go to prison during their lifetime.[50] Powell's accuser, on the other hand, is not a white woman, but an African American girl historically constructed as the oversexed counterpart to the mythical chaste white woman endangered by the violence of the mythical black rapist; that construction served, during slavery and after, to efface the reality of black women's systematic rape and continues, even today, to deny the fact of the ongoing sexual assault of African American girls and women.

Still the question remains: after the silence, what are we to say?

Retelling: Listening for the Differend

It is perhaps too early to speak. To speak now would mean to speak in Quashana's place without trying to hear what she cannot say. It would mean to speak in the old idiom, before finding the next phrase whose meaning, referent, and structure of address will be different. Finding the next phrase in a different idiom requires, first, what Foucault calls in *The Courage of Truth* an ethical *parrhesia* (frank speech) that includes not only the courage to speak but also, more importantly, the courage to listen.[51] This means listening not simply for what is said—the factual description of the wrongful act or perhaps the expression of a feeling—but for that which remains unarticulated—the narrative gap, the silence. This form of listening to Quashana's story—rendered as a dialogue from the transcript of her testimony at the trial—might then begin to reveal possibilities for other forms of relation as well. As we listen, once again, to Quashana's words, what can we hear?

Q. Now, while he was licking your vaginal area, what were you doing?
A. I was crying.[52]

In testifying about an act of sexual violation, Quashana participates in what Foucault might call a "procedure for telling the truth of sex" (HS1 57). In Lyotardian terms, her speech is rendered through the cognitive regime of propositions whose only stake is truth. Relayed through the particular discursive field of power known as sex law, Quashana's story about sexual violation becomes a propositional truth quite different from the harm she experienced that night on the couch in Powell's apartment. What the law hears in Quashana's story is not rape or sexual violation, but rather what Georgia defined through its sodomy statute as a consensual "sexual act involving the sex organs of one person and the mouth or anus of another."[53] This "truth" of sex is *all* the law is able to "hear"; indeed, this technique for producing the "truth of sex" allows the state to redefine Powell as a sodomite and causes Quashana to disappear.[54]

Of course, the original harm (of rape, of nonconsensual sodomy) remains, but only as a trace, as that which has been effaced by the truth-producing procedures of the legal framework in which the complaint was heard. Thus the original harm is doubled by the law's discursive erasure of both the harmful act (nonconsensual sex) and the complaint that attempts to speak it. This unsaid remainder whose stake is something other than the law's truth can be read, as a trace, in the phrase from Quashana's testimony that signals a feeling precisely at the moment of evocation of the historically unspeakable sodomitic act. This is, significantly, the moment of Quashana's erasure and the moment that marks the law's violation of her: "I was making a sound, but it wasn't a loud cry. It wasn't an outcry." As that which, in language, "can scarcely be grasped,"[55] this moment in Quashana's testimony marks what Sfez describes as the "sharp pain of language" where "the real . . . is fissured by the differend."[56]

As a fissured real, the differend thus signals, above all else, the need for multiple levels of reading. On one level, "I was crying" and "I was making a sound" can reasonably be read as indications of nonconsent, narrative signals of unwanted sex the prosecution was simply unable to prove. This was also, apparently, the judge's reading of the testimony, since Powell was ultimately found guilty and sentenced to prison, albeit for a different crime than the one originally brought before the court. However, this reasonable reading points to the fissure—the law's duplicity in convicting Powell—for in sentencing Powell the law both hears and doesn't hear Quashana's lack of consent. The law hears Quashana by punishing Powell; it doesn't hear her by refusing to acknowledge the encounter as nonconsensual. Further, this privileging of what is heard as the truth of sex—an act of sodomy—over what the law cannot hear—crying as nonconsent—hardly leads, as logic would dictate, to Quashana's conviction, along with Powell, as a consensual sodomite. Indeed, reading Quashana's testimony unmasks the incoherence of the legal production of a truth where rapist and plaintiff are transformed by the law into the "sodomite" and his illegible other.

Read this way, the production of Powell as a "sodomite" serves to ensure the erasure of the affect phrase that is part of Quashana's story. Further, in *Lawrence* the transformation of a story about sexual violation into a story about illegitimate state intrusion into a private sphere of consensual sex repeats a contemporary and historical denial—the experience of black women as victims of rape—and thereby reproduces the double erasure of the wrong and the complaint that is the differend. Even more insidiously, as a citation in *Lawrence*, *Powell* wrongly becomes part of a redemptive story about the state where the law gallantly corrects its own violent history of illegitimate criminalization by overturning *Bowers* in *Lawrence*. From this perspective, the redemptive story about the decriminalization of sodomites masks both the ongoing interpersonal sexual violence previously "covered" by sodomy laws and ongoing forms of state violence.[57]

This reading of the phrases "I was crying" and "I was making a sound" as indicative of nonconsent produces a believable, coherent narrative about the historical imbrication of rape and sodomy and serves as a cautionary tale about the dangers of governmentality. It is a reading that should not be dismissed. However, the situation of the differend produces other possible levels of reading as well, where something other than the truth of propositions is at stake. As Lyotard reminds us in *The Differend*, phrases "can have stakes other than the true."[58] Indeed, the eventual transformation of the phrases—"I was crying," "I was making a sound, but it wasn't a loud cry. It wasn't an outcry"—into the celebratory overturning of *Bowers* in *Lawrence* dramatically marks language's instability and exposes the ruse of the law's truth games. If language is unstable—that is, resistant to truth telling in any clear or simple way—then reading itself becomes complex and multilayered, its stakes something other than truth.

So what would it look like to read these affect phrases not for what they mean in the truth-seeking language of litigation (consent or nonconsent), but rather, as Lyotard suggests, for what they *signal* as feeling? This is not a matter of reading "I was crying" and "I was making a sound" as *expressions* of a feeling that we could isolate and name, although to do so is tempting: they could mean, for example, fear, sadness, or shame. Such a reading would resubmit the phrase to a cognitive regime where feeling translates as a discernible truth. To read the phrases as the narrative signals of something other than a truth the law can know requires a different protocol of reading and one that is generally unwelcome in the context of the law and even, I would argue, in most academic discourse, especially in this neurologically driven, scientistic moment. However, I want to reassert the necessity of this nontruth-seeking protocol, a form of reading that requires listening for what remains unspoken, the gap in the narrative that speaks something other than a rationally knowable truth. Reading Quashana's words—"I was crying," "I was making a sound, but it wasn't a loud cry. It wasn't an outcry"—opens a narrative gap because the phrases cannot link, in the context of the law, to another phrase that would allow us to know in legal terms what really happened that night in Powell's apartment. Rather, as negative phrases that signal an inability to speak, the phrases link to silence, thereby pointing beyond themselves to an event that remains unknowable as a legal truth and as a feeling that cannot be named in the law's idiom.

The idiom of the law thus remains inadequate to a rendering of the event's reality: Quashana's idiom and the idiom of the law are incommensurable. This is not because Quashana uses language poorly, but rather because the event itself resists articulation in the idiom of the law: a trial with rules of proof to be matched against a code of punishable transgressions. In the collision between the event and the law, the law redefines the event by reducing "what happened" to a choice of words: *forcible rape, aggravated sodomy,* or, finally, *consensual sodomy.* None of these words match the event; the law's language remains inadequate to it: "the silence indicates that phrases are in abeyance of their becoming event" ("en souffrance de leur événement").[59] Quashana's words begin to say it, as narrative signals that mark a feeling: "the feeling is the suffering of this abeyance" ("le sentiment est cette souffrance").[60] But the words do not speak in the law's idiom. No linking can occur that would allow the law to hear the harm and respond, ethically, as justice.

After the Silence: What Is There to Say?

Paradoxically, it is precisely the privation of the ethical—this failure of justice in Quashana's case—that brings the matter of the ethical into view. Correspondingly, it is precisely the collision that occurs within the law between the law's idiom and an event that remains inarticulable that brings into view the incommensurability of the two idioms and the instability of language: this is the differend. In view of the privative nature of the ethical, the question then becomes: what can we do? Lyotard says: find the next link, the next phrase, the next thing to say. "Politics," writes Lyotard, "is . . . the question of linkage."[61] Thus ethical questions about justice raise the specter of politics precisely at the point where the incommensurability of the two idioms comes into view. That incommensurability presents us with an obligation, a thing to do: to "give the differend its due."[62] But what does this mean? For the law? For feminists? For queers?

The answer to this question—what does it mean?—will not be found in a formula for political practice or a how-to manual that will allow all progressives to agree about what to do. But the ethical obligation revealed by the differend does point to the necessity for future investigations—for a variety of actors in different fields—into the various forms that new political interventions might take. If the differend signals what the law cannot hear, there are at least two conclusions to be drawn from that signaling. First, as a truth-telling discourse of propositions with a certain performative and therefore policing force, the law is severely limited in its capacity to redress wrongs and to carry out justice. Quashana's situation is just one example of that fact. This suggests that the next thing to do is not simply to find some other means, within the law, for achieving justice by conforming to its cognitive regime of truth. That cognitive regime, Foucault reminds us, is also a field of power. To redeploy the language and logic of the law is to participate in its disciplinary, subjectivating power. This means, in Lyotardian terms, that the next phrase cannot be in the idiom of the law. New idioms—new meanings, new referents, new forms of address, new narrative structures—must be found.

Second, because both feminist and LGBT movements for sexual justice have relied heavily on the formal workings of the law, we need to challenge activist strategies so deeply invested in identity, legalism, and politics-as-policing. This is not simply because a "queer" victory (*Lawrence*) hides a "feminist" defeat (*Powell*). There are other defeats here, including queer ones, as Franke, Ruskola, Puar, and others have argued. A challenge to legalistic political strategies must address, more broadly, the question of the interplay between power and the differend that I have unraveled in *Powell* and *Lawrence*. Put simply, although this analysis has focused on Quashana, there is more than one differend at work here. If the celebratory discourse about *Lawrence* erases Quashana's violation, it also erases the myriad ways in which queers have been, and continue to be, beaten and battered not only by the law but even more importantly by all the indirect, extralegal apparatuses through which sexuality is regulated. The Court's decision in *Lawrence* will hardly change that fact. As Nan Hunter puts it in Foucauldian terms: "*Lawrence v. Texas* marked a dramatic milestone in efforts to limit state power to control homosexuality, but the product is likely to be a different regulatory regime rather than a libertarian utopia."[63]

Even more broadly, this exposure of the multiple differends masked by a legal victory that claims to produce justice also uncovers a Foucauldian network of power of which one ever diminishing strand is the formal legal system. If *Powell* in *Lawrence* reveals fundamental rifts between feminist and queer conceptions of power—again, where feminists tend to rely on what Foucault describes as "repressive" power while queers tend to adopt an antinormative understanding of power as "productive"—ultimately the liberatory and ethical aims of both feminists and queers will be thwarted by a legal system that brilliantly manipulates this double face of power, where repressive power and productive power play off each other in a game of justice that obscures what is happening between the lines and behind the scenes. Even with *Lawrence,* the law as a strand of governmentality has the capacity to wound, and "our collective social body will continue to bleed."[64] To fail to challenge an almost exclusively litigious and legislative political strategy—a strategy that characterizes much LGBT and feminist activism today—is to participate in the proliferation of subjectivating, sometimes violent forms of discursive and nondiscursive power. As Foucault puts it in *History of Sexuality,* volume 1: "power is tolerable only on condition that it mask a substantial part of itself. Its success is proportional to its ability to hide its own mechanisms" (86). So again, returning to a Lyotardian language, we might choose, as the next thing to do, something other than a phrase in the language of litigation. "Politics," says Lyotard, "is the threat of the differend. It is not a genre, it is the multiplicity of genres, the diversity of ends, and par excellence the question of linkage."[65]

So what is the next thing to do, to say? If politics is linkage, what makes intervention possible? I want to end this chapter's reflections here, as the starting place for new forms of thinking in new idioms, with another plea (not new, but necessary today) for the ongoing value of antifoundationalist critique, rifts, and disagreements. "To give the differend its due" does not mean we can use the law to bring justice to Quashana or even that we can use legal scholarship to give her a voice where before she remained voiceless. The problem of the differend cannot be addressed by a legal discursive field that itself produced the problem. Rather, the eruption of the differend points to the importance of working through legal problems in arenas not constrained by strictly legal forms of interpretation that function, in Thomas's words, "as an agency, accessory, and instrument of violence."[66] This long-standing critique of the law as a place for thinking is thus also a challenge to think and feel differently and to ask where that different thinking-feeling might lead. This was Nietzsche's challenge as well as Foucault's and Lyotard's. It can, perhaps must, be ours as well. For both feminists and LGBT activists, to what extent does our investment in the law as a discourse that will bring about political change also, inadvertently, reproduce the silencing of the differend? How might antifoundationalist critique interrupt the law as the place that determines our thinking and feeling, thus reconfiguring the discursive frames for our theoretical and political practice?

This intertextual reading of *Powell v. State* and *Lawrence v. Texas* has shown that the emancipatory narrative generated by *Lawrence* occludes the workings of a discursive system of power that, as Foucault puts it, "hides its own mechanisms" (HS1 86) and underwrites violence. It also denies the fracturing eruption of the differend precisely at the point where political identities attempt to consolidate themselves through coherent narratives about progressive struggles toward justice and freedom. Through a close reading of one particular disclosure of the differend, I have tried to show the costs—both ethical and political—of that project of consolidation. Those costs reveal the folly of a unilateral investment in the law to bring about political remedies for the ongoing harms that women, queers, and people of color continue to suffer. Such unilateral investments not only distort the actual, extralegal workings of power but also foreclose other possibilities for political change: new linkages to new phrases for "the opening up of common (which does not mean consensual) worlds."[67]

5 One-Handed Reading

These last four chapters explore the possibility of an erotic queer feminism by bringing the term *lesbian* back into the picture. Although lesbian feminism played a constitutive role in the development of feminist theory and politics in the 1970s, it was largely occluded with the rise of the anti-identitarian politics and thinking that characterized the queer over the course of the 1990s and early 2000s. This chapter and the next three revisit that history in order to challenge an identitarian conception of lesbian with an alternative ethical account that redefines lesbian as an event of marginalization that is erotically charged. Although this conception of lesbian is not limited to the texts I explore, I focus in particular on an angry, kinky mostly francophone lesbian feminist tradition that has not been taken up by the primarily Anglo-American practioners of academic queer feminism. Remembering my Irigarayan point, developed in chapter 1, about a forgetting of sexual difference that has itself been forgotten, the essays in this latter part of *Are the Lips a Grave?* explore the stakes of a forgotten lesbian jouissance whose forgetting, like sexual difference, is itself forgotten. In this chapter, "One-Handed Reading," I focus specifically on Violette Leduc's *The Bastard* (1964) in order to re-engage the problem of "difference" as it relates to lesbian sexuality and sexual pleasure as jouissance. In doing so, I rethink the ethical problem of the other through the narrative performance of a lesbian erotic ethics.

Masturbating Dykes

In *The Indelible Alison Bechdel*, the creator of the popular comic strip *Dykes to Watch Out For* gives her readers a rare glimpse of the "real life" behind her fictional lesbian world by recounting her own coming out story. Having acknowledged but not yet acted upon her newly discovered lesbian desire, Bechdel narrates the climactic moment of the homoerotic journey through which the self-as-dyke is produced. Significantly, this climax is depicted as a moment of reading.

Indeed, Alison has already devoured *Desert of the Heart, Rubyfruit Jungle, The Well of Loneliness*, and Joyce's *Ulysses* by the time we meet her in the first frame of the sequence. Having discarded Joyce, Alison embarks on another kind of adventure: "My full academic passion was reserved for a *different* odyssey . . . the quest for my *people*." This sapphic journey of self-discovery occurs not across the sun-dappled seascape of some Homeric voyage, but rather among the rumpled sheets and billowing pages of Alison's own book-strewn bed. Her quest is both erotic and epistemological: "an insatiable hunger" for a "knowledge" that is at once literary, corporeal, and female. By the third frame this quest appears to

FIGURE 5.1   Alison Bechdel, *Dykes to Watch Out For*

have reached its fulfillment: we find Alison, still in bed, fully engaged in that practice of "one-handed reading" which Bechdel, less delicately, calls "whacking off."

The tone, message, and audience of Bechdel's story appear to be worlds away from the theoretical preoccupations of this book thus far, as it does from the high-culture heroines I will treat in this chapter: Hélène Cixous, Luce Irigaray, and Violette Leduc. But I use Bechdel here to focus on a queer feminism that stands outside established academic feminism and queer theory as they have been institutionalized since the 1980s. In this section I make a case for the ongoing importance of lesbian feminist, literary, and cinematic rewritings of sexuality for ethical debates about sex. In that context Bechdel's masturbation story brilliantly serves up, pop culture–style, some of the central preoccupations of the antifoundationalist academic feminist theory so deeply influenced by what problematically used to be called French feminism.[1] More specifically, within the nexus of issues narrated by Bechdel's comic strip, the links between autoeroticism, knowledge, and relationality can be explored more fully in terms that resonate with feminist and queer theory's concerns about gender, sexuality, and subjectivity. Put somewhat differently, Bechdel helps us to think about queer feminist subjectivity by figuring it visually as the one-handed reading of a masturbating dyke.

In what might be seen as an emerging genealogy of literary lesbian masturbators, Hélène Cixous exemplifies the 1970s theoretical terms through which masturbation, sexuality, and writing are yoked together to produce a celebratory concept of female difference. In her 1975 feminist manifesto, "The Laugh of the Medusa," Cixous famously defines the now much derided concept of *écriture féminine* as a masturbatory activity. Writing, she proclaims, is nothing less than "a systematic experimentation of the bodily functions . . . [a] practice, extraordinarily rich and inventive, *in particular as concerns masturbation*, [that] is prolonged or accompanied by a production of *forms*."[2] She goes on to contrast this coming age of gynocentric invention with the prefeminist days when women didn't write at all or, if they did, only in conditions of deep secrecy and shame: "you've written a little, but in secret . . . as when we would masturbate in secret, not to go further, but to attenuate the tension a bit, just enough to take the edge off."[3] In Cixous's opening evocations of female self-stimulation, then, masturbation marks both the frustration of uninspired, purely mechanical acts of sexual release and, at the same time, the latent promise of the potentially transformative, orgasmic production of ever new forms.

Indeed, in the ecstatic, breathless pages that follow, Cixous seems to make good on the transformative promise: "The Laugh of the Medusa" virtually explodes into an orgasm of deliciously erotic abandon, the female text as body emerging into a volcanic eruption of a jouissance worthy of Bersani's anal-erotic queer self-shattering.[4]

Moving behind Cixous to an earlier time, this chapter explores masturbatory jouissance in the work of Violette Leduc in order to ask about an always already queer feminist antifoundationalism that has been occluded with the rise of queer theory out of feminism. I begin with Cixous in order to distinguish between the masculine psychoanalytic tradition out of which queer jouissance is born and the almost illegible queer jouissance we find in Leduc's masturbatory writing. Cixous is helpful in the distinction she makes between feminine and masculine economies of masturbation as metaphors for writing. In what she calls the "classic" masculine economy of phallic sameness, "the act of writing is the equivalent to masculine masturbation"; further, she adds, "the woman who writes cuts herself out a paper penis."[5] This masculine economy of masturbation is not necessarily attached to men: its conception of masculine and feminine is nonidentitarian. As Cixous suggests in her description of the flimsy penis that "the woman who writes" cuts out for herself like a paper doll, both women and men participate in masculine forms of whacking off. Even more pointedly, in the Freudian economy of representation, masculine creative production often dons the disguise of female masturbation; in other words, men who whack off end up looking like masturbating women. As Roland Barthes reminds us in *S/Z*, written just five years before Cixous's manifesto, the paper penis as text is also a "braid": "text, fabric, braid" ("texte, tissu, et tresse"), Barthes writes, "are the same thing."[6] For Barthes, the illusion of the singular voice of poetic expression represses the complex workings of "*écriture*" or writing, which can only be released through the transformative powers of the hand: "the hand intervenes to gather and intertwine the inert threads."[7] This image of writerliness as the manual manipulation of threads, or weaving, thus achieves its force, paradoxically, by appropriating as its own the female work of weaving through which the text as *tresse* is created. As Barthes puts it: "We know the symbolism of the braid: Freud, considering the origin of weaving, saw it as the labor of a woman braiding her pubic hairs to form the penis she lacks."[8]

To be sure, this image of female weaving as creative production is hardly new, any more than the gesture through which the masculine

artist appropriates weaving as a symbol of his own artistry. The mytholog-
ical and literary examples of this topos of artist as weaver range from the
stories of Arachne, Philomela, Ariadne, and Penelope to the thirteenth-
century *chansons de toile* to Paul Valéry's "La Fileuse."[9] No one articulates
the stakes of masculinity in this braided logic of representation more
baldly than Lacan, who, as a faithful reader of Freud, weaves his own story
of the phallus as signifier by invoking the familiar notion of femininity as
masquerade. Readers may recall this particularly knotted Lacanian story:
if the text can never be anchored in the illusion of the presence of the thing
itself, as Lacan would have it, that means the penis is always a phallus,
and the phallus is always missing. But because sexual difference derives
from the internal divisions of language through which the illusion of the
phallus marks the other as lack, woman must stand in that place of lack.
Thus she is always the Barthesian masturbating weaver, endlessly creating what will never be there. However, her female difference is just the
mask, the veil, the weaving, or disguise that hides her status as nothing
more than the lack that is man's desire. Remember, Lacan defines desire
as the result of the subtraction of satisfaction from need; thus woman as
the figure for man's desire is no more than the place of infinite loss that
erases her, the empty result of man's libidinal operations of subtraction.[10]
This concept of desire allows Lacan, at the end of "The Signification of
the Phallus," to imply that femininity as masquerade upholds meaning
itself; desire as lack takes "refuge" in this "mask" of femininity. The result
is that representation—a universalizing phallic erection of truth—makes
its appearance through the veil of femininity: "in the human being, virile
display itself appears as feminine."[11]

Most important here is the point Lacan makes about the relationship
between masturbation, visibility, and gender: visibility itself, what Lacan
calls "virile display," appears as feminine. This can be explained further
through the linking of visibility to the notion of writing, the text as *tresse*
or braid that comes into appearance through masturbatory reading. To
use Barthes's image: the multivocality of an *écriture* whose artistic mer-
its are revealed through an invocation of femininity—"woman braiding
her pubic hair"—masks the operations of a phallic desire whose subject
is always masculine. In other words, masturbation serves to reveal writ-
erly jouissance as masculine in the structural, nonidentitarian sense of
the term.

So the question becomes: how do queer lesbians masturbate (write)
differently? Let me leave Barthes, Lacan, and Cixous for a moment in or-

der to briefly consider one other theoretical model before returning to my reading of Leduc. In her famous reading of Freud's lectures on femininity in *Speculum of the Other Woman*, Luce Irigaray insists on the impossibility of female masturbation within the Freudian psychoanalytic model.[12] In her deconstruction of Freud, Irigaray focuses on the role of the clitoris for female self-stimulation. Of course, Irigaray hastens to add, it is hard to understand why we should limit ourselves to the clitoris alone, just as it is equally hard to accept Freud's insistence that the clitoris be "given up" in favor of the vagina precisely at the moment femininity is "formed." Clitoris and vagina can never be substituted one for the other, Irigaray insists, and both play a role in woman's jouissance. In other words, since for Freud the clitoris is the inadequate copy of its stately masculine model, any pleasure a girl might derive from clitoral masturbation alone can only be conceived, in Irigaray's view, as a masculine pleasure.

Irigaray also insists in *Speculum* on Freud's construction of female homosexuality as arrested development in the clitoral, phallic phase. While "normal," fully realized women go on to accept the vagina alone as the site of a pleasure that, in fact, was never theirs to begin with, for Freud lesbians remain stuck in the masculine phase. Thus, as Irigaray puts it, just as female masturbation is impossible, so too is female homosexuality, except as "hommo-sexuality, with the double *m* of *l'homme*, or man, where the female masturbator, like the lesbian, is no more than an inadequate copy of the real thing: a little penis, a little man. As I argued in chapter 1, Irigaray's concept of *hommosexuality* is not homophobic, as some have charged. Rather, it reveals an antifoundationalist critique of homosocial bonding that allies her with antimasculinist self-shattering projects like Bersani's. And yet, just as Freud freezes women in his reading of masturbation as the construction of a penis, so too queer theorists freeze Irigaray's antifoundationalism, recasting her jouissance as cultural feminist essentialism (and therefore an inverted phallic tumescence).

This brings me to a crucial anatomical point with surprisingly far-reaching theoretical implications. Although many feminists—from Anne Koedt in "The Myth of the Vaginal Orgasm"[13] to Naomi Schor in *Breaking the Chain*[14] to Elizabeth Lloyd in *The Case of the Female Orgasm*[15]—have wanted to reclaim the clitoris as the privileged site of female pleasure and thus the specificity of female difference, Irigaray insists, as we saw earlier, that the clitoris and the vagina are inseparable. In other words, as she makes clear in her famous essay about female masturbation and lesbian desire, "When Our Lips Speak Together," the concept of difference is more appropriately figured as *lips*.[16] Again, as I argued in chapter 1, it is possible to read the Irigarayan lips as the heterotopian figures for the new forms of relation of an erotic ethics.

Irigaray's insistent question in the lips essay—"How can I say it?"—can thus be read as another form of my earlier question: How can we masturbate (or write) differently? The answer to that question has no clear form as a cultural product or thing to be named, but rather lies in the relation I call reading. Irigaray describes difference as an ongoing process of connection and rupture. As I argued in chapter 1, the Irigarayan lips are not a form at all; rather, they narratively perform both self- and other-oriented forms of lovemaking in the infinite and funny combinations of mouth to mouth, mouth to labia, labia to mouth, labia to labia, inner labia to outer labia, outer labia to mouth, outer to outer, inner to inner, outer to inner, to mouth, to labia. . . . Irigaray's lips are not a noun—what she calls the "dead skins" of the postcoital phallus—but rather a series of verbs, where the lips open and close, become red, "pinks, browns, blonds, greens, blues . . . luminous"[17] then red again: "They're stirring, moving, they want to speak."[18] As "Luce" herself puts it in act 3 of "*Luce et veritas*": "How can we say it? I know, you're talking about love . . . funny, lesbian, outrageous love. An ethics of lips, making love.[19]

Luce's insistence here on "an ethics of lips, making love" dramatizes the radical potential of Irigaray's lips as a model of subjectivity and reading that is both nonutopian and productive of an ethics of difference. Irigaray uses the two lips to theorize and perform a relational model of subjectivity that refuses the closure of truth, allowing the irreducible difference of alterity to emerge. It is that attention to alterity and the emergence of difference that characterizes the antifoundationalism so often attributed to a postfeminist, queer philosophical position. As I showed in chapter 1, Irigaray's antifoundationalist destabilization of epistemic certainty both echoes and predates the emergence of queer theory.

Leduc's Erotic Ethics

This chapter explores how, in literary writing, we encounter a queer feminist antifoundationalism that echoes and predates Irigaray herself. That writing is the work of Violette Leduc. No one, to my mind, dramatizes the attention to the erotic undoing of the subject and the emergence of alterity better than Leduc in her 1964 autobiographical novel, *La*

Bâtarde. As Elizabeth Locey explains, "Leduc played an important role in removing erotic literature, and particularly erotica written by women, from the obscurity in which it had lurked for so long."[20] I want to examine this little-read, sometimes ridiculed, bastard writing to analyze how one female literary masturbator—Violette Leduc—symbolically redeploys the conventions of authorship to inscribe herself as the lovemaking lesbian writer of difference hinted at in Irigaray's theory.[21]

If we imagined, for a moment, a twentieth-century lesbian trajectory that would link Colette's Gomorrheans to Violette Leduc's bastard to Alison Bechdel's present-day dyke, we could link lesbianism and masturbation through the autobiographical act itself. In this model, to write the self as lesbian would be, by definition, a self-reflective and therefore masturbatory process. To say "I am a lesbian" would be to masturbate. Insisting on the queerness of this lesbian writing, we could add to this corpus Eve Kosofsky Sedgwick's autobiographical comments at the beginning of her "Jane Austen and the Masturbating Girl." In that essay Sedgwick implicitly says "I am queer" by recounting the story of her battle against her right-wing enemies in the culture wars. This battle elevated Sedgwick's title—which Roger Kimball had gleefully plucked from the pages of an MLA convention program—to the status of an icon of the "mental masturbation" of those postmodern, "PC" intellectuals who, for Kimball and others, epitomized the degeneracy of academic discourse in the humanities in the 1990s. In this right-wing narrative, sexuality and autobiography converge to produce the horrific figure of the *still* illegitimate female intellectual—revealed to be nothing more than a masturbating girl.

I'm not going to describe all the ways in which similar forms of self-disclosure on the part of speaking subjects who occupy more solidly hegemonic positions—stories about one's wife and kids, for example—are resolutely *not* marked as masturbatory. Rather, I want to follow Sedgwick's example in the case of Jane Austen and reclaim masturbation as an activity of which we can be proud. To be sure, when compared to the European and Anglo-American medical practice of clitoridectomy, which violently policed the masturbatory impulses of our nineteenth-century "hysterical" sisters, modern attitudes toward masturbation seem relatively benign.[22] However, as Sedgwick points out, our modern views tend to place masturbation "in the framework of optimistic, hygienic narratives of all-too-normative individual development" (109), thus leaving it untapped as a potentially disruptive practice. And although Foucault warns us about the positivist underpinnings of our modern obsession

with masturbation, this does not mean we can simply ignore it for its potentially strategic redeployments.[23] Extending Sedgwick, who sees in masturbation "a reservoir of potentially *utopian* metaphors and energies for
independence, *self-possession*, and a rapture that may owe relatively little
to political or interpersonal abjection" (111), I want to pursue the possibilities of one-handed readings as ways into the *heterotopian, desubjectivating*
spaces imagined by Foucault.

Violette Leduc's autobiography functions, for me, as one such reservoir for metaphors of one-handed readings. In an early scene that begins, like Bechdel's comic strip masturbation story, with a description of
reading, Leduc opens her notebook to a passage about a woman on her
wedding night: "she was comparing the sexual organ of a man to an eel
inside a woman."[24] Violette cannot understand this seemingly horrific initiation into heterosexual intercourse except as an image of monstrosity: "I
couldn't imagine it at all, or I imagined it too well. I could see the eels on
the fishmongers' stall; I envisaged the serpentine virility beneath the trou-
sers, writhing down from the navel to the ankle. My fist tapped against
my temple, and every time I whispered: it's impossible, the cover of the
notebook replied: it is possible" (LBE 22–23, translation modified; LBF 37).

This terrifying plunge of reading into the imaginary of heterosexual
intercourse is immediately followed by a masturbation scene that, extending across alternating moments of bedtime reading and sleep, serves to
restabilize Violette's fragile sense of self: "Often I walked my fingers down
under the bedclothes and stroked them up and down between my lips;
later on I often twisted the hair around them with one finger as I lay in
bed, reading, before going to sleep. I continued to do so without climax-
ing until the age of eighteen. It was a pastime, a verification. I breathed
in my fingers, breathed in this extract of my being to which I attached no
value" (LBE 23, translation modified; LBF 37)[25]

Less an image of Sedgwick's "utopian metaphors and energies for
independence, self-possession, and rapture," Leduc's narrative corresponds more in tone to Alison Bechdel's image of a repetitive, mechanical "whacking off" that, for Violette, ends not in utopia or even orgasm,
but rather reshapes the self as "an extract" of herself. Although Violette's
jouissance is not a false semblance of orgasm, Leduc's nonorgasmic experience shares some of the features Annamarie Jagose associates with
"fake orgasm" as a "counterdisciplinary practice."[26] Like fake orgasm, Violette's experience "gives rise to an internal alterity that . . . functions as
a breach in the usual fiction of self-continuity."[27] Immediately after this

episode, Violette discovers the pleasures offered "down there" through the clumsy fondling of an adolescent boy: "His hand moved lightly up inside my skirt. Aimé Patureau was raking his fingernails against my skin with the grace of a page" (LBE 23, translation modified; LBF 37).[28] Violette summarizes her masturbatory experience as one of subjective expansion: "The stroking fingers helped me grow up" (LBE 23; LBF 37).[29] In yet another episode of manual manipulation, the roles are reversed with an older neighbor named Estelle: "She took my hand, she guided it over the dry hair that felt like brittle hay, she forced my fingers inside the folds of her flesh" (LBE 25; LBF 39).

So what are we to make of this strange, rather troubling series of events that some might view as examples of interpersonal abjection? How can we read them in relation to the masturbatory ethics of love hinted at by Irigaray? I propose reading these scenes as part of a journey—a "finger-walk"—that, like Alison Bechdel's "different odyssey," is as much about a desubjectivating practice of freedom in relation to others as it is about the discovery of sexual pleasure. While Violette's travels begin with her own fingers between her own lips, the scenes that follow describe an alternation where the masturbatory hand shuttles back and forth between the self and the other. We might think of these scenes about the awkward, inadequate pleasures of youth as allegories of the process of learning to read, where the masturbating hand that ontologically inscribes and decomposes the self into an "extract"—"a verification . . . an extract of my being"—becomes the writing hand that reaches out toward the other in order to read and be read.

From this perspective, it becomes possible to interpret Violette's later, more mature foray into the realm of sexual pleasure—specifically the love-making scenes at the boarding school with Isabelle—as a story that also allegorizes the dream of an ideal reading. Unlike the previous episodes with Aimé and Estelle, Violette's passionate connection with a body that mirrors her own frees her to simultaneously affirm her own subjectivity and, at the same time, allow the subjectivity of the other in her difference to emerge: "The caress is to a shudder what twilight is to a lightning flash. Isabelle was dragging a rake of light from my shoulder to my wrist; she passed with her five-fingered mirror over my throat, over the back of my neck, over my back. I followed the hand, I could see under my eyelids a neck, a shoulder, an arm that didn't belong to me" (LBE 74; LBF 84).[30]

Brought into being through the reflective caress of the hand that promises an eventual frisson of luminous bliss, Violette's body crosses and recrosses the temporal, crepuscular border whose anticipations of pleasure illuminate the mirror in which the lines and shapes of Isabelle's body both repeat and disrupt Violette's form; across the twilit border of the mutual caress, the reflective bodies of Violette and Isabelle become, at one and the same time, both the body of the self and the body of the other.

In this and subsequent lovemaking scenes, Leduc metaphorizes a process of writing where the caressing hand traces shapes and meanings across the multiple, overlapping surfaces of self and other that undo the subject-object relation in which they are epistemically and ontologically bound. Most important, this movement of writing can only take place as the interpretive movement across textual borders that we call the practice of reading. It is only here, through the hand of the other, that the self is released into the desubjectivating ethical space of the coextensive subject: "The hand moved up again: it was drawing circles, overflowing into the void, spreading its sweet ripples ever wider around my left shoulder, while the other lay abandoned to the darkness streaked by the breathing of the other girls. I was discovering the smoothness of my bones, the glow hidden in my flesh, the infinity of forms I possessed" (LBE 83; LBF 92).[31]

Significantly, this self-undoing comes about through a relational corporeal experience. Lack is reinscribed as circles repeat circles to delineate a play between absence and presence that is never resolved, but, rather, continues to unfold in the asymmetrical movement of a shoulder abandoned to a collective breathing. This complex movement between self and other, absence and presence, establishes a correspondence between the symbolic process of making and unmaking meaning and the corporeal acts of making love. It is only in the relational acts of crossing—between self and other, absence and presence, meaning making and making love—that the relational queer experience of a desubjectivating reading can be said to occur.

In this view, Leduc's bastard novel both stages and enacts the theoretical operations through which eroticism, knowledge, and ethical transformation as *relational* processes are linked. Through that transformation, the proverbial act of one-handed reading proliferates into a multiplicity of hands and meanings; in that sense the figure of the masturbating dyke is never singular but participates in a relational ethics of self-transformation as a practice of freedom. Indeed, self-and-other forms of lovemaking go hand in hand, so to speak, in their figuration of a relational model of writing and reading that, like Irigaray's lips—mouth to mouth, mouth to labia, labia to labia—allows the self-undoing alterity of difference to emerge. In staging that process as a scene where the ideal lover, Isabelle, is also the ideal reader, Leduc narratively performs the paradoxical moment of simultaneous connection and rupture where the genital illusion of woman's lack—and of being itself—is rewritten. Both Leduc and Irigaray's writings about female reading as female pleasure point, therefore, not to the frozen utopian forms of Cixous's reversals, but rather to the heterotopian possibilities of difference *within* sameness. In the continual movements of writing and reading, rewriting and rereading, circle with circle and lips with lips, this textual practice of masturbation inscribes alterity at the heart of a queer feminist erotic ethics.

Ultimately, this narrative about "female" masturbation also moves us away from seemingly endless feminist debates about female subjectivity as positionality or agency that appear to have little connection with queer theoretical concerns. Indeed, the question of agency in particular has plagued feminist theorists at least since *The Second Sex* (1949), where Leduc's mentor and friend, Simone de Beauvoir, inscribed women's agency within a Sartrean understanding of subjectivity, but also, in eroticism, began to challenge it as well.[32] Interestingly, while Beauvoir's phenomenological model of subjectivity cannot quite let go of conceptions of the subject as substantival and endowed with consciousness, her pages on the mutuality of the erotic experience in the later chapters of *The Second Sex* begin to undo the common claim that Beauvoir simply valorizes transcendence over immanence. In "Sexual Initiation," for example, Beauvoir writes: "The erotic experience is one that most poignantly reveals to human beings their ambiguous condition; they experience it as flesh and as spirit, as the other and as subject."[33] Leduc exploits this ambiguity to further destabilize erotic subjectivity in her narrative rendering of an abject but ultimately transformative corporality. We find Leduc, over a decade before Irigaray's important formulations, rewriting relationality and the process of othering. I read this rewriting as an important articulation of a queer feminist ethics of eros. In this sense Leduc reconfigures the existentialist, humanist models of subjectivity with which Beauvoir is struggling: she juxtaposes, without resolving, the philosophical reductions through which selves acquire meaning in their transcendence with the self-undoing practices of bodies in their immanence. This is, as Debra Bergoffen argues, Beauvoir's erotic ethics.[34] So too Leduc, in her masturbatory writing, suggests that meaning making is not just an individual philosophical operation but also a reciprocal process: a kind of "making love" in which subject and other are transformed.

I know: it's hard to think about love, much less talk about it in public, because it seems impossible to escape its schmaltzified, narcissistic, possessive structures. But a different genealogy of a masturbatory queer dyke-love seems a good place to start to ask the key questions—about mutuality, reciprocity, and respect for difference—that would weave together a new ethics of love.

6 Queer Lesbian Silence
Colette Reads Proust

In considering how to situate the topic of this chapter—"Queer Lesbian Silence"—I keep thinking back to a poster I used to have hanging on my office door, year after year, to commemorate LGBT people with a "Day of Silence." The poster encouraged us to promote awareness of the silence imposed on lesbian, gay, bisexual, and transgender people by refusing to speak for an entire day. "Why do you use silence to end silence?" the poster asked. It went on to deplore the silencing that homophobia and heterosexism create in our society, arguing for the increased voice and visibility of queers.

Along similar lines, Adrienne Rich reminds us in her poem, "Cartographies of Silence," about the lives lost in the carefully constructed silences of history:

Silence can be a plan
rigorously executed

the blueprint to a life

It is a presence
it has a history a form

Do not confuse it
with any kind of absence.[1]

I begin this chapter with an invocation of silence as a way of signaling the paradox of queer lesbianism simultaneously made legible and
marginalized by a speech-inciting sexual *dispositif:* mediatized versions of
lesbianism notwithstanding (think Ellen DeGeneres or lesbian chic), to
speak about lesbianism is to speak about silence. Indeed, it could be that
the most faithful tribute to lesbian existence would be not to redeploy a
machinery of cultural representation that never seems to get it right but,
rather, as the poster suggests, to use silence to end silence. And yet, even
our symbolic moments of silence usually feel "not quite right." My feelings about a "Day of Silence" were always vexed, and I think they pointed
to that quality of "not quite rightness" that is a hallmark of representation
itself and includes silence as representation. As Rich so eloquently puts
it: Silence "is a presence / It has a history a form," yet cannot be fully
rendered.

That said, it's also important to remember that speech and silence do
not exist in a vacuum, but rather as the temporally shifting effects of a
process of reading in time. In the context of this book, I engage lesbian
silence in a queer feminist, postidentitarian landscape that no longer
quite knows what to do with this word *lesbian,* whose complementary
relation to its brother term, *gay,* reveals the asymmetrical logic of gender
identified by Beauvoir, where *gay* occupies the position of both the positive and the neutral.[2] Following Beauvoir's logic, lesbian "is the negative,
to such a point that any determination is imputed to her as a limitation,
without reciprocity."[3] Refracted through the lens of different readers in
different times, pursuing this asymmetrical figure of negativity is more
than a project of reclamation—more than a geological excavation where
falsity is replaced with truth and silence is replaced with the voice of
identity and the restoration of an agency whose source is Lesbos, Sap-
pho, or even the separatist movements of the 1970s. Rather, I conceive
of this project of engaging the queer lesbian in the context of silence as a
process that brings into view the complex, diachronic, permutating dance
between text and interpreter that I've called reading. It is within such a
frame that this chapter stages a scene of reading: the lesbian reading the
lesbian in Proust.

I've positioned Colette in this chapter as a lesbian reader, for reasons
that I hope will become clear. Both during Colette's lifetime and today,

over fifty years after her death, readers of Colette have been fascinated by the spectacle of her seemingly limitless libidinal proclivities, the vision of a polymorphous sexuality whose range included, at the very least, heterosexual, same-sex, and intergenerational desire. I put it this way because, as Elisabeth Ladenson points out in an important essay on lesbianism in Colette, the complex construction of subjectivity in her work does not allow us to simply "out" her, either as an "authentic" lesbian or as the "real" author behind the textual "I."[4] Rather, she sits on the border of the categories themselves—man and woman, straight and lesbian, character and author—refusing any reductive equivalence that would consign her to one camp or the other: queer. Colette describes her position as reader in her most elusive but important book about sexuality, *The Pure and the Impure*, situating herself in "the place of a spectator . . . one of those choice seats that allow the spectator, when excited, to rush out on the stage and, duly staggering, join the actors."[5] As Ladenson quite aptly puts it: "Colette's seat is ringside . . . at once inside and outside the fray."[6] Both as a subject of speech and a subject of desire, then, Colette quite explicitly positions herself within the "between" space of the border.

It is this "not quite in/not quite out" position that makes Colette, in my view, an ideal queer reader of lesbianism in Proust. When I call Colette a queer reader of Proust, I am not only referring to her famous remarks about Sodom and Gomorrah in *The Pure and the Impure*, analyzed in chapter 2, where Colette contrasts the dazzling truth of Sodom with its apocryphal copy, Gomorrah. In invoking Colette as a reader of Proust, I mean to also invoke her *position* as a reader, using her as a model of relationality that opens up new ways of engaging Proust's text and his place in queer theory.[7] Just as the desire to "out" Colette in some simple way is continually thwarted, so too the desire to "find" the truth about sexuality in Proust's text is ultimately misguided. And yet, as Sedgwick points out in *Epistemology of the Closet*, it is precisely the thwarting that makes Proust such a perfect figure for a modern Western epistemology which frames knowledge and ignorance as sexual.

More specifically, there's more to the figure of the lesbian in Proust than the typical psychobiographical "transposition" theory would suggest, where the most important lesbian character, Albertine, has been repeatedly read as a fictional stand-in for the real-life object of Proust's desire, Alfred Agostinelli. While the transposition theory suggests that Albertine, along with the other *jeunes filles en fleurs* are, as Ladenson puts it in *Proust's Lesbianism*, "male characters in textual drag . . . a series of hairy thugs in sundresses,"[8] Colette's readerly position suggests something more complex than a theory that amounts to transphobic slapstick. Questions about historical accuracy or authenticity—Was Proust really gay? Is Albertine "really" Agostinelli? Does Albertine look like a real lesbian to you?—are, for Colette, beside the point. Unlike some critics, I argue here that when Colette points to Proust's depiction of "Gomorrah" as "apocryphal" and says, "there is no Gomorrah," she is not making a judgment about authenticity, a textual faithfulness to some authentically lesbian extratextual referent. Rather, Colette's comments on Sodom and Gomorrah model a kind of reading where the figure of lesbianism functions as a cipher for the multiple gaps, displacements, and silences at work in Proust's text and, by extension, in queer theory. Particularly important is the fact that these comments occur in a work, The Pure and the Impure, that explicitly links aesthetics with ethics by thematizing the relationship between pleasure and morality, what she calls in La Jumelle noire [The Black Twin] "the edge of the precipice where human morality crumbles, lightly touches the fragile limit that separates the pure and the impure."[9]

Having introduced Colette as a reader of "lesbianism" in Proust, I want to contrast her here with another famous reader in order to flesh out my thinking about the broader ethical and aesthetic issues signaled by that lesbian absent presence. In his 1947 article on ethics in Proust, "The Other in Proust," Emmanuel Levinas, like a number of Proust critics, focuses on Albertine as the quintessential "other" in Proust's novel.[10] Levinas argues that the absolute alterity of the other in Proust allows for the emergence of the complex interior life that is so widely celebrated as uniquely Proustian. For Levinas, it is precisely the unsolvable mystery of the other that allows for the articulation of the self's internal alterity, the "I"'s infinite otherness to himself. Problematically, Levinas dismisses any specifically ethical parameters for thinking about the question of the other in Proust. Without much explanation, he simultaneously asserts and excuses Proust's "amoralism" in the name of magic, thus trumping ethics with aesthetics: "magic begins," Levinas writes, "like a witches' Sabbath, where ethics leaves off."[11]

Behind this dismissal of ethics in Proust, one might dimly perceive a Levinas who betrays a discomfort with the particular kinds of alterity we find in this queer novel. Obliquely justifying his position, Levinas alludes to the permutations of Proust's characters over the course of the Recherche, transformations that he calls "highly unlikely," but which somehow "feel completely natural in a world that has reverted to Sodom and Gomorrah."[12] Levinas's insistence on unlikely things feeling natural signals, indirectly, the cultural consignment of Sodomitic and Gomorrahesque relations into that "utterly confused category" of unnatural acts.[13] Given their "against nature" status, for Levinas Sodom and Gomorrah can only be perceived as natural through a lens that brackets the realm of "moral rules." In other words, the sexual alterity marked by the "amorality"[14] of Sodom and Gomorrah can only work for Levinas if it is evacuated, "giddily" (162), from the realm of the ethical into an aesthetic dimension. The "glittering extravaganzas" (162) of Proust's "fairies" have no place within the realm of "the moral rules" that proclaim "Proust's amorality" (162). Having dismissed ethics as irrelevant to Proust, Levinas can then reclaim and interiorize this troubling "amoral" alterity as a fantastic, miraculous otherness within the self: "Everything takes place as if the self were constantly doubled by another self," Levinas asserts, concluding that "the mystery in Proust is the mystery of the other" (163). And that mysterious other is no other than the poetic self.

Levinas's bracketing of ethics in his reflections on the Proustian other is all the more troubling given the specifically social claims of his essay. He describes Proust as a "sociologist" (161), claiming him as "the poet of social reality" (163). And yet what are we to make of this poetry of the social when the social can no longer be considered in ethical terms, in relation to the frame of "moral rules"? What is the status of this sociality without ethics, a sociality that is purely aesthetic? If Levinas justifies this "amoral" universe in the name of the beautiful and mystical realm of magic, what is at stake in that gesture? Might we read Albertine as a figure who, in her ungraspable otherness, constitutes a warning to those who would obliterate difference and thereby dismiss ethics in the name of aesthetics? Further, might there be something to say beyond the usual clichés about Albertine as mystery, Albertine as nothingness, Albertine as absent presence, Albertine as empty figure for the absolute alterity of the other? In posing these questions, I want to point not only to the limits of Levinas's particular reading of Proust but, more important, to a more widespread critical refusal to see difference as singular, a difference that is not effaced into a general category of otherness. And if there is something to be said beyond the clichés about Albertine's opacity, perhaps one path lies in looking at her specificity as a lesbian or, in Proust's terms, a Gomorrhean other, rather than reading her either as Agostinelli in textual drag or, in the case of Levinas, as a manifestation of the inner life of heterosexual Man, what he celebrates as "the way inner life looms forth from an insatiable curiosity about the alterity of the Other that is both empty and inexhaustible" (163).

How to describe the event of that lesbian singularity? Again, we might take our clue from Colette who, inadvertently perhaps, politicizes Proust's gendered rendering of the Sodom and Gomorrah opposition. When Colette declares Gomorrah to be nonexistent, she makes her assessment in relation to the constructed existence of Sodom. Let's read one passage, then, in Proust's rendering of Sodom, through the "reading glasses" provided by Colette. In many ways, Colette's chapter on male homosexuality in Proust can be read as an extended commentary on the following passage from the *Recherche*:

> All the shameless Sodomites were allowed to escape, even if, on catching sight of a boy, they turned their heads like Lot's wife, though without being on that account changed like her into a pillar of salt. With the result that they engendered a numerous progeny with whom this gesture has remained habitual. . . . These descendants of the Sodomites, so numerous that we may apply to them that other verse of Genesis: "If a man can number the dust of the earth, then shall thy seed also be numbered," have established themselves throughout the entire world; they have had access to every profession and are so readily admitted into the most exclusive clubs that, whenever a Sodomite fails to secure election, the black balls are for the most part cast by other Sodomites, who make a point in condemning sodomy, having inherited the mendacity that enabled their ancestors to escape from the accursed city.[15]

It is important to note here that while the Bible justifies God's destruction of the cities by emphasizing the wickedness of the inhabitants, the Proust passage I just cited rewrites the Bible's justification of a heterosexual, procreative, and in fact incestuous logic by appropriating a verse referring to Lot and his descendants (Genesis 13:16) and applying it to the Sodomites' ubiquitous presence in the most exclusive and privileged circles of society.[16] I can't help but read this as a cynical, somewhat twisted harbinger of a queer slogan made popular in the 1990s: "We are everywhere." In addition, Proust emphasizes the mendacity and deception that characterizes the Sodomites' ability to survive. It is only through hypocrisy and the betrayal of their own people that the Sodomites both escaped from the biblical city and continue today to enjoy the privileges of economic security and social inclusion.

Colette, on the other hand, transforms Proust's image of slanderous, hypocritical, lying Sodomites into a phallic pillar of truth: "intact, enormous, eternal." The Gomorrheans, by contrast, become "puny counterfeits" or, in another passage, "preoccupied with men, their bitter and apocryphal detractors."[17] By explicitly inscribing the Sodom/Gomorrah opposition in terms of truth and its apocryphal copies, Colette politicizes Proust's aesthetic rendering of the gendered pair. Colette's rewriting reveals the asymmetry of an apparently symmetrical opposition between Sodom and Gomorrah, wicked men and wicked women, what some today might call gay men and lesbians. And that asymmetry has to do, again, as Beauvoir pointed out, with a differential system of power that constructs the existence of the one through the eradication of the other. And while Eve Kosofsky Sedgwick sees this clearly enough in her subtle reading of Albertine in *Epistemology of the Closet*, this logic of exclusion that Levinas fails to address is the same logic that makes Albertine illegible to queer theory. As Sedgwick puts it in *Epistemology of the Closet*, despite the fact that "within or around Albertine there are erotic possibilities that mark a potentially regenerative *difference from* the spectacularized [male homosexual] plot," Albertine remains unheard, unread, a moment of forgetting that is itself forgotten: "the chalky rag of gender pulled across the blackboard of sexuality, the chalky rag of sexuality across the blackboard of gender."[18] And, in the context I've sketched out, this "cloudy space from which a hidden voice can be heard to insist" delineates the site of an ethical failure as well.[19] In the terms I sketched out in chapter 2, this failure happens as a failure to read *an inscriptional relation to another*. So while Proust cries out: "We (read, men) are everywhere," Colette points out, in Irigarayan fashion, that there is no sexual difference here. As she puts it quite bluntly: "there is no Gomorrah."

If Albertine and the "vice" she represents remain opaque, nowhere is this more true than in the volume that literally contains her lesbianism—*The Captive*—which, with the exception of Sedgwick's pages in *Epistemology of the Closet* and Elisabeth Ladenson's *Proust's Lesbianism*, also remains among the least commented pages of Proust's corpus. This is not a question of bringing light to the dark or of making transparent an otherwise opaque lesbianism. Rather, it is a question of reading Albertine "against the grain," through a Colette-like border vision. I agree with Sedgwick and Ladenson that one of the things that makes Albertine so appealing to Marcel is precisely her inaccessibility, her status as an *être de fuite* whose desire is always elsewhere. That said, I want to briefly look at the one part of the novel where Albertine is "pinned down," so to speak. Albertine's captivity in *The Captive*, we may recall, is the result of the narrator's anguish after the discovery, in *Sodom and Gomorrah*, of her earlier association with Mlle. Vinteuil. That association harks back to the famous scene of voyeurism at Montjouvain in *Swann's Way*, where Vinteuil's daughter theatrically acts out her lesbian proclivities while profaning her dead father's memory as the young narrator looks on through the window. As Sedgwick points out, this scene and other important scenes of voyeurism in the novel point to the Proustian linking of visual perception with truth. And while vision is for the Proustian narrator, as well as all of Western philosophy, the primary mode for apprehending the truth, we also know that ultimately the novel is about epistemological failure: the errors of vision, the gaps in recognition, the inability to understand through the workings of the gaze. To put this more specifically in ethical terms: while seeing is the primary mode of reading social signs, when it comes to exploring the depths of the other, seeing falls short and truth fails.

Returning to *The Captive*, we can see that by imprisoning Albertine within the domestic space of his Paris apartment, Marcel both locks her into a heterosexual space and, at the same time, freezes any possibility of the other desire that was so threateningly unleashed not only in the multiple associations with Montjouvain but also in the numerous scenes involving Albertine and her friends at the seaside resort, Balbec. Symptomatic of that simultaneous confinement and paralysis are the lengthy passages describing Albertine asleep, who becomes a "plant" (84), an "unconscious thing" (88) deprived of her "humanity" (84), a kind of "mute nature" (88) animated only by the "unconscious life of vegetables, of trees" (84).[20] Constructed as the interiority of what Beauvoir calls woman's immanence, the specificity of Albertine's desire as well as her social location are mystified as the organic matter of nature itself.

In fact, her condition as a "vegetable" in *The Captive* is a cultural construction resulting from an opposition between the domestic and public spheres. Proust renders that opposition obsessively throughout the volume, where the interior, static, controlled space of Marcel's apartment where Albertine is held captive contrasts with the street sounds of the social world just outside the window. I'm interested in that opposition not only because it tells us something about the gendered construction of Albertine "pinned down" but also because it can provide some insights into what Levinas calls the "sociological" aspects of Proust's novel. Levinas paints a picture of Albertine as other in order to demonstrate a sociality without ethics, a sociality that is purely aesthetic. In *The Captive* Albertine becomes an object, a mute thing, victimized, aestheticized, internalized as grist for the mill of Proust's art. And just as the social specificity of each *cri de la rue* outside Marcel's window is transformed into the lines of a Gregorian chant, so too Albertine's social particularity is sucked into the aesthetic machinery of Proust's imagination.

In other words, like those anonymous *cris de la rue* as Gregorian chants, Albertine's construction as an aesthetic object of heterosexual desire masks her insertion into a social fabric and, more specifically, mystifies the specificity not only of her "different" sexuality but also of her class status. This masking, in turn, displaces ethical questions into the realm of sensation, feeling, and desire and thus obfuscates the political workings of the text. On this view, Albertine's opacity becomes a signifier for the dismissal of both ethical and political questions in the name of aesthetics, exemplified by Levinas's reading of the other in Proust. Further, it hardly seems coincidental that there is a historical correspondence between the separation of the aesthetic as an autonomous sphere and the rise of the bourgeoisie. Art and, more broadly, the entire sphere of perception and sensation became autonomous because of their integration into a capitalist mode of production. As Terry Eagleton explains: "When art becomes a commodity, it is released from its traditional social function within church, court, and state into the anonymous freedom of the marketplace."[21] It is precisely that anonymous, capitalist marketplace status of the aesthetic object which is so threatening to the narrator of the *Recherche*, the would-be artist who wants to put all his ontological eggs in the aesthetic basket. It is also no coincidence that the object of desire whom he literally imprisons is squarely a member of the middle class, unlike the aristocratic Duchesse de Guermantes or the innumerable working-class girls—*boulangères*, *cremières*, and so forth—who also incite his libidinal and therefore aesthetic desires. Indeed, Albertine's opacity is the opacity of the commodity, the sign of a sign that has no referent, the absolute autonomy and utter alienation of the object in capitalism.

Thus, to return once again to Colette's ethical reading of the other in Proust, the declaration that "there is no Gomorrah" can be seen to mark Albertine's opacity as an aesthetic commodity, the sign of a sign that has no referent. Albertine is not only "othered," she is also eradicated through the aesthetic machinery of Proust's novel. This eradication is not just ontological, but takes on the specifically social dimensions that are inherent to the realm of the ethical. Albertine as the other marks the betrayal of the ethical in the name of the aesthetic, revealed in the progressive effacing of Albertine's class status and, more generally, the question of the social per se in the novel.

I asked earlier: Might we read Albertine as a figure who, in her ungraspable otherness, constitutes a warning to those who would obliterate difference and thereby ultimately dismiss ethics in the name of aesthetic self-transformation? We could return to that question with a hypothetical answer: Yes, we might read her as a warning. Which is to say, if Albertine-Gomorrah is the figure of absolute alterity, the other who, in her otherness, literally does not exist at all, it is from her place that we must read, from her place that we must ask the ethical question, the question of the other, because it is she who is obliterated by the aestheticizing moves of representation. What Levinas fails to see in his reading of Proust is that we can never bracket the ethical question in the name of the magic of the aesthetic, because the two in fact are inseparable.

The ethical failure marked by the aestheticization of the other as object of love can also be expressed in political terms. As Marx might see it, Albertine's interior captivity and aestheticization points to a tension between an aesthetic ideal—the interiority of the creative act—and a political reality—the exteriority of class society that, in the *Recherche*, remains unresolved. Indeed, the aestheticization of the ethical sphere is depicted here as the interiorization of the messy otherness of the outside world. This process of aestheticization and interiorization is one that effaces the outside otherness, thereby rendering it nonexistent. So Colette has a point, and it remains, for me, a queer feminist one, in a reading we might compare with Irigaray's famous interpretation of Plato's parable of the cave discussed in chapter 1. When it comes to inscribing Gomorrah as the place of the other, Proust relies on a Platonic structure. Like the prisoners shackled in the darkness of the cave whose exclusion upholds the building of the republic, Albertine as Gomorrah remains the prisoner of a Platonic specular economy that literally x-es her out.

So, to end at the beginning, in Genesis, with the proverbial gesture of return: the Bible says the wicked were destroyed. Proust says no; they used deception to get away, and now "we are everywhere." To both Colette says: that may well be, but the gesture of obliteration continues, even among those who were originally targeted but managed to escape.

Among the "we" who are purportedly "everywhere" are those who in fact fall outside the "we" into nonexistence. So how might those others, like a trace or a ghost, come forward again, with a difference?

If Albertine-Gomorrah remains unread, and if we take this unreading seriously not just as an epistemological failure but also as an ethical one, then our task becomes twofold. Not only must we read, yet again, that which remains unread, but we must read the processes and structures that produced a forgetting that was itself forgotten as well. The category of the unread, the unheard, the illegible is not the static result of a finite movement of reading or hearing, but the perpetually produced fallout of obliterating interpretive acts. This fallout takes the form of multiple, modulated silences over time, which brings me, once again, to the image of the poster that used to hang, for years, on my office door. "Why do we use silence to end silence?" The question is a profound one. As this example of the performative deployment of silence makes clear, those who speak from the place of the other are, in fact, not silent at all, but unheard. Colette's statement—"there is no Gomorrah"—marks the complexity of a "rigorously executed" unhearing that is constitutive of cultural intelligibility itself. Our challenge then, is to attend to the silence of Gomorrah, not as absence, but as the restoration of a fissured ground whose promise is a different history.

7 What If Hagar and Sarah Were Lovers?

A Story

Several years ago, my partner Tamara and I were babysitting our then one-year-old godchild, Charis, when we decided to run to the grocery store to pick up some things for dinner. As we approached the checkout line, the white teenage clerk looked up, smiled, and commented on how cute Charis was with her wispy blond hair and big blue eyes. Then, addressing me, she said with conviction: "She looks just like you."

"Actually, she isn't mine," I replied.

"Oh," said the clerk, scanning my pale skin, blue eyes, and straw-colored hair. "I assumed you were the mother." She glanced over at Tamara, confidently interpreting her dreadlocks and brown skin: "And I thought you were the nanny."

Feeling Tamara stiffen at my side, I vaguely understood that this reading of her in a place like this—an upscale Italian grocery store in the heart of a wealthy white New Haven neighborhood—was something she had encountered in similar contexts a thousand times before.

"No," Tamara replied, glaring at the clerk, then pointedly looking at me. "She's not the mother, and I'm not the nanny."

Secretly I was relieved that Tamara had spoken, allowing me to take the groceries and leave the store as if nothing had happened. And yet, even in that moment of saying nothing, I was aware that something fragile had just been punctured. Somehow the clerk's failure to read us as family shattered the intimacy that moments before had safely bound us together. Even more acutely, my own failure to speak sharply threw into question an implicit trust between Tamara and me, an unspoken faith in each other without which our relationship could not continue.

Afterward, in the car, Tamara and I talked about what had happened, perhaps trying to stave off the threat of trust irrevocably broken. We examined our feelings of anger and sadness at the quick and unexpected intrusion of racism in a day-to-day encounter; Tamara's feeling that she should have said more and that I, her lover, should have said *something*; my own sense of having betrayed Tamara by not speaking at all.

"I didn't know what to say," I said meekly. "I was just so taken aback by what she said."

Tamara glanced at me impatiently. "You could have turned it around, asked her why she would make such a comment." She paused. "At least get her to question her own assumptions."

I knew she was right, that I should do better. Yet even in that moment of self-recognition, shame gave way to a wave of self-pity. I started to cry. Suddenly, just for an instant, I saw myself—my tears, my paralysis, my leaden silence—through someone else's eyes, the eyes of someone non-white, perhaps even Tamara as she saw me in that moment. And from that other perspective, I was a cliché—the Weepy White Woman—and I hated myself for it.

If Levinas's ethical failure in the previous chapter could be described as an inability to hear the silence of the other, my silence in this scene could be described as an example of another kind of ethical failure: an inability to speak when speech is called for—not incited speech, but speech that is called for as an ethical demand. In this case the other is not an abstract category but my life partner, who has just been racially interpellated in a way that, while numbingly stereotypical, also draws out a painful historical truth about what the womanist theologian Delores Williams calls the social role surrogacy of women of African descent.[1] Here the nanny stereotype points to a history of racial and economic subordination that stretches from Hagar in the Bible to the southern mammy of American slavery to the present-day Caribbean immigrant women who leave

Trinidad or Haiti to push white children in strollers down the fashionable streets of New York City. Indeed, the "you must be the nanny" comment speaks to Tamara's personal story about her own mother who left Jamaica when Tamara was a child to work as a nanny for a wealthy white family on Long Island.

To be sure, this is not only a story about ethical failure as a failure of love. Tamara and I are still partners, and just as she and I continually learn how to move together through these everyday stories of division, so too, in a broader sense, we can all attempt to link our slips and silences to less violent practices of social belonging.

A Feminist Ethics of Vulnerability and Care

This chapter's opening story about a grocery store encounter can be read in at least two ways: 1) as a personal love story or 2) as a moral tale about trust, accountability, and responsible action. It's not your typical story, either as love plot or moral tale. Not only is the heterosexual love plot transformed to focus on a relationship between two women, but the story revolves around the moment where love falters. This focus on love's inadequacies parallels the ambiguity of the narrative's moral function. Although things will get better between the two lovers beyond the frame of this particular tale, the central ethical problems raised by the story—silence, passivity, and betrayal—remain unresolved. In that sense the story narrates the possibility of love's failure, despite the fact that the relationship continues. Because love fails to heal the betrayal, the story's ethical meaning—either as exemplary model or cautionary tale—remains unclear.

The narrative's ambiguous ethical status makes it well suited to my purposes in this chapter: to explore queer love in the context of a feminist ethics of care and the concept of vulnerability to which it gave rise. Many of feminism's most revered tenets—commitment to global sisterhood, attention to the particularity of women's lives, the critique of domination and violence—are implicitly grounded both in a strong sense of justice and in a belief in women's benevolence and capacity for love. However, because the ethics of care was first articulated as a critique of traditional theories of justice, feminist morality often produces a dichotomous view of justice versus care and love.[2] The ethics of care is famous for asserting an ethically superior commitment to love, care, and connection in opposition to the abstract, rule-bound requirements of justice. In recognizing the value of care and love in establishing and maintaining human relations—what Eva Kittay calls "love's labor"[3]—the ethics of care thus sometimes inadvertently reinforces the public versus private dichotomy that frames this binary view of justice versus love.

To be sure, some work in the ethics of care has in fact recognized the mutual imbrication of love and justice.[4] Emerging as a field in the early 1980s, the ethics of care raised critical questions about many of the assumptions underlying traditional moral philosophy. Specifically, the ethics of care argued for a shift away from a conception of ethics as a universal list of norms to one where moral judgments would be adumbrated by an acknowledgment of the contingent, context-bound nature of human relationships of care. Now an established field of feminist scholarship, the ethics of care has significantly changed the way society as a whole views moral decision making, equality, and the relation between self and other. Central to this work is a recognition of dependency as a crucial dimension of human existence where "human vulnerability and frailty" are fully accounted for "in our very conceptions of ourselves as subjects and moral agents."[5] In acknowledging human dependency, some feminist philosophers and legal scholars have revised traditional concepts of justice and the good life, replacing the ideal of individual autonomy with a weblike ideal of interdependency based on vulnerability, love, and care. As a result, the ethics of care has not only shaped contemporary philosophical debates about moral commitments and relations but has also profoundly influenced policy issues ranging from welfare reform to reproductive rights to neoliberal economic practices.[6]

After the establishment of feminist care ethics in the 1980s, the implicit association between love and care in this field was challenged from the perspective of justice, most notably by feminist analyses of the political, legal, and economic structures underlying the work of care.[7] This line of argument not only saw justice and love as inextricably connected but asserted that questions of justice can be found at the heart of care as well. Martha Fineman's more recent work in vulnerability studies goes even further to replace the concept of dependency in care ethics with that of vulnerability. Asserting the universality of vulnerability, Fineman argues that the vulnerable subject opens up possibilities for formal equality and justice not afforded by either the Lockean liberal subject or the dependent subject of care ethics. In a slightly different vein, Judith Butler's Levinasian turn toward ethics has involved her in a growing engagement with questions of vulnerability, the Other, and what she calls "precarious life."[8] And, although Butler would probably not see herself as part of a feminist ethics of care tradition, her writings on precariousness repeat the language of interdependence and mutuality that characterizes much of that work. As Butler puts it in *Frames of War*: "the subject that I am is bound to the subject I am not. . . . We are bound to one another in this power and this precariousness. In this sense, we are all precarious lives."[9]

Whether in its earlier iteration as care or its later conception as vulnerability or precariousness, an important strand of the work I'm engaging critiques the ways in which liberal feminism has relieved the burden of caregiving traditionally consigned to all women as a class—child-rearing and domestic chores, care for the sick, those with disabilities, and the elderly—by replacing the unpaid work of upper- and middle-class wives and mothers with the poorly paid work of nannies, maids, home health aides, and other domestic workers. Many feminists have argued that, while this move has increased opportunities for some women in the public sphere, shifting the work of care to another group of women has not furthered the feminist goals of equality and justice. Rather, the gap of inequality produced by the traditional gendered division of labor that divided upper- and middle-class men from women has simply shifted to reveal the ever growing gaps that divide economically and racially privileged women from nonwhite, poor, and working-class women. Significantly, that gap increasingly has global dimensions, with what Arlie Hochschild calls "the importation of love from poor countries to rich ones" (17).[10] At the same time, the feminist focus on care, vulnerability, and love as the cornerstones of a new ethics rooted in dependency has sometimes obscured the economic dimensions of the poorly remunerated, often exploitative work of care. The feminist recognition of care and vulnerability thus sometimes inadvertently masks other inequalities and injustice among women. This problem of inequality at the heart of care is summed up succinctly, in Joan Tronto's words, as "injustice justified by care."[11]

Thus feminist reflection on love and care remains haunted by a problem of justice: the continuing inequality among women as a whole. This ethical problem of injustice at the center of the feminist quest for justice and equality is hardly new; indeed, it can be linked to a long-standing intersectional tradition of self-critique within feminist theory and practice that precedes the development of a feminist ethics of care. As I argued in the introduction, at least since the early 1970s, women excluded from a narrow but universalized Western liberal feminist conception of "all women" have challenged the classist, racist, and heterosexist underpinnings of mainstream feminism. As a result of that intersectional challenge, feminist theory has come to recognize the importance of differences among women and has clarified the ways in which those differences translate into social and political inequalities. Drawing on that recognition of differences, some feminists have further argued not only that some women are more privileged than others, but that many liberal feminist successes have been achieved at the expense of other, less privileged women. More than a mere recognition of the differences among women, this deeper admission puts forward the challenging claim that increasing inequality between women is a result of the gains of liberal feminism. As Elsa Barkley Brown puts it: "We need to recognize not only differences but the relational nature of those differences. Middle-class white women's lives are not just different from working-class white, Black, and Latina women's lives. It is important to recognize that middle-class women live the lives they do precisely because working-class women live the lives they do. White women and women of color not only live different lives but white women live the lives they do in large part because women of color live the ones they do."[12]

A few simple personal examples can clarify this point. As a white, middle-class feminist scholar, I am able to pursue the relatively satisfying intellectual work I do because another woman cleans my office every day, while yet another set of women descends on my house every other week to perform the domestic chores of sweeping, vacuuming, and scrubbing that traditional gender roles would have consigned to me were it not for the gains of liberal feminism. And if I were a parent, still another woman or group of women would take on at least some of the burden of raising my child. All these tasks constitute strands of a web of dependency that feminist scholarship has massively elucidated over the past thirty years. However, when responsibility for "love's labor" is transferred from mother and wife to nanny and maid, the feminist goal of equality is undercut by the intrinsically unjust structure of domestic work.[13] This injustice constitutes a betrayal of feminism's grounding commitment to love and further reveals a fact often overlooked by the ethics of care: namely, that the analytic separation of justice and care belies the reality of their mutual imbrication with each other.

My purpose in this chapter is not to rehash structural arguments about inequalities among women that are all too familiar to feminist scholars. I proceed from the assumption that such inequalities exist and concur with the additional claim that upper- and middle-class feminists have benefited from the exploitation of other women.[14] Feminist ethics, therefore, must take seriously the fact of inequality not only as a failure of Lockean liberalism, as Fineman does, but also as a failure of feminist justice and feminist love. This recognition of failure is neither a call for feminist guilt nor a prescription for postfeminist despair. Rather, I offer the acknowledgment of failure as an invitation to rethink the complexity of some of feminism's most cherished ethical ideals: justice, mutual respect, reciprocity, and, especially, queer love.

The rethinking I have in mind here derives not from the architecture of philosophical argument, but from the textured detail of overlapping stories whose capacity for transformation lies in the kind of narrative performance I theorized in chapter 2. For the sake of clarity, I focus in these stories on moments of betrayal like the one I described in the grocery store. These moments of betrayal function symbolically to mark the ongoing fact of injustice as a political and ethical burden that queer feminism must continue to carry. I wield the admittedly harsh word *betrayal* here both as a sign of injustice and as a tool of demystification; I use betrayal to expose the painful truths about relations between women that are sometimes obfuscated by a feminist focus on love and care or a queer focus on pleasure. Betrayal names the gap that continues to divide economically privileged women from poor and working-class women, white women from women of color, and women in industrialized nations from women in the developing world. And, since injustice will continue to inhabit the feminist struggle for access to opportunities and power as long as structural inequalities remain, there is no reason to believe that this betrayal will not remain part of queer feminism's story as well.

The pain of betrayal I explore here also speaks, indirectly, to the problem of feminist solidarity and the exclusion of exclusion I discussed in the introduction. In Irigarayan terms, betrayal points to the logic of the Other's Other, where the maternal absence at the source of our symbolic system exposes the aggressions that rupture ideals of harmonious feminist belonging. From this perspective, the diagnosis of betrayal that shadows feminist discussions of intersectionality—either as angry accusation or guilty complicity—might be viewed less as a moral condemnation that reinvokes normative politics than as a recognition of a constitutive structure of othering that makes love hurt.[15]

Love cannot heal the rift of betrayal, as my grocery store narrative makes clear. And yet, queer loving relations between women continue.

Although love does not conquer all, neither does betrayal. Rather, love and betrayal—care and injustice—coexist, each at the heart of the other. This is where my stories dwell and the place to which I return, again and again, through stories: to that fraught nexus of queer love and betrayal. Having been there, already, in my own everyday story about racism and nannies, I move there again through the biblical tale of Hagar and Sarah, a narrative I had never really noticed until I read a short story by the contemporary British writer Sara Maitland about Abraham, Hagar, and Sarah. In this chapter, then, I retell a story of betrayal between women; the result of the retelling is not only a deeper understanding of the complexity of love as it relates to justice in feminist ethics. It is a tribute as well to the abiding force of the queer practices of relation that reshape the present and allow us to rethink our own pasts.

This strategy of tracing a feminist ethical story through a series of repeated retellings not only draws attention to queer love at the heart of feminist ethics but also reinforces the importance of intertextual narrative performance explored in chapter 2. In so doing I want to highlight the interplay between the given and the new in the work of theorization. My emphasis on retelling stems from the conviction that neither feminism nor queer theory can simply spring free from what is given to begin ex nihilo with a brand new story. Rather, queer feminist thought, like queer feminist stories, must start with the given in order to find their way toward something new: new stories, new ways of being, queer new ways to love.

My attention to the interplay between the given and the new also relates to the historical situatedness of these particular stories. Although thematically similar, the grocery story narrative and the biblical story about Hagar and Sarah are far removed from each other in space and time. Reading my own story through the Hagar and Sarah story resituates the earlier narrative in ways that appear to ignore the historical specificity of the biblical setting. Indeed, a historian might argue that history itself is thus effaced in the process of retelling. However, from another perspective, the process of retelling invites new ways of thinking about the narrative dimension of history and the ways in which ideas or events from the past sustain multiple stories. This does not mean that the past is nothing more than stories or that old stories can give birth to an infinite number of new stories. Indeed, I am less concerned about questions of historical veracity here than I am about the process of retelling itself. In rewriting the given, retelling draws attention to the dynamic interplay, once again, between *what is* and *what might be* theorized in chapter 1, where the given is both acknowledged and transformed. In this way retelling both opens the original narrative of the given to interpretive doubt and, at the same time, makes visible the specifically narrative dimension of a genealogical process of imaginative rupture and transformation.[16]

Hagar and Sarah

Growing up with inconsistent exposure to church and Sunday school, I never paid much attention to Abraham and Sarah, and never even noticed Hagar at all. Years later, I rediscovered this particular biblical tale through a short story I read during one summer vacation: "Triptych," by Sara Maitland, from her collection, *Angel Maker* (1996). Maitland's story led me back to the Bible, which in turn led me to reflect on my relationship with my partner in the larger context not only of feminist ethics but of a history of telling stories. My own queer love story, then, led me circuitously to other love stories, and it is through those stories that I accessed new ways of understanding not only my personal narrative but a theoretical story about feminist ethics. Thus storytelling itself reshaped the way I was able to think about specific conceptual and political problems within feminism. Without storytelling, the process of reconceptualization would not have occurred. Significantly, that process landed me in a place I had not been seeking—at the Bible's beginning in Genesis. I did not seek it out, and yet, as both a founding text of the three monotheistic religions—Christianity, Judaism, and Islam—and what Phyllis Trible calls one of patriarchy's "texts of terror," the story of Abraham, Hagar, and Sarah was exactly where I needed to be, both for the grappling I was doing with my own personal struggles and for my thinking about feminist ethics.

The biblical narrative about Hagar and Sarah begins in Genesis 16, after Abraham, Sarah, and, presumably, Hagar, have lived in Canaan for about ten years. Unable to bear children herself, Sarah offers Abraham her "Egyptian slave-girl whose name is Hagar" (Genesis 16:1) as her surrogate.[17] "Go in to my slave-girl," Sarah says, "it may be that I shall obtain children by her" (Genesis 16:2). Then Sarah "took Hagar the Egyptian, her slave-girl, and gave her to her husband Abram as a wife. He went into Hagar, and she conceived; and when she saw that she had conceived, she looked with contempt on her mistress" (Genesis 16:3–4).[18]

Angered by Hagar's contemptuous look, Sarah banishes her and sends her into exile. In the wilderness Hagar is addressed by the angel of the Lord, who convinces her to return to her mistress, assuring Hagar that she will have many offspring. Obeying God's command, Hagar returns to Sarah, fulfilling her function as surrogate mother by giving birth to Ishmael: "Hagar bore Abram a son; and Abram named his son, whom Hagar bore, Ishmael. Abram was eighty-six years old when Hagar bore him Ishmael" (Genesis 16:15–16). Thus begins the patriarchal reign of Father Abraham, whom God had promised numerous progeny: "Look toward heaven and count the stars. . . . So shall your descendants be" (Genesis 15:5). This patriarchal frame of the Genesis story is developed and reinforced over the course of the remaining chapters, which recount the founding of Abraham's family. Highlights include the institution of circumcision according to God's command that all foreskins be cut as a sign of the covenant between God and Abraham and all his male descendants (Genesis 17:9–14); God's promise that, incredibly, the postmenopausal Sarah will bear Abraham a son, Isaac, who will displace Ishmael as recipient of God's covenant (Genesis 17:15–22); God's destruction of Sodom and Gomorrah (Genesis 19:24–26); and the especially edifying story of Lot, who, having been mercifully forewarned by God of the impending destruction, flees the cities to settle in a cave in the hills where he impregnates both his daughters, thereby assuring his status as another ancestral father of generations of descendants (Genesis 19:30–38).

Meanwhile, ninety-year-old Sarah gives birth to a son whom Abraham, now one hundred, names Isaac (Genesis 21:1–3). Isaac grows older, is weaned, and becomes the playmate of his older brother, Ishmael, Hagar's son. Once again, Sarah is complicit with patriarchal family and inheritance laws; having already brutalized Hagar through forced surrogacy and exile years earlier, once again Sarah becomes the agent of Hagar's dispossession: "So she said to Abraham, 'Cast out this slave woman with her son; for the son of this slave woman shall not inherit along with my son Isaac'" (Genesis 21:10). Abraham casts out Hagar and Ishmael according to Sarah's wishes, leaving them to wander "in the wilderness of Beer-sheba" (Genesis 21:14). Exiled, hungry, and alone with her dying son, Hagar lifts up her voice and weeps (Genesis 21:16): "And God heard the voice of the boy; and the angel of God called to Hagar from heaven, and said to her, 'What troubles you, Hagar? Do not be afraid'" (Genesis 21:17).[19]

As the Bible presents it, this story more than adequately demonstrates the limits of love by exposing the inequality, injustice, and betrayal that characterize the relationship between Hagar and Sarah. Not only is Hagar structurally subordinated to Sarah in her status as Sarah's slave, but Sarah is the direct agent of Hagar's subordinate role as surrogate mother in forcing her to conceive and give birth to Ishmael. This key aspect of the relationship between Hagar and Sarah—where Hagar performs, for Sarah, "love's labor"—links the biblical story to the problem of inequality at the heart of care.

Both traditional biblical scholars and feminist theologians have generally interpreted this story as a tale about women's hostility toward each other, but have tended to ignore Sarah's complicity with a patriarchal system that subordinates one woman to another. An exception to this trend in biblical scholarship is *Sisters in the Wilderness*, where Delores Williams reinterprets Hagar's story as the black "community's analogue for African-American women's historic experience" (SW 4) in the context of white domination and oppression in the U.S. For Williams and other African American Christians, the story functions transhistorically as a narrative about "the brutal or cruel treatment black women have received from the wives of slave masters and from contemporary white female employers" (SW 3). Williams draws on Hagar as "surrogate" mother, wet nurse, as well as namer of God to describe the historical construction of women of African descent under slavery in the U.S., where "the relation between the slave-owner's wife and the slave woman is, like Sarah and Hagar's relation, built upon the exploitation of the slave woman's body and labor" (SW 36). The various forms of black women's "social role surrogacy" described by Williams include, during slavery, the southern black mammy as surrogate nurturer, the field-worker as surrogate male laborer, and the sexually promiscuous "Jezebel" figure as surrogate partner of the white man whose sexual "pleasure" is founded in the systemic rape of his female slaves. With emancipation, black women's surrogate roles continue, according to Williams, as domestics employed by white families, as single heads of households, and as "breeders" in the growing surrogacy industry in North America.

From a perspective that insists on historical accuracy, the objections to be leveled at this kind of ahistorical, racialized reading of "Hagar the Egyptian" are obvious, especially since race itself is a modern concept. But Williams's reading works as an example of the dialectical play between the given and the new inherent in the process of retelling, where historical situatedness is both marked and transcended in the cultural transformation of the original story.[20] Thus, while Williams fails to offer an empirically grounded reading of the biblical story, as a symbolic interpretation her reading expresses a communal emotional truth and opens the Bible to the "something new" of a nonliteral reading, thus bearing witness to what Kelly Oliver might describe as "that which is beyond recognition in history."[21] In that perspective, the "poetic" reading of Hagar as black and Sarah as white has much to offer my argument here about the mutual imbrication of love and justice in contemporary feminist ethics.

First, Williams's reading allows the Hagar story to function as a lense through which to reread my opening grocery store narrative about a black woman and a white woman trapped in sedimented layers of inequalities that are connected both to slavery and to the contemporary nanny industry evoked by the clerk's statement to Tamara: "You must be the nanny." As an allegorical text with symbolic meaning, the Hagar story thus paradoxically uncovers the historical baggage that makes love fail, at least in that moment of rupture and betrayal.

Second, because Williams insists on reading Hagar not only as a surrogate mother and wet-nurse working for Sarah but also as a figure for black care workers employed by white families, her interpretation of the story sheds light on my central concern about love and betrayal, or the injustice at the heart of care. More specifically, Williams's ahistorical reading demonstrates the analogical structure that links Sarah-as-wife to the wives of slave masters in the American south to "contemporary white female employers." Attention to those links reveals the role of "love's labor" in relation to patriarchal power. In each case, the increased power of the "white" woman is a function both of her loyalty to patriarchy (either as wife or as a man-like employer) and her derogation of female care work to a subordinated other. This transhistorical, structural reading thus suggests that "injustice justified by care" is not simply a contemporary liberal feminist phenomenon.

In this allegorical sense, then, Williams's interpretation of the Sarah-Hagar story as a tale about domination, injustice, and betrayal between women is "true." At the same time, as a symbolic reading it also opens the door to other, less familiar readings. As the tradition of Midrash and, especially, its Jewish feminist appropriations show, new readings of old stories can reveal the transformative potential hidden in the fissures of narratives about marginalization and violence.[22] Like cracks in granite, these fissures expose alternative stories, new configurations of meaning that serve both to acknowledge and resignify injustice and victimization. Read differently, these chapters in *Genesis* where Hagar and Sarah reside might tell a story not only about domination, betrayal, and complicit silence, but also about love.

So how might we reread the story of Sarah and Hagar? To be sure, the project of desperately seeking love in a story of hate is rife with contradictions. The well-known ethical dangers of sugarcoating or whitewashing are all too apparent in any transformative interpretive gesture that imaginatively moves us from terror and division to joy and connection. These dangers are brought to the fore when we acknowledge that the social structures that produced the terror and division are still in place, despite our ongoing collective desire for imaginative revisioning. In other words, genealogical transformation cannot happen in a vacuum, in the absence of a political contestation of the economic forces and institutional structures that continue to pit the Sarahs against the Hagars of the world.

At the same time, the project of opening new heterotopian spaces can nourish the more specifically political work we might do. In that spirit we might choose to look for love in a text of terror as part of a queer feminist political struggle within and against the systems through which that terror is produced. Within this context I am particularly interested in the project of rewriting as a queer feminist endeavor whose purpose is to expose and rethink the explicitly ethical and political meanings of some of Western culture's founding texts. Authors such as Angela Carter, Jeanette Winterson, Monique Wittig, and, in my analysis here, Sara Maitland rewrite myths, fairy tales, and biblical stories in order to dramatize a feminist resistance to some of these texts of terror. This contestational intertextual practice reveals the ideological gaps between the original texts and their rewritten versions. In that process the rewritten narratives can be seen to function not only as new interpretations of old stories; as heterotopias, they both register harm and performatively enact alternative visions of the social order.

Bible Study

In her short story, "Triptych," Sarah Maitland queers the Bible by rewriting the story of Hagar, Sarah, and Abraham not only as a parable of misogynist, racist, homophobic, and patriarchal violence but also as a tale about the ethical ideals of mutual respect, reciprocity, and love. Maitland's narrator is a decentered subject, as the story is refracted into three distinct narrative voices: first from Hagar's perspective, then Sarah's, and finally from the perspective of Abraham. Actually, Maitland's plans for Abraham's story are never realized. As the narrator puts it at the beginning of the third section of the triptych, "Abraham": "I thought, I really did, in all sincerity, that I would write Abraham's story too. I thought I would write it here, like the others, trying to recreate it, enter into it, understand it; tell it. But I'm not going to. . . . I can't be bothered" (198). Besides, she says, almost everybody already knows the story of the first patriarch anyway. For those who don't know the story, she advises, just "sneak into almost any second-rate hotel. . . . Open the drawers of the bedside cabinets, and in one of them you will find . . . a fairly bulky hard-covered book. This is entitled *The Holy Bible* and has been placed there by a charitable organization which holds Abraham's version of this story dearer to its heart than I hold it to mine" (198–199). The story "held dear" is a story of the origin of nations, as God says to Abraham: "As for me, this is my covenant with you: You shall be the ancestor of a multitude of nations" (Genesis 17:4). In Maitland's rewriting, Abraham's story embodies the beginning of "patriarchy," in the feminist, critical sense of the term. As her narrator puts it: "Father Abraham is, frankly, a real bastard" (200). This too, Maitland implies, is something everyone knows, but doesn't want to admit, since Abraham's virtue constitutes the founding ethic of both the Jewish and Christian story.

What everybody doesn't know is the other, suppressed story, another narrative whose traces can be discerned, according to Maitland, in "the abiding emotional reality of Sarah and Hagar" (200). This is how Maitland rewrites the story of Ishmael's birth:

> Sarah's breasts soft and warm against her head and shoulders, Sarah's voice gentle and determined: breathe push relax push push breathe breathe down the baby, said Sarah's voice, breathe out the baby strong strong and gentle and steady and Ishmael suddenly rushing down on the strength of her muscles and Sarah's sweet calm. Sarah's hands untiring, loving, washing her with a soft cloth after the labor, washing tenderly and happily, all over, hands like cool honey all over her, mother, friend, lover. Sarah.
>
> (186)

The emotional power of Maitland's rendering of this "text of terror" as shared queer maternal bliss is undeniable, at least for me. And, one could argue, if we only read for the Biblical plot line of Sarah's horrific

treatment of Hagar, the "abiding emotional reality" of more hopeful textual and historical possibilities is lost. However, it could also be argued
that while Maitland's version of the story may be powerful, its distance
from the original biblical narrative about the slavery, betrayal, cruelty, and
dispossession of one woman at the hands of another opens it to the same
kind of criticisms that postcolonial critics have leveled at a feminist rhetoric of love which obfuscates continuing inequalities among women.[23] In
that sense, my framing question might seem not only queer but ethically
and politically suspect: what if Hagar and Sarah were lovers?

Let me be clear: the jolt of that question, in all its dimensions, is not to
be underestimated, particularly if we consider the historical resonances
of this archetypical relation between a privileged white woman and her
dark-skinned slave. What would it mean for Hagar and Sarah to love each
other? What kind of love could that possibly be? Maitland herself hints at
the dangers of honey-coated love. In a scene that foreshadows Ishmael's
circumcision, Maitland describes Hagar's nightmares of violent silencing and bodily mutilation: "Sarah had woken [Hagar] from recurrent
nightmares in which the little bronze knife cut away her tongue, or her
breasts," but "Sarah had held her in her arms and promised, promised,
promised that never never never would she let that happen to her" (187).
And yet, when the nightmare becomes the reality of Ishmael's circumcision, Sarah's tenderness toward Hagar becomes not a sign of fidelity to
her promise but, rather, the mark of her betrayal: "Now she said, it will
not hurt, it will not hurt, Abraham would do nothing, never, that would
hurt his precious manhood; and she had led Hagar away gently into the
depths of the tent and covered her with a blanket and kissed her ears
and eyes and mouth and genitals so that she would not have to hear the
screams of her mutilated child. . . . But why had Sarah not spoken, why
had Sarah kept silent in the tent, smothering Hagar with kisses rather
than challenging the madness that grew in Abraham?" (187).

In this haunting scene a gesture of erotic love—the kiss—becomes
a symbol of betrayal and the smothering of the other. Most important,
the kiss represents a refusal to speak, the visible sign of Sarah's silence.
This point is crucial, because it complicates a familiar feminist politics of
voice, where woman's oppression is marked by silence and her liberation
heralded by an emergence into voice. However, Sarah's refusal to speak in
this scene points to a more complex understanding of silence not only as
a mark of oppression, which is the case for Hagar, but also, for Sarah, as

a mark of privilege.[24] Sarah's privilege vis-à-vis Hagar allows her to choose silence, and it is her silence that directly leads to Hagar's marginalization. Further, the complexity of the voice-silence dichotomy is rendered even more poignant because, like Judas with Jesus, the betrayal is masked by an act of tenderness.

Sarah's gestures of love set the scene for her ultimate betrayal of Hagar and Ishmael, when Sarah agrees that they shall be exiled in the wilderness. Maitland underscores the sense of Sarah's, not Abraham's, betrayal when Hagar finally sees "that it was Sarah, that *it was love, which had betrayed her*, which had given her child over to the desert dogs to maul in the darkness" (192, my emphasis). Although Abraham possessed the patriarchal authority to cast out Hagar and Ishmael, Maitland's retelling makes it clear that the responsibility lies with Sarah. Despite the kisses, the honey coating of love, betrayal cuts through the surface of intimacy to reveal at its core an irredeemable ethical failure: "Sarah had chosen. Understanding was pointless, was too expensive, was unaffordable, when you were the black slave girl and she was the wife" (192). From the visible signs of love in fondling and embracing comes forth a silent but definitive hailing that, once and for all, fixes the asymmetries and abuses of illegitimate power. "Sarah had now called her slave and had used that power over her" (189).

In the context of this rewriting of the story as injustice and betrayal at the heart of love, let me pose, once again, the queer question of this chapter's title: what if Hagar and Sarah were lovers? Read through the lens of Maitland's retelling of the biblical story, the question points to two of narrative performance's most important ethical functions. The first is the acknowledgment of damage and injustice, what one might call narrative's unmasking capacity to articulate harms. The second involves narrative's more heterotopian, transformative function. That is, Maitland's queer retelling of a biblical story opens the given toward the proleptic transformations of genealogical retellings, thereby instantiating the ruptures in the present that register the ethical force of genealogical excavation.

In this way narrative performance can lend itself to the project of developing a queer feminist ethics of eros. Specifically, a focus on stories complicates an overly simplified approach to feminist ethics as justice versus care and a queer disinterest in ethics as moral norms. This approach to retelling as genealogical moves queer feminist ethics toward an acknowledgment of the mutual imbrication of freedom and constraint, justice and care, love and betrayal. These tensions reveal themselves in all their complexity through the ongoing interplay between the given and the new, the already written and the yet-to-be-written: *what is* and *what might be.* Correspondingly, queer feminist ethics cannot be located in one place or the other—either the acknowledgment of love or the recognition of betrayal—but rather emerges in the nexus of the two, in the place where already plotted stories encounter their own narratives of resistance. Thus the old—Sarah and Hagar as mistress and slave—become the new— Sarah and Hagar as lovers. But the new identities hardly cancel out the old ones; rather, the two coexist uncomfortably, even agonistically. It is precisely in that space of uncomfortable coexistence—where competing stories and contradictory identities resist each other—that new (unknowable) possibilities emerge.

No one can predict, before they happen, what those new possibilities will be. The agonistic pairings that have shaped this chapter—injustice and care, betrayal and love—will most likely continue to inhabit not only our own individual lives but the unfolding lives of queer feminism as well. In the symbolic space that joins Sarah with Hagar, Lynne with Tamara, rich with poor, white woman with woman of color, the feminist struggle for justice will have successes, no doubt, but will also continue to confront its own failures. No ethics can emotionally soften or intellectually sublate those failures. But a queer feminist ethics might begin to practice love as a political act of working through, where our collective "shadows and histories, scars and traces" become always ready to transform themselves into surprising new forms of connection.[25]

Coda: Other Stories

For a long time now, I've been scanning my memory, trying to come up with another story. I'd like to write about Tamara and Lynne triumphantly overcoming the failures of queer love. But the more I search the more I realize there is no final story. What I find, instead, is a series of snapshots over time. Each snapshot is a singular story; at the same time, each story is another story retold.

Spring 1997. Tamara and I talk about having children of our own. We don't discuss the nanny question. Instead, I've been reading the memoir of a white mother of black sons, and race weighs heavily on my mind.

"There are things about raising a black child that scare me," I tell her. "I'm afraid of my own inadequacies. Growing up white, I was never taught those safety skills that a black child needs to learn." I look at Tamara. "You learned things about keeping yourself safe in a racist society that I never had to learn."

"You can learn them too," Tamara says. "If we had a black child, you'd have to."

I imagine myself as Jane Lazarre, the white mother of a black son, Khary:

> I am hearing a story about common, everyday racism from one of my sons. It is a prototypical story of young Black maleness in an American city, 1990s. Khary's friend has rung the bell one night and is waiting for him to come downstairs. The friend, also Black and nineteen years old, drives the family car, a Toyota. We live on a racially mixed street in a racially mixed neighborhood, yet when Khary comes downstairs, he finds three cops surrounding his friend who is spread-eagled on the front of the car, being searched. Suspecting he had stolen the car, the cops approached him while he was standing against it, and when he objected, turned him around roughly and began their search. I am outraged and shout: "This is unbelievable!" "Unbelievable?" my son says angrily. "Unbelievable, Mom? It happens to me all the time."[26]

What lesson, I think, closing the book, would have protected her child from this?

Fall 1997. Together Tamara and I visit the fertility clinic in the Yale–New Haven hospital to discuss our options for my insemination. I'm thirty-seven years old; we know we can't wait forever. When we meet with the doctor, we tell him we want a black donor. He says nothing, but his eyes betray his disapproval.

In the end we don't go through with it. The time isn't right, and more and more the baby looks like something to fill the holes in our life: loss of a job, the death of a friend after a long struggle with AIDS. Not good reasons for having a baby.

Fall 1999. Having moved to Houston, our priorities change. Work, friends, and political activism become more important than ever. We decide not to have children after all. The decision feels right, but I grieve it hard, this loss of a thing that never was.

In less than a year I'll be forty.

Spring 2004. Tamara and I are here in the hospital the day Zoe is born. Zoe and her birth mother, Catherine, are black. Her adoptive mother, Jennifer, is white. Holding open a space we call family, Tamara and I welcome them in: Zoe, Jennifer, Catherine.

Summer 2011. Atlanta, Georgia. At home it's usually just the two of us. Things grow simpler, quieter, as we age. Now we have chickens along with the ever multiplying brood of cats. This interspecies family feels right. Still, sometimes, I am haunted by the stories that bring ancient violences into the present moment of our everyday lives. "And she had led Hagar away gently into the depths of the tent and covered her with a blanket and kissed her ears and eyes and mouth and genitals so that she would not have to hear the screams of her mutilated child."[27]

I cover Tamara with a blanket at night, kiss her ears and eyes and the comet-shaped birthmark on her left shoulder. There are no babies—no Ishmael, no Isaac—to wake us with their screams.

Other violences live here, though; we just can't hear them. Our house sits on land that was bloodied by the Civil War. In a more recent history, Tamara's life is forever separated from that of her mother in a chain of care that implicates us all. I can only imagine it: how Tamara must have stood there, frozen, only five years old, as her mother left her, felt her mother's love extracted for someone else's child. The words I use to describe this common yet mostly unspoken form of loss—love and betrayal, injustice and care, the failure of ethics—don't begin to say it. I feel trapped by this story that remains untold. It is, in this sense, a constitutive silence. And yet it belongs in this genealogy, only partially voiced, here with Hagar and Sarah.

Part of me would like to remove us forever from what the world usually reads as Abraham's story: edit out the betrayals, rewrite us as lovers once and for all in an imaginary queer utopia. But there is, thank goodness, no once and for all: no utopia, and no easy ending to this chapter. Our story unfolds, becomes other stories. I can only continue to seek out the stories, especially the queer ones, that point us toward love: a renewed commitment, impossible but necessary, to begin again.

8   After Sex

Prologue: Streetwalker

Although generally unknown in the U.S., the contemporary French novelist and filmmaker Virginie Despentes became something of a celebrity during the early 2000s after the appearance of her controversial film, *Baise-moi*.[1] The film tells the story of prostitute Nadine (played by Karen Bach) and sex actress Manu (played by Raffaëlla Anderson), who meet by chance after arguments with their boyfriends and the violent rape of Manu on the banks of the Seine outside Paris. In a plot that Linda Williams sums up as "a bloody buddy/road movie" that could be titled *Thelma and Louise Get Laid*,[2] their encounter leads to a killing spree punctuated by sexual romps with their unsuspecting victims. But, unlike its more mainstream buddy film model, *Thelma and Louise* (1991), *Baise-moi* ends not in a transcendent leap into the otherworldly canyon lands of the American West but with the abject death of Manu after her botched hold-up of a convenience store. The equally anticlimactic arrest of Nadine by a provincial police force only seals the viewer's sense of a depressing realism. As Linda Williams points out, it's hardly high art.

Despentes tells the story of how she became a celebrity in her quasi-theoretical *Bildungsroman*, *King Kong Theory* (2006). Her story begins with

FIGURE 8.1   Karen Bach as Nadine in *Baise-moi*

violence: "I hitch-hiked, I was raped, I hitch-hiked again."[3] She gives us a few details: age seventeen, July 1986. "There are two of us, both wearing mini-skirts, I have on stripy tights and red Converse" (KKE 25). Despentes and her friend are raped in a car by three men while hitchhiking near a gas station somewhere on the periphery of Paris: nature-culture, the border space where the domestic woman becomes the streetwalker. We are reminded here, by "Virginie D.," what it means to be "just" a woman: "The rapist comes to an agreement with his conscience—there was no rape, just a little slut who didn't know what she wanted, and for whom a little persuading was all that was needed" (KKE 28). A few pages later we find her again, this time holding a weapon: "During that rape, I had a flick-knife in the pocket of my red and white Teddy—a gleaming black-handled, perfect action, long, thin blade, polished, shining and sharp. A flick-knife I used to pull out at the slightest provocation, in that muddled time. . . . I didn't even think about using it. . . . But at that precise moment, I felt female, disgustingly female. . . . It was rape that turned me into a woman again" (KKE 37–38).

Valerie and Virginie

Virginie Despentes is, in many ways, a third-wave version of the bad girl of second-wave feminism, Valerie Solanas. In the story of Solanas's infamous crime against Andy Warhol, we find an allegory of the feminist taking out the queer man who refuses to see or hear her. New York, New York. June 3, 1968: Valerie shoots Andy Warhol three times with a .32 caliber automatic as he's talking on the phone. Pronounced clinically dead, Andy revives after five hours of surgery. Valerie attacks him not because he's raping her, at least not literally, but because she's pissed off at the way she's been exploited. Andy had promised to produce her play, "Up Your Ass," then lost the manuscript and gave her the cold shoulder. The Factory is no longer open to her, so Valerie shoots Andy while he's on the phone: "Click . . . Click . . . Click . . . phone, gun, film, clicking in her head, shooting . . . Click . . . Strangely, shooting him [is] connecting with him, becoming his addressee."[4]

Most people will say that Valerie was just crazy. Not only did she shoot Andy, but she founded a society of which she was the only member, a feminist society whose only trace is scum. SCUM: SCUM Manifesto. But Valerie's crazy ways may have something to teach us about the possibilities of a queer feminism. Valerie wrote from the gutter, the place of scum, but not as a victim. Like Virginie Despentes, she wrote with a vengeance, jabbing with the blade of her acronym: SCUM. Society for Cutting Up Men. Like Virginie, Valerie comes out of the gutter carrying a weapon.

Valerie may have succeeded in shooting Andy Warhol, but this hardly means she succeeded in a feminist act of just retribution any more than Virginie who, with her shiny switchblade, was able to vanquish her rapist enemies that night on the periphery of Paris. Success and failure are difficult to measure, especially when it comes to revenge. All feminist Valerie wanted was to become a writer. But queer Andy threw her script in the garbage. Twenty years later she died a lonely death, long before her time, homeless and forgotten. "Valerie Solanas was a loner," Avital Ronell writes. "There is something poignantly American about the way she handled the self-acknowledged loser life with which she was saddled. . . .

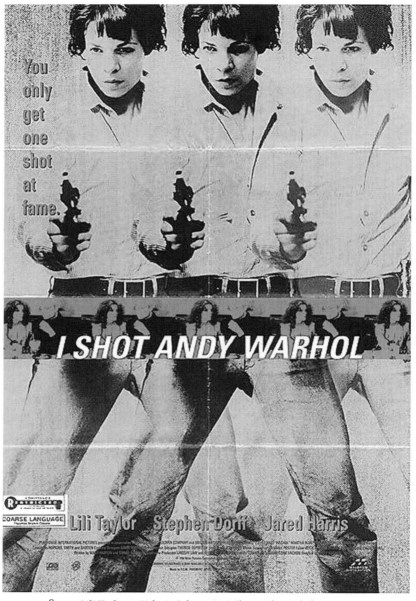

FIGURE 8.2   Lili Taylor as Valerie Solanas in *I Shot Andy Warhol*

Valerie was not meant to have disciples or spawn a new breed of revolutionaries. She offered the uniquely American dead-end-one-warrior-revolution spinning on its own determined axis" (AR 9).

From a certain perspective, the French third-wave Virginie succeeds where the American second-wave Valerie failed. Not only a writer but a film director, Virginie lives a life of scripting, shooting, cutting, montage, and splicing that Valerie could only dream of. Ronell writes: "'Cutting up' no doubt conjures castrative glee, insinuating carving up, morcellating men. Yet it also opens other semantic possibilities of which Valerie was fond: laughter, montage, editing" (AR 11). When we're reading about Solanas it's hard not to think about Lorena Bobbitt, who in 1993 notoriously cut off the penis of her abusive husband. But Valerie's real dreams weren't all that bloody: they were creative, technological, symbolic. They are the dreams that Despentes is able to realize.

Born in 1969, the year Valerie was sentenced to three years in prison for shooting Andy, Virginie Despentes takes over where Valerie left off: "I'm writing *as* an ugly one *for* the ugly ones : the old hags, the dykes, the frigid, the unfucked, the unfuckables, the neurotics, the psychos, for all those girls that don't get a look-in in the universal market of the consumable chick" (KKE 1).[5] Like Valerie, Virginie writes from the gutter, the place of SCUM. Like Valerie, Virginie despises "passive, rattle-headed Daddy's Girl," the ultimate target of the SCUM manifesto: "ever eager for approval, for a pat on the head, for the 'respect' of any passing piece of garbage," she will grow up to become "Mama, mindless ministrator to physical needs, soother of the weary, apey brow, booster of the tiny ego, appreciator of the contemptible, a hot water bottle with tits."[6] Virginie's comrades are those, like Valerie's imaginary guerrilla girls, "who by the standards of our 'culture' are SCUM" (SM 61). "So I am writing from here," Virginie says in 2006: "As one of the left-overs, one of the weirdos, the ones who shave their heads . . . the fat tarts, the skinny sluts, those whose cunts are always dry, those who have big bellies, those who would rather be men, those who behave as if they were men, those who think they're porn queens, who don't give a damn about guys but who are interested in their girlfriends, the ones with big asses and thick, dark body hair they don't wax, brutish, noisy women" (KKE 4, translation modified).[7] This is her queer feminist commitment, her SCUM perspective: "The character of the loser in the femininity stakes doesn't just appeal to me: she's essential" (KKE 2, translation modified).

Baise-moi

In *King Kong Theory* Virginie Despentes writes: "In 1993, *Baise-moi* was published. The first review was in *Polar* magazine. A guy's review. A three-page indictment. It's not that the guy doesn't thnk the book is good, according to his criteria. In fact, he doesn't talk about the book at all. His problem is that I'm a girl, representing girls in this way" (KKE 104–105). Are the "girls like that"—Nadine and Manu—the incarnation of Valerie's SCUM dream to "keep on destroying, looting, fucking-up and killing until the money-work system no longer exists" (SM 77)? These post-poststructuralist antiheroines give corporeal form to the heady proclamations of France's antihumanist (male) philosophers of the second half of the twentieth century, from the Foucauldian prediction that man will disappear to the Derridean deconstruction of man to the Deleuzian man's body without organs. In a shooting spree that leaves dozens dead, Despentes's duo literalizes the "Ends of Man" that Cerisy made famous in the 1980 colloquium based on Derrida's 1968 essay. They seem to be "hastening the day" (SM 73) that Valerie predicted, when "males, like the rats following the Pied Piper, will be lured by Pussy to their doom" (SM 73). But in 1993 Despentes's Ends of Man does not go over with the same acclaim as its earlier poststructuralist version.

Unlike Foucault, Derrida et al., Despentes stages rape as being "at the center, the heart, the foundation of our sexualities" (KKE 40). Like Irigaray before her, who was expelled from the École Freudienne in Paris for exposing "this sex which is not one," so too Despentes pays a price for depicting the brutality of a rape that, in the eyes of its perpetrators, "is not actually a rape" (KKE 27). In *Baise-moi*'s famous rape scene, Manu endures the attack on the banks of the Seine by not moving or crying out at all. "Feels like I'm fucking a corpse" (BME 50), one of the attackers says. And his friend replies: "Look at her, she isn't even crying, she's not even a woman. . . . They're trash" (BME 50–51). Manu's lack of interiority has less to do with a Deleuzian critique of psychoanalysis than it does with the lived, gendered reality of the streetwalker, the *asphalteuse*. As Manu inimitably puts it: "I don't give a fuck about their poor jerk-off cocks and because these aren't the first and because they can go shit on themselves. It's like a car that you park in the projects, you don't leave anything valuable in it 'cause you can't keep it from being broken into. I can't keep assholes from getting into my pussy, so I haven't left anything valuable there" (BME 52).[8]

In a society where men "don't know the difference between [a] cunt and [a] garbage chute" (BME 50), this sex which is not one—the symbolic no-place, without value, of the Irigarayan "nothing to see," the stripped-down car parked in the projects—becomes the site of a creative, performative violence that shares in the SCUM manifesto's "gutter perspective."[9] After her real-life rape on the periphery of Paris, Despentes becomes an occasional prostitute—"a crucial step in rebuilding myself after the rape" (KKE 61)—and then a writer. "I start working as a hooker in late '91," Despentes says, "and write *Baise-moi* in April '92. I don't think this is a coincidence. There is a real connection between writing and prostitution" (KKE 72–73). Before becoming a prostitute, Despentes describes herself as "an almost transparent girl, with short hair and dirty sneakers" (KKE 53, translation modified). Then "suddenly I had become a creature of vice. Classy" (KKE 53). Like Manu and Nadine, who become larger-than-life gangsters, Virginie is "Wonder Woman spinning around in her phone booth and coming out of it as a superheroine" (KKE 53).

It is as a whore-writer—the streetwalker—that Virginie is able to recycle woman as trash into something other. Variously labeled "pornography," "erotic literature," "rock novel," "trash," and "underground" literature, *Baise-moi* has to date sold over one hundred thousand copies and has been translated into eighteen languages. The novel's success has been heightened by its even more famous film version, directed by Despentes and former porn star Coralie Trinh Thi, released in France in the summer of 2000, and subsequently banned after an intense campaign from the extreme right. Eventually the French government reached a compromise by awarding the film an "X" certificate, the mark of the pornographic or, perhaps, the x-ing out of the place of woman: a cinematic garbage dump. An X rating has concrete effects: the film can no longer be shown in regular movie theaters and its producer has to pay back the subsidies that French filmmakers otherwise receive. In Canada the film was also banned by the Ontario Review Board following walkouts at a Toronto Film Festival screening, and a viewer at the Theatre Parisien in Montreal broke into the projection room and tore the film out of the projector.

In *King Kong Theory* Despentes writes: "So three porn actresses and an ex-hooker must be forbidden from shooting a film about rape. Even a low-budget, genre film, even a parody. It's important. As if we were threatening state security" (KKE 108). Despentes's insistence on *Baise-moi*'s parodic dimension—"it's important"—is something that should give us pause, for the stubborn refusal to hear the ring of irony in Despentes's work puts members of the Front National—who had the film banned—and tone-deaf feminists—who tore the film out of the projector in Montreal—into an all-too-familiar alliance. Indeed, in *King Kong Theory*, Despentes's theoretical recycling of the media's caricature of the "baise-moi girls"—"three hard-core stars and an ex-whore"—only underlines her penchant for repetitive, redoubled, performative reworkings of earlier forms, even of herself. And, as critics have noted, both the novel and the film versions of *Baise-moi* exaggerate their own performative strategies, recycling an array of objects from high and low culture, from Baudelaire's "Femmes damnées" (Damned women) to grunge music, B movies, video games, comic strips, pornography, the Hollywood psychothriller, rape revenge narratives, the road buddy film, and popular literary subgenres such as roman noir, gore, and gothic novels. Numerous film critics have linked *Baise-moi* to Gaspar Noé's *Seul contre tous* (1998), which plays on a TV screen in one of *Baise-moi*'s early scenes while Nadine has sex with one of her clients.

FIGURE 8.3 Rafaëlla Anderson as Manu in *Baise-moi*

Indeed, as Linda Williams puts it, "the film's punk ethic is laced with a cineliteracy that makes it easy for viewers to place it in the context of its predecessors (28)," including among its other explicit cinematic intertexts *Bonnie and Clyde* (1967), *Thelma and Louise*, and, in the sex club scene where Manu makes a man get on all fours and grunt before shooting him in the ass, the "squeal like a pig" scene in John Boorman's *Deliverance* (1972) and its parody in Quentin Tarantino's *Pulp Fiction* (1994).

This strategy of recycling is not unlike that of Solanas in the SCUM manifesto, whose "regurgitation of the familiar and the idiomatic operates as a kind of sewage system appropriate to the resuscitation of SCUM."[10] The strategy requires an artistic process of cutting up, reorganization, suturing, and splicing, which makes Solanas's acronym, SCUM (Society for Cutting Up Men), appropriate for Despentes's bloody art as well. Like Solanas, Despentes's "embrace of scum . . . resuscitates the dirty, the lowdown, and the marginalized."[11] From that no-place among "the ugly ones," Despentes takes the car parked in the projects without "anything of value in it" (BME 52) and transforms it into something "precious" (BME 52, translation modified).

Porn Writers

Paris, France. January 28, 2005. Karen Lancaume, also known as Karen Bach, dies after ingesting a massive quantity of sleeping pills in a friend's apartment in the 14th arrondissement. Born in Lyon in 1973, Karen began her career as a porn actress in 1996, and appeared in X-rated features such as Christian Lavil's *La Mante religieuse* (1997), Alain Payet's *La Marionnette* (1999), Fred Coppula's *Niqueurs nés* (2000), and Mario Salieri's *Le Calvaire de Monica* (2001). But her greatest notoriety came when Virginie Despentes cast her as Nadine in *Baise-moi*. What was it like being a porn star? Here's what Karen had to say: "Double penetration at 5 degrees, followed by an ejaculation. Covered with sperm, soaked, freezing cold, no one offered me a towel. Once you've shot the scene you're not worth anything."[12] Is this why she ended her own life? A fan wants to know: "Did she find being a porno star degrading? Was she depressed about what her life had come to? Had a romance gone bad? Was she a drug addict? Perhaps she'd discovered that she had a fatal disease? I wish I knew more. —Michael."[13] There are no answers to Michael's questions. A suicide note Karen left for her mother says, simply: "too painful."

FIGURE 8.4 Karen Bach as Nadine in *Baise-moi*

Despentes writes in her blog, after hearing about Karen's death, February 1, 2005: "The words don't go together, the one about your death and the memory of you."[14] In November Karen had sent Virginie the first pages of her book. Rafaëlla Anderson, who played Manu, had published the autobiographical *Hard* in 2001, and Coralie Trinh Thi had published her first novel, *Betty Monde*, in 2002.[15] Karen was the only one of the "baise-moi girls" who had not yet written a book. "It seemed right to me," Despentes writes in her blog, "that she would start writing hers. Especially because, in fact, not one of us had told the entire story of *Baise-moi*. She wanted to tell her story, in its entirety."[16] But unlike Virginie, who, as prostitute-writer, was able to reconstruct herself as Wonder Woman, Karen couldn't save herself. No amount of cutting, suturing, and recycling can resuscitate her after her death. Perhaps writing wasn't really her thing, as Despentes admits in her blog: "She's the only girl I know, really, whose big dream was to be a housewife. The first time she told me that,

I wanted to put it aside, but in getting to know her better, I understood that this existed, as a life dream. That was her thing. Sometimes we don't do what we want."[17]

In *Baise-moi* Nadine—Karen Bach—is no housewife: "I'm no homebody. I'm a woman of the streets. Time to take a walk" (BME 77), she says. Nadine is the whore, "the streetwalker, the one who takes over the streets" (KKE 67), not only by going out, but by watching porn, like a man:

> Nadine's sitting in front of the TV, wearing a suit, pushing fast forward to get past the credits. . . . On-screen is a fat blonde, trussed to a wheel, her head at the bottom. . . . There's a guy in glasses energetically masturbating her with a whip handle. He calls her a fat, dirty pig and she chortles . . . Offscreen a woman's voice bellows: 'And now, bitch, piss your brains out.' Urine gushes out like a show of holiday fireworks" (BME 5). Change of scene. A man's voice. "You'll see, you'll end up loving my cock, they all end up loving it."
>
> (BME 6)

Of course the porn-rape fantasy that we witness through Nadine's eyes—that they all end up loving it—is mocked by *Baise-moi*'s "perverse aesthetic"[18] which combines, in the rape scene, the stock close-up porn shot of penis and vagina—"they're really doing it" (Williams 29)—with the emotional realism of the rape-revenge genre. Similarly, in the "condom scene," Despentes reverses porn's classic ejaculatory "money shot" when Manu vomits on a man's semi-flaccid penis before she and Nadine kick him to death for wanting to use a condom. Recycling porn, *Baise-moi* is different, as Karen Bach once put it in describing her experience as a hard-core star: "Porn, it's guys getting off in girls' mouths, women who get a full load. *Baise-moi* is the opposite."[19]

If *Baise-moi*'s perverse aesthetics produce a porn dystopia of "fucking murderers of assholes in rubbers" (BME 202), how to make real what Manu calls the "mind-blowing choreographies [they] can invent together" (BME 135): "looking for our lucky star" (BME 114), letting "the naughty-by-nature side of our soul do its thing" (BME 114)? How to remake the Irigarayan nothing-to-see into something precious? In a hotel room Nadine spends the day listening to her Walkman and looking at porn while Manu paints her toenails. Nadine is especially captivated by "the blond with the waxed pussy" (BME 139): "her small labia are decorated with brilliant gems, there's a gold ring through her clit" (BME 138, translation modified). Do the glossy pages turn the empty car in the projects into a jeweled treasure? Karen as Nadine watches herself as she flips the pages or pushes the buttons on the remote control, the porn star trying to give back to herself what others have taken. "Walkman soundtrack saturating her eardrums: *Here comes sickness.* She's wedged the pillow under her stomach and masturbates against it while she looks at the photos" (BME 137, translation modified). Empty pleasure. The day passes. Manu vomits after eating too much MacDonald's and drinking too much beer. "Empties herself" (BME 139, translation modified). Life is empty. After a while, Nadine looks at the ceiling, her arms crossed behind her head.

"*Suicidal tendencies*" (BMF 141).

"DEATH ROW. HOW LONG CAN YOU GO" (BMF 131).[20]

Queer Feminism After Descartes

Despentes's version of the "ends of man" leaves no doubt, post-Descartes, that the mind-body split is fatal. She writes, cuts, sutures, and splices—like Solanas—in the face of an apocalyptic future. To be sure, if Despentes has a politics we might call feminist, it's not the same as the late-sixties radicalism we find in the rhetoric of a Valerie Solanas whom Norman Mailer dubbed "the Robespierre of feminism" (in AR 10). But for all their differences, both Solanas and Despentes stage a rage that, although directed at men, consumes the entire planet. As Manu puts it: "I shit on all of them" (BME 46). Manu "truly believes she's capable of covering the entire neighborhood with one bout of diarrhea" (BME 46). From Solanas's "peasants in rice paddies" (SM 77), her cold war "Bomb" (SM 62), or her "grown-up world of suburbs, mortgages, mops, and baby shit" (SM 61) to Despentes's evocations of collective rape during American slavery and the Algerian War, this feminist rage targets everyone in a society created by what Solanas calls patriarchy's "negative Midas touch—everything [man] touches turns to shit" (SM 45).

In that apocalyptic vision, sexuality is the major preoccupation and distraction of a society that, managing life, moves closer and closer to planetary death. But the response to biopower's sex as death is not the age-old prudishness of our Victorian feminist forebears or modern-day reformers like Catharine MacKinnon. As Solanas puts it in one of the most cited passages of the SCUM manifesto, "you've got to go through a lot of sex to get to anti-sex":

> Unhampered by propriety, niceness, discretion, public opinion, "morals," the respect of assholes, always funky, dirty, low-down SCUM gets around . . . and around and around . . . they've seen the whole show—every bit of it—the fucking scene, the dyke scene—they've covered the whole waterfront, been under every dock and pier—the peter pier, the pussy pier . . . you've got to go through a lot of sex to get to anti-sex, and SCUM's been through it all, and they're now ready for a new show; they want to crawl out from under the dock, move, take off, sink out. But SCUM doesn't yet prevail; SCUM's still in the gutter of our "society," which, if it's not deflected from its present course and if the Bomb doesn't drop on it, will hump itself to death.
>
> (SM 61–62)

"You've got to go through a lot of sex to get to anti-sex": this is certainly one of the lessons of *Baise-moi*, where both sex and violence are a constant source of empty but spectacular pleasure. After having sex with a man in a garbage-filled alley, "[Manu] thinks about what she'd rather do here, fucking or carnage. While the guy was at it, she'd thought about what happened that afternoon, how she—Manu—had exploded that woman to pieces against that wall, how the gun had destroyed her. Bestial, really. As good as fucking. Unless it's that she likes to fuck as if it's a massacre" (BME 125–126).

But if the recycled violence, like Solanas's regurgitated shit, is aggressively parodic, the story's conclusion marks the seepage of real endings, in all their banality, beyond that which can be aesthetically regurgitated. There is no Thelma-and-Louise-like "jump without a bungee" (BME 206) into an elsewhere of sisterly union. Rather, Manu dies—offscreen, unglamorously, and alone—after being shot by a convenience store clerk, "the head separated from the trunk by a gleaming wound" (BME 231). Cartesian. And Nadine's subsequent attempt to heal the split by giving the tale a tragic form also ends in—not necessary—failure. After burning Manu's body—"this precious cadaver" (BME 232)—Nadine attempts a Romeo-and-Juliet-like final gesture that will allow her to embrace her friend beyond death: "She's ready, surprised at feeling so peaceful. She takes the gun from her pocket, she's soaked with sun. She'll think of Manu as the gun goes off, they'll stay together" (BME 244). But her suicide is thwarted as the police arrive and disarm her before she is able to pull the trigger.

"Porn is made with human flesh, the flesh of actrices" (KKE 102), Despentes writes. Behind spectacular death with its Bonnie-and-Clyde bravado, the end comes quietly, behind closed doors and, in the worst cases, unnoticed. Valerie Solanas, Karen Bach: alone and desperate, "they drag around at the end, stuporous, drained, shivering in near autistic spheres of solitude. Their language shivers still" (AR 31). No more "girl Nietzsche" (AR 17), no more "warrior of negativity" (AR 24), just "Valerie's weariness" and Karen's pain: "Nietzsche slumped over" (AR 31). Sex as we know it is "too painful," "the refuge of the mindless," as Solanas puts it. "The nicer she is, the more sexual she is. The nicest women in our 'society' are raving sex maniacs" (SM 60). And Despentes writes:

> Those of us at the top are those of us who have become the allies of the powerful. These are the women most able to keep quiet when betrayed, to stick around when scorned, and otherwise flatter the male ego. . . . The most stylish women, the most charming, the friendliest to men. . . . Women in power are the allies of men, those of us the best able to submit, and to smile in their subjugation. To pretend that it doesn't even hurt. The others—the enraged, the ugly, the strident—are stifled, dismissed and invalidated. Non grata among the nobs.
>
> (KKE 110)

It is not porn per se, or even rape, that is the object of this feminist outrage, but rather the grinding, repetitive, systematic, never-ending thwarting of life as eros—the denial of the choreographies invented together. The outrage is against what Virginie felt that night in 1986 on the outskirts of Paris: "it isn't penetration that's terrifying me, but the thought that they're going to kill us. . . . I can remember very precisely that fear of death. A white fear—time stopping, no longer existing, already not existing" (KKE 43–44).

"You've got to go through a lot of sex to get to anti-sex, and SCUM's been through it all, and they're now ready for a new show" (SM 61). What will the new show look like? Where will it be? On an island, perhaps, "that doesn't feature on the map" (KKE 99), will we find ourselves in the form of King Kong who "has neither cock nor balls nor boobs" (KKE 100), "neither male nor female" (KKE 100), "hybrid, before the imposition of the binary" (KKE 100)? Despentes writes in *King Kong Theory*: "Unless we step into the uncharted territory of the gender revolution, we know exactly where we will be regressing. An all-powerful State that infanta-lizes us" (KKE 21). Will Despentes's "gender revolution" bring down a state heading toward what she calls a "fascist regression" (KKE 18)? How to be feminist—or simply a *baise-moi* girl—without becoming one of the "personal assistants" (KKE 127) who,[21] like Solanas's Daddy's Girls, re-main caught in the trap Monique Wittig called "the familiar cul-de-sac of 'it's-wonderful-to-be-a-woman'" (KKE 126)?

We know, of course, that the answer cannot come from a creature on an island that exists on no map. Like the woods, it is a utopian no-place whose creature, inevitably, is conquered: "Then the men in uniform, the world of politics, of the State, intervene to kill the beast. Scaling build-ings, fighting with planes that come at him like mosquitos. Only the sheer number of them allows them to kill the beast" (KKE 102, translation modified). What remains is not violence but an unexpected tenderness: "the beauty and the beast . . . are sensuously tender" (KKE 100, translation modified). Such tenderness comes after an apocalyptic rape that is "obses-sive" (KKE 44), not because it is man against woman—the beast against the beauty—but because of its proximity to death and "their inhuman hatred" (KKE 44). It is a tenderness that seeps from beneath the written surface of rage. Can it teach us, perhaps, a different way of reading the marks left behind by a history of violence?

What I find in *Baise-moi*'s violence, unexpectedly, is tenderness. It is a fleeting tenderness that appears intermittently, like a palimpsest or the scars Manu reads on Nadine's back: "like a fresco that's been furi-ously crossed out" (BME 96), "upsetting hieroglyphics raging through the flesh" (BME 96). "I have a hard time understanding that," Manu says, touching Nadine's scars. "But it's kind of pretty, like abstract art or something" (BME 97). This *Baise-moi* tenderness is what might be taught, in a queer feminist mode, as a lesson from the streetwalker, out of the space—raging and vulnerable—of a prostitute writing that unwrites sexuality in the face of a world "heavy with humanity, fragility, distress" (KKE 55). Despentes writes about turning tricks:

My clients . . . were nice to me, attentive and tender. Much more so than in real life in fact. If I remember rightly, and I think I do, it wasn't their aggressiveness that was hard to handle, or their contempt, or any of their preferences, but their individual loneliness, sadness, their pasty skin and unhappy timidity, the flaws they displayed under the mask, the weaknesses they showed. Their oldness, their desire for young flesh next to their old men's bodies. Their pot bellies, small dicks, flabby buttocks or yellow teeth. It was their fragility that made the thing difficult. . . . In my small experience the clients were heavy with humanity, fragility, distress. And it hung around afterwards, stuck on me like remorse.

(KKE 54–55)

This is the place where queer meets feminist and feminist meets queer: in the fragility of bodies coming undone, in a space of tenderness, after sex.

Afterword

Queer Lives in the Balance

I know the title of my afterword sounds dire: queer lives in the balance. To be "in the balance" is to be in an undetermined, even critical position, and the idiom of my title—queer lives in the balance—delivers the punch of a life-and-death situation in the mode of Al Gore's book, *Earth in the Balance*. Yet I want to end here with an everyday problem, one I face even now as I'm writing: our relentless failure to achieve work-life balance. My title might appear to make the stakes of such a problem seem relatively minor: a high-class concern for two-career families or the policy makers of human resources departments. The queer lives of my title seem to inhabit a more perilous landscape than the one peopled by the balance-seeking mothers and fathers, still employed, who live at the tip of an economic iceberg. Poised, as they are, at the edge of life itself—a question about biopower—queer lives in the balance appear to have little to do with a mundane, repetitive, individualist work-versus-quality-of-life calibration.

Indeed, the dire resonance of my title is meant to telegraph my own discomfort with the bucolic but also strangely bureaucratic ring of that phrase: work-life balance. I deploy the phrase not because I like it, but because I want to reframe its familiar contours through the lens of queer feminism.[1] More important, I hope to bring into relief how thin the separation is between the harmonious-yet-bureaucratic ideal of being *in balance* and the risky state of being *in the balance*, how infinitesimal the line that differentiates a well-ordered sense of equilibrium from an undetermined but ever present condition of danger. That condition of danger is one, I would argue, that characterizes not only our times but perhaps all times. As Foucault famously remarked: "My point is not that everything is bad, but that everything is dangerous, which is not exactly the same as bad."[2] Is anyone "in balance" and not "in the balance," out of the way of danger, guaranteed to avoid the risk of falling? Some of us may occupy the tip of the iceberg of privilege, but the iceberg itself is melting—think collapsed economy, think literal icebergs: the real places where polar bears are drowning.

Let me also add, on a personal note, that I'm caught up short by the phrase *work-life balance* because I've never, ever had it, not even once in my life. Shall we interpret this failure of mine as a feminist lesson about the need for structural changes in the work-domestic relation? Or should we read this failure as a queer manifestation of edge-seeking libidinal excess? As I hope the pages of this book have shown, the conceptual division that undergirds these two alternatives limits our ability to respond creatively to the problem Kathi Weeks calls "getting a life."[3] If work-life balance has been consistently framed as a feminist issue, my impulse to bring queer lives into the picture is an attempt to unsettle the queer-feminist opposition rather than to reinforce it.[4]

As a number of writers have demonstrated, the modern imperative to achieve a perfect balance between life and work has repeatedly ended in failure. The more we strive, the more we fail. Indeed, as Amy Allen explains in her discussion of the "Mommy wars," our social and economic arrangements are structured to make us fail: we have embraced "economic policies and social institutions that set up systematic obstacles to women working outside of the home" while, at the same time, professing a belief in equality for women.[5] And while Allen's feminist call to change the structural conditions within which individual life choices are made is important, I want to approach work-life balance from a slightly different perspective.

The gap between an ideal balance and the structural constraints that thwart us—between the blinding light of Platonic balance and the murky reality of our cave-dwelling lives—is captured by that Foucault-inflected word: *dangerous*. The structure of the ideal masks a violence, and for Foucault, Irigaray, and many of their antihumanist contemporaries that violence has to do with the status of the subject. Foucault called it man, but today, in large part due to feminist efforts, we can call that "self" man and woman, fathers and mothers whose working selves are threatened, wobbly, unraveling at the edges.[6] In *The Problem with Work*, Kathi Weeks asks: "Why do we work so long and hard?"[7] In her book-length response to that question, Weeks proposes a utopian postwork politics to address the threats that have made us increasingly wobbly. And while I share Weeks's sense that framing the work-life problem in "the register of individual belief and choice" is not the solution, I depart from her concluding dismissal of ethics "with its focus on practices of the self and encounters with the other" in favor of a collective politics.[8] While we certainly cannot dismiss politics, if the selves that constitute collective bodies remain unchanged, it is unlikely that our political efforts will change much either. And, if ethics is involved in practices of the self in relation to others, as Weeks claims, such a formulation must be conceived as part of the desubjectivating project that marks Foucault's work from start to finish. As both Foucault and Irigaray have shown, rhetorically dismissing ethics in the name of politics hardly means that ethical questions won't continue to plague us.

As I've argued throughout this book, my ethical question is the question of the subject: the modern, moral, Western subject that lurks behind most everything we do, even when we try to dismiss him. Doesn't our pursuit—individual or collective—of a utopian integration of work with life mask that harmonious, coherent, masculine self, promoted to what Leo Bersani calls in "Is the Rectum a Grave?" "the status of an *ethical ideal*"?[9] This is my most insistently Foucauldian, "everything is dangerous," queer lives in the balance question. For if work-life balance or simply "getting a life" fails to challenge the status of the self as an ethical ideal, what happens to the abjected residue of that utopian ideal: the queer, the oblique, the incoherent, and indeed, the erotic?

I've never achieved Platonic balance, and I have specifically queer feminist questions about this failure of mine—this condition of being out of balance, living on some sort of edge: falling, scraping my knees, then getting up only to find myself tripping, flailing, or tipping over again. I say I have specifically queer feminist questions because the layers of scar tissue that pad my knees do not tell the story most often told in the neoliberal work-life balance literature: a story about selves who struggle to juggle the demands of work with those of family. Work-life balance means work-*family* balance in the vast majority of writings on the matter.

As Weeks points out, this way of framing the work-life problem is "singularly inadequate" and yet remains pervasive.[10] But what is family? I, for example, have no children or elderly parents to care for. I have a partner-lover-significant other who watches me with an array of reactions ranging from bemusement to anger, as I do my "out of balance, edgy" thing, day in and day out, sometimes happily, sometimes miserably.

At this point my insistently antifoundationalist question—what is the relation of the balanced-self ideal to the queer excess it both excludes and produces—can be extended with a second question, one that emerges in that gap between my queer feminist "life" and the "life" of the work-life balance literature: What are the possible "lives" to be imagined and explored both within and to the side of the "life" of work-life balance? What does it mean to inhabit, pursue, or name those lives as queer? I've reviewed a lot of work-life balance publications from the last five years or so, analyses and reports published in venues I normally don't frequent, like *Journal of Human Behavior in the Social Environment, Gender, Work and Organization, Social Policy and Administration, Cultures and Organizations, Journal of Marriage and Family, Journal of Feminist Family Therapy,* and *HR* publications of various kinds. With very few exceptions, there is virtually nothing on "queer lives" as they relate to work-life balance. When "queers" are included, it is usually as lesbian or gay parents trying to find a balance between work and family. So, again, the overwhelming preponderance of the literature not only equates "life" with "family," as I have previously mentioned, but also most often equates "family" with "children." "Life" equals "family" equals "children."

Don't get me wrong: there's nothing wrong with having children. To paraphrase Foucault: I'm not saying it's bad. But it might be dangerous. And surely there must be other ways of thinking about life.

And, indeed, there are. In the realm of queer theory, these ways of living tend to be explicitly nonreproductive. Unlike the literature on LGBT families, queer theory tends to articulate ways of life that are almost entirely divorced, it would seem, from systems of kinship or what Foucault calls in *Sexuality One* the *dispositif* of alliance. These lives are sexual in the explicitly Foucauldian, "proliferation of perversions," "incitement to speak" sense of the term. This is, of course, epitomized in the antisocial thesis strand of queer theory, begun by Bersani and developed in Lee Edelman's 2004 *No Future*, where Edelman argues that "*queerness* names the side of those *not* 'fighting for the children,' the side outside the consensus by which all politics confirms the absolute value of reproductive futurism."[11]

In a slightly different vein, Judith Halberstam argues in her book, *In a Queer Time and Place* (2005), "that there is such a thing as 'queer time' and 'queer space,'" where queerness involves "strange temporalities, imaginative life schedules, and eccentric economic practices" of lives "unscripted by the conventions of family, inheritance, and child rearing."[12] Halberstam names, specifically, "ravers, club kids, HIV-positive barebackers, rent boys, sex workers, homeless people, drug dealers, and the unemployed" as "people [who] could productively be called 'queer subjects' in terms of the way they live (deliberately, accidentally, or of necessity) during the hours when others sleep and in the spaces (physical, metaphysical, and economic) that others have abandoned" (10).[13] Other examples of antiheteronormative queer challenges to reproductivity abound. These queer lives live in very different neighborhoods than those I've encountered in the vast literature on kinship and work-life balance.

So what is the point, you might ask, of putting them in conversation with one another? Again, the work-life-as-work-children balance question has spurred me to add queer lives to the picture and ask how we might think about those lives in that context. Specifically, the *what about the queers* question I'm bringing to this long-standing feminist issue exposes, once again, another rift between feminist and queer conceptions of sexuality, ethics, and forms of belonging that this book has explored. I have examined this rift in an attempt to transform the queer feminist opposition itself, one that is not only foundational for queer theory but that has been insistently repeated.

Here I want to ground the theoretical questions in pragmatic concerns about everyday life: to explore how the rift reveals itself here, at home, hidden within the family problem of work-life balance. Framing the question as a biopolitical question about life—about lives in balance or lives in the balance—I want to turn again to Foucault in *History of Sexuality*, volume 1 to focus the question—what is a queer life?—in the context of families and work-life balance. Foucault's take on life and its implications for queer life can help us to see how the bucolic-bureaucratic ideal of "lives" in balance masks the dangerous intensification of life called biopower that places life itself in the balance.

Foucault sets up his argument about biopower in *History of Sexuality*, volume 1 in his 1975 course, *Abnormal*, where in his March 5 and March 19 lectures he describes the role of the family in the modern production of sexual subjects.[14] Specifically, Foucault argues that in the modern period childhood functions as the primary instrument for the universalization of psychiatry and what he calls the "immobilization of life" around the figure of the child (Ab 301). That immobilization takes shape primarily through the constitution in the late eighteenth and nineteenth centuries of a new family body Foucault calls the "kangaroo family" (Ab 244), with the child's body as the nuclear element of the family body. That self-enfolding and self-replicating family space is an autoerotic space of surveillance (Ab 245). "What is now being constituted," Foucault writes, "is a sort of restricted, close-knit, substantial, compact, corporeal, and affective family core: the cell family with its corporeal, affective, and sexual space entirely saturated by direct parent-child relationships" (Ab 248). At the same time, "at the very moment that the cellular family is enclosed in a dense, affective space"—the space of "life" in work-life balance—"it is endowed with a rationality that . . . plugs [the family] into a technology" that opens the family to "medical and hygienic intervention" (Ab 250). Thus, Foucault writes, "the psychiatrist becomes the family doctor" (Ab 147), the rational voice of well-adjusted selves, the voice of a psyche-logos who can intervene to both name and manage those sexuality-saturated lives within families distributed across a grid that differentiates the normal from the abnormal. Foucault writes: "a medico-familial mesh organizes a field that is both ethical and pathological," and "the family becomes not only the basis for the determination and distinction of sexuality but also for the rectification of the abnormal" (Ab 254). What Foucault calls the "medicalized" family "functions [then] as a source of normalization" (Ab 254).

In *History of Sexuality*, volume 1 Foucault develops this logic of the family as it relates to sexuality. The family occupies the space of the overlap between an older system of alliance—based on juridical codes and a symbolics of blood—and a newer *dispositif* of sexuality "which [is] superimposed on the previous [system]" but does not completely supplant it. Sexuality—which concerns itself with sensations of the body, the quality of pleasures, and the nature of impressions (the "stuff" of queer theory)—is "born" and takes shape in a technology of power "that began on the fringes of familial institutions" (HS1 110), but that, since the seventeenth century, "gradually becomes focused on the family" (HS1 110).[15] In the modern period, sexuality continues to operate in conjunction with alliance and to depend on it for support. But the relations of power that both produce and sustain sexuality are new.

These new relations of power are guided by a logic whose stakes are life itself. The power of deduction—"a subtraction mechanism," the right to extract taxes, labor, and blood, what Foucault calls the right to "take" life (HS1 136)—becomes merely "one element among others" in a newer, more complex mode of power that incites, monitors, optimizes, organizes: "a power bent on generating forces, making them grow, and ordering them" (HS1 136). This "life-administering power" evolves in two basic forms, around a "great bipolar technology" (HS1 139): disciplinary power at one pole and biopower at the other, an anatomopolitics of the human body and a biopolitics of the population. The second form of power, biopower, comes somewhat later and is focused specifically on the "species body."

That species body is, in my view—and this is my admittedly polemical point—the body at issue in work-life balance discourse. For isn't the body of work-life balance—the body that gives birth, raises children, and cares for its elders—that same body Foucault describes as "the body imbued with the mechanisms of life and serving as the basis of the biological processes: propagation, births and mortality, the level of health, life expectancy and longevity, with all the conditions that can cause these to vary" (HS1 139)? Isn't work-life balance language part of what Foucault calls the "supervision . . . effected through an entire series of interventions and regulatory controls: a biopolitics of the population" (HS1 139)? Isn't even the phrase *work-life balance* a manifestation of what Foucault describes, in biopower, as an "attention to the processes of life—characterized by a power whose highest function is perhaps no longer to kill, but to invest life through and through" (HS1 139)? When viewed through this lens, "life" loses some of the dreamy qualities it takes on in the work-life balance equation, where "life" as family means healthy relationships, parental intimacy and well-behaved children, warm soup on cold nights, the quiet pleasures captured by the phrase "all in the family."

I'm not suggesting that those who have invested time and energy into creating more balance (more pleasure?) in workers' lives are motivated by a logic that Foucault ultimately links to modern dangers like "the atomic situation" and genocide and to which we in the twenty-first century might add drowning polar bears and the death of the planet. What I am suggesting is that work-life balance is still operating under an old logic that is gradually being supplanted: the old logic of the *dispositif* of alliance for its understanding of family and the old logic of deduction for its understanding of workers within systems of power. When we try, and fail, again and again, to "take back" our time, to "take back" the energies of our own vital bodies, we are still functioning within an understanding of power as what Foucault calls the sovereign, juridical "right of seizure: of things, time, bodies, and ultimately life itself" (HS1 136). This is why Foucault writes, in *History of Sexuality*, volume 1, that "in political thought and analysis, we still have not cut off the head of the king" (HS1 88–89).

So let me end with some lingering questions. For those who struggle with the "life" of social reproduction, is it sufficient to try to become better selves who make better choices without looking at the violence of subjectivity itself in a modern regime where to be a subject is to be a sexual subject, with all sexuality's disciplinary and biopolitical implications? Might Irigaray's diagnosis of the absence of a maternal genealogy help us to reframe social reproduction in its relation to capital accumulation as both a material and symbolic problem? And for those whose struggles involve miseries of the childless variety, is it sufficient to inhabit what Foucault calls the "reverse discourse" of perverse sexuality by extolling the pleasures of no future or the antiheteronormative? Isn't it true that the more we praise our own perversions, the more we fall into the trap Foucault illuminated for us: the belief that in "saying yes to sex" we are saying "no to power?" And might the relational ethics of eros I have traced over the course of this book help us to practice, in the here and now, new modes of living and political belonging? Are we in balance or out of balance in the work-life calibration? Let me end here, channeling Foucault but altering him slightly, in a queer feminist resonance that I hope will reverberate beyond these pages: the irony of this question is in having us believe that our liberation, and not our life, is in the balance.[16]

Notes

Introduction

1. Foucault, *The Order of Things*, xxiv.

2. Foucault, "On the Ways of Writing History," 289–290.

3. Ibid.

4. Ibid.

5. Foucault, "Lives of Infamous Men," 160. For the French original, see "La vie des hommes infâmes" (1977), in *Dits et écrits*, 2 vols. (Paris: Quarto Gallimard, 2001), 240 (2:237–253).

6. Foucault, "On the Ways of Writing History," 294.

7. Deleuze, *Nietzsche and Philosophy*, 1.

8. Throughout the book I use the term *queer feminist* without a hyphen to indicate the paradoxical nexus as split that the queer feminist conjunction names. As a queer feminist, I speak from a position that both bridges the rift between queers and feminists and, simultaneously, acknowledges the differences that continue to divide us. In that sense the queer feminist position is not self-identical.

9. For a detailed elaboration of this point in relation to Foucault's *History of Madness*, see Huffer, *Mad for Foucault*.

10. Nietzsche, *Daybreak*, 103.

11. For a more detailed explanation of this point, see Maudemarie Clark and Brian Leiter, "Introduction," ibid., vii–xxxiv.

12. Margaret Whitford, *Luce Irigaray: Philosophy in the Feminine* (London: Routledge, 1991), 76.

13. Ibid., 78.

14. As Foucault puts it in a 1976 lecture: "The disciplines are the bearers of a discourse. . . . The code they come to define is not that of law but that of normalization. . . . It is human science which constitutes their domain, and clinical knowledge their jurisprudence." See Michel Foucault, "Two Lectures," in *Power/ Knowledge: Selected Interviews and Other Writings, 1972–1977*, ed. Colin Gordon (New York: Pantheon, 1980), 106–107.

15. See Rubin, "Thinking Sex"; see also Sedgwick, *Epistemology of the Closet*. For a reappraisal of Rubin's essay, see the "Rethinking Sex" issue of *GLQ: A Journal of Lesbian and Gay Studies* 17, no. 1 (2011). For recent reflections on this history, see especially Love, "'Oh, the Fun We'll Have'"; and Robyn Wiegman, "Telling Time" (chapter 2), in *Object Lessons*, 91–136.

16. Halley, *Split Decisions*. Hereafter cited in this chapter as SD.

17. For an approach to queer feminism that is more foundationalist than mine, see Marinucci, *Feminism Is Queer*.

18. Jagose, "Feminism's Queer Theory," 160.

19. Wiegman, "'Dear Ian,'" 94. For an extended version of "'Dear Ian'" and its discussion of the queerfeminist split, see Wiegman, "Telling Time."

20. Although Halley describes both feminist and queer divergentist projects, her examples of the former are overwhelmingly convergentist and her strongest endorsements obviously go in the direction of queer divergentist projects. Halley offers parts of the Combahee River Collective Statement and Gayatri Spivak's essay, "Can the Subaltern Speak?" as examples of feminist divergentism, but critiques both for not pushing their divergentist impulses far enough. In *Object Lessons* Wiegman makes a similar critique of Halley: "Halley does not take divergence far enough" (27).

21. Rancière, *Disagreement*. For an analysis of feminism in the university that draws on Rancière's conception of politics as disagreement, see Bouchard, *A Community of Disagreement*.

22. Although other definitions of politics include policing in their purview, I follow Rancière here in offering a more restricted definition of politics: "I now propose to reserve the term politics for an extremely determined activity antagonistic to policing: whatever breaks with the tangible configuration whereby parties and parts or lack of them are defined by a presupposition that, by definition, has no place in that configuration—that of the part of those who have no part" (Rancière, *Disagreement*, 29–30). And further: "Modern politics holds to the multiplication of those operations of subjectification that invent worlds of community that are worlds of dissension; it holds to those demonstration devices that are, every time, at once arguments and world openers, the opening up of common (which does not mean consensual) worlds where the subject who argues is counted as arguer" (ibid., 58).

23. On Sedgwick's nondualism, see especially *Touching Feeling*. For a prodivergentist feminist argument, see Wiegman, *Object Lessons*. Although Wiegman explicitly adopts a divergentist position, her critique of Halley ends in a

paradoxical position that is not too far from Rancière's: "what we share the most," Wiegman writes, "begins and ends in divergence" (136). Although even here divergence trumps convergence, Wiegman also admits to being "confronted with the difficulty of maintaining [her] own commitment to divergence" (324).

24. Wiegman, *Object Lessons,* 93.

25. See Nietzsche, *On the Genealogy of Morals;* also see Deleuze, *Nietzsche and Philosophy.*

26. Although Robert Hurley's published English translation of Michel Foucault's *Histoire de la sexualité* (three volumes) renders the title as *The History of Sexuality,* I have removed the definite article (*the*) in my references to the title to conform to the ambiguity of the title without the article in the French original. I also occasionally refer to volumes 1, 2, and 3 as *Sexuality One, The Use of Pleasure,* and *The Care of the Self,* respectively.

27. See Foucault, *History of Madness;* also see *Histoire de la folie à l'âge classique.*

28. Foucault, *The History of Sexuality,* vol. 1: *An Introduction,* 146.

29. At the end of ibid. Foucault writes: "The rallying point for the counterattack against the deployment of sexuality ought not to be sex-desire, but bodies and pleasures" (157). Many queer theorists have interpreted this statement as a formula for resistance to sexual normativity through BDSM and other radical sexual practices. See especially Halperin, *Saint Foucault.* For a more nuanced view that includes a genealogy of "bodies and pleasures," see McWhorter, *Bodies and Pleasures.*

30. See Freud, *Civilization and Its Discontents.*

31. Rajchman, *Truth and Eros,* 108.

32. Bartsch and Bartscherer, "What Silent Love Hath Writ," 2.

33. For a contemporary articulation of ethics as a manner of living, see Williams, *Ethics and the Limits of Philosophy.*

34. On eros in Nietzsche, see Pippin, *Nietzsche, Psychology, and First Philosophy.*

35. On the problems with the label "French feminism" as applied to Irigaray, Cixous, and Kristeva, see Delphy, "The Invention of French Feminism."

36. See Wiegman, "'Dear Ian'"; also see Wiegman, "Heteronormativity and the Desire for Gender." For a more extended version of Wiegman's interrogation of gender, see "Doing Justice with Objects" (chapter 1), in *Object Lessons,* 36–90.

37. For the earliest naming of intersectionality as a concept, see Crenshaw, "Demarginalizing the Intersection of Race and Sex" and "Mapping the Margins." The subsequent literature on intersectionality is too vast to list in a single note. For influential overviews, see especially McCall, "The Complexity of Intersectionality"; and Berger and Guidroz, *The Intersectional Approach.* For a critical view see Nash, "Re-thinking Intersectionality"; and Robyn Wiegman, "Critical Kinship" (chapter 5), in *Object Lessons,* 239–300.

38. Wiegman, *Object Lessons,* 240.

39. Butler, *Gender Trouble,* 3. Butler does not cite Crenshaw.

40. For a detailed argument about the differences between Butler's identity ruptures and Foucault's unraveling of subjectivity, see Huffer, *Mad for Foucault,* especially chapters 2 and 3.

41. Butler, *The Psychic Life of Power*, 98.

42. See Puar, "'I would rather be a cyborg than a goddess.'"

43. Muñoz, *Disidentifications;* and Ferguson, *Aberrations in Black.*

44. Rodríguez, *Queer Latinidad*, 5 (emphasis added).

45. Halberstam, "The Politics of Negativity in Recent Queer Theory," 824.

46. Muñoz, "Thinking Beyond Antirelationality and Antiutopianism in Queer Critique."

47. Edelman, "Antagonism, Negativity, and the Subject of Queer Theory," 821 (emphasis added).

48. Muñoz, for example, excoriates antisocial queer theory as "nothing more than rote invocation of poststructuralist pieties," but approvingly aligns his own utopian readings of culture with Sedgwick's reparative reading practices. See Muñoz, *Cruising Utopia*, 12.

49. See Puar, *Terrorist Assemblages.*

50. See especially McWhorter, *Racism and Sexual Oppression in Anglo-America,* who makes a similar claim (although not addressing intersectionality per se in any detail [15]).

51. Wiegman, *Object Lessons,* 248.

52. For a critical race perspective on Foucault's claims about the demise of sovereign power in modernity, see especially Falguni Sheth, "The Violence of Law: Sovereign Power, Vulnerable Populations, and Race" (chapter 2), in *Toward a Political Philosophy of Race,* 41–64. For further reflections on sovereignty and race, see Sheth, "The War on Terror and Ontopolitics."

53. Foucault, "Two Lectures," 106.

54. Ibid.

55. Ferguson, "Reading Intersectionality."

56. Yuval-Davis, "Intersectionality and Feminist Politics."

57. For an incisive analysis of the institutionalization of women's studies as a field founded on the ideal of what Samuel Weber calls "the exclusion of exclusion," see Bouchard, *A Community of Disagreement.* For Weber's original analysis, see Weber, *Institution and Interpretation,* 138.

58. See Bouchard, *A Community of Disagreement,* 10, for a similar articulation of this point.

59. Crenshaw famously describes the experience of a black woman seeking legal redress for discrimination through an "analogy to traffic in an intersection" where "an accident happens." See Crenshaw, "Demarginalizing the Intersection of Race and Sex," 149.

60. Nash, "Re-thinking Intersectionality," 8.

61. Alexander-Floyd, "Disappearing Acts." Although Alexander-Floyd does not focus on Nash, she views Nash's critique of intersectionality as having been enabled by the disappearance of black women in Leslie McCall's influential essay.

62. Brown, "The Impossibility of Women's Studies," 130.

63. To be sure, intersectionality has been the object of extensive discussion over the years. But most of the debates have revolved around questions of meth-

odology or application of the paradigm. Questioning the usefulness of the paradigm itself has not been at the forefront of this literature.

64. Brown, "The Impossibility of Women's Studies," 122.

65. See Irigaray, "When Our Lips Speak Together"; and Bersani, "Is the Rectum a Grave?"

66. See Foucault, "The Return of Morality," 473.

67. Foucault, *The History of Sexuality,* vol. 2: *The Use of Pleasure,* 9.

68. Barthes, *A Lover's Discourse,* 15.

1. Are the Lips a Grave?

1. Bersani, "Is the Rectum a Grave?" Hereafter cited in this chapter as "RG."

2. Irigaray, "When Our Lips Speak Together." Hereafter cited in this chapter as "Lips."

3. For the earliest (1984) articulation of the need for sexuality studies separate from feminism and gender studies, see Rubin, "Thinking Sex." A more recent iteration of the queer split from feminism is Halley, *Split Decisions.* Hereafter cited in this chapter as SD.

4. For a challenge to the rigidity of overinterpretations of these splits and a similar recognition of a shared queer feminist antifoundationalism (although Irigaray is not mentioned), see Jagose, "Feminism's Queer Theory."

5. For another articulation of this problem see Huffer, "Weird Greek Sex."

6. To my knowledge, only three essays have been written on Irigaray and Foucault, including Braidotti, "The Ethics of Sexual Difference"; Winnubst, "Exceeding Hegel and Lacan"; and my "Weird Greek Sex."

7. Foucault, "Final Interview," 10.

8. In his later work Foucault describes "ethics" as a subset of "morality," which he divides into three categories: 1. a moral code; 2. the conduct of those who follow the code; and 3. "subjectivation," or "ethics": the way individuals constitute themselves as subjects of the code. Foucault argues that every morality includes both behavioral codes ("code-oriented moralities") and subjectivation ("ethics-oriented moralities"). See Foucault, *The History of Sexuality,* vol. 2: *The Use of Pleasure,* 30. Hereafter cited in this chapter as UP.

9. For a book-length treatment of this question, see my *Mad for Foucault.*

10. For a useful overview of moral philosophy, see *The Blackwell Guide to Ethical Theory.* See especially Schroeder, "Continental Ethics," for the Continental exception to the philosophical conflation of ethics as morality.

11. Michael Warner's book-length argument against attempts "to control *someone else's* sex life" is framed in terms of autonomy. Following Warner, Tim Dean's "impersonal ethics of alterity" in the context of bareback culture combines a psychoanalytic theory of disidentification with a relational autonomy ("freedom from interference"). See Warner, *The Trouble with Normal,* 1; and Dean, *Unlimited Intimacy,* 25.

12. For Bersani, see "RG" and *Homos,* especially the final chapter, "The Gay Outlaw," on an antisocial ethics of evil and betrayal. Also see Lee Edelman's death-driven negative ethics in *No Future.* For a different reading of Bersani as a sweet "moralist" in his and Adam Phillips's more recent *Intimacies,* see Berlant, "Neither Monstrous Nor Pastoral," 271.

13. Butler, *Giving An Account of Oneself,* 10.

14. On ethics as a manner of living, see Williams, *Ethics and the Limits of Philosophy.*

15. On the "prevailing moralism" of contemporary sexual theory, see Sedgwick and Frank, "Shame in the Cybernetic Fold," 5.

16. In *On the Genealogy of Morals* Nietzsche famously calls for a transvaluation of values; in his earlier book, *Daybreak* (103), he links moral transvaluation to a different thinking and feeling.

17. On ethics as the relation between subjectivity and truth, see Foucault, "The Ethics of the Concern for Self as a Practice of Freedom." Hereafter cited in this chapter as "ECS."

18. On the "land of morality," see Nietzsche, *On the Genealogy of Morals,* 21.

19. Barkley Brown, "'What Has Happened Here,'" 272–286.

20. As Foucault puts it in *The Order of Things,* "utopias afford consolation" (xvii).

21. Foucault, "Different Spaces," 179. Hereafter cited as in this chapter as "DS."

22. Irigaray, *Speculum of the Other Woman.* Hereafter cited in this chapter as S.

23. On this point, see especially Edelman in the MLA debate on the antisocial thesis in queer theory, in "Forum: Conference Debates."

24. General overviews of queer theory tend not cite Irigaray at all. She makes one appearance in the 1991 issue of *differences* (vol. 3, no. 2) devoted to queer theory, in reference to hommo-sexuality, in the opening introduction by Teresa de Lauretis. Neither Beemyn and Eliason's *Queer Studies* nor Corber and Valocchi's *Queer Studies* give even a single reference to Irigaray. Although Annamarie Jagose has written extensively and insightfully about Irigaray in *Lesbian Utopics,* when she writes about queer theory specifically, in *Queer Theory,* Irigaray disappears. Turner's *A Genealogy of Queer Theory* does not mention Irigaray, despite Turner's claim that "the originators of queer theory are all feminist scholars" (34). In her *Critical Introduction to Queer Theory,* Nikki Sullivan briefly mentions Irigaray, but only in the context of feminist poststructuralist thought. In Warner's *Fear of a Queer Planet,* Irigaray appears in two places: parenthetically, alongside Wittig and Kristeva, in his introductory aside about French feminism, and, as a footnote, in Diana Fuss's explanation of mimicry in her essay on female homosexuality in Freud. In a retrospective overview of queer theory, a 2005 issue of *Social Text* (84–85), "What's Queer About Queer Studies Now?" there are no references to Irigaray; the same is true of the 2006 *Transgender Studies Reader* edited by Stryker and Whittle. The only "queer" anthology in which she does appear with any frequency (in five articles) is in a volume explicitly devoted to

the relation between feminism and queer theory, Schor and Weed's *Feminism Meets Queer Theory*, where she is cited approvingly by some (Judith Butler, Biddy Martin, and Rosi Braidotti) and castigated by others (Trevor Hope and Carole-Anne Tyler). Three exceptions to this absence are Butler's early books, especially *Gender Trouble* and *Bodies That Matter*; Stockton's first book, *God Between Their Lips*; and Salamon's *Assuming a Body*.

25. Foucault, *The History of Sexuality*, vol. 1: *An Introduction*, 154 and 103.

26. Sedgwick, "Privilege of Unknowing," 49.

27. Sedgwick, *Tendencies*, 49; and Owens, "Outlaws," 223.

28. Hope, "Melancholic Modernity," 228.

29. Solanas, *SCUM Manifesto*, 60.

30. Irigaray develops her argument about hommosexuality in *Speculum*, especially 98–103.

31. Although beyond my focus here, this argument implicitly contests the charges made by Owens, Sedgwick, and others that Irigaray's hommosexuality is homophobic and heterosexist.

32. Irigaray, *Conversations*, 160. Hereafter cited in this chapter as C.

33. See Irigaray, *I Love to You* and *Sharing the World*.

34. Grosz, "The Hetero and the Homo," 344.

35. Deutscher, *A Politics of Impossible Difference*, 190.

36. See Winnubst, *Queering Freedom*, 106.

37. See Willett, *The Soul of Justice*, especially 123–156; and Chanter, "Irigaray's Challenge to the Fetishistic Hegemony," 217.

38. Grosz, "Irigaray and the Ontology of Sexual Difference," 103. While I agree with Grosz that Irigaray is elaborating a new ontology, I disagree that this elaboration is "a new metaphysics," as Grosz claims. Irigaray's indebtedness to the Heideggerian dissolution of the metaphysical foundations of ontology seems to be at odds with Grosz's claim.

39. Deutscher, "Conditionalities, Exclusions, Occlusion," 252 and 249–250. Hereafter cited in this chapter as "CEO."

40. For an articulation of this Heideggerian argument vis-à-vis the feminine in Irigaray, see Mortensen, "Woman's Untruth and *le féminin*."

41. Irigaray, *Sexes and Genealogies*, 19.

42. As Irigaray puts it in Speculum: "The vagina . . . functions like the anus, the rectum" (S 24).

43. Huffer, "*Luce et veritas*," 38. Hereafter cited as "Luce."

44. Irigaray, "The Return."

45. Irigaray, *Speculum de l'autre femme*, 454.

46. Van Leeuwen, "An Examination of Irigaray's Commitment to Transcendental Phenomenology." Irigaray's most explicitly Heideggerian books include *The Forgetting of Air*, *The Way of Love*, and *Sharing the World*. For investigations of Irigaray's engagement with Heidegger, see, in addition to Mortenson and Van Leeuwen, Hodge, "Irigaray Reading Heidegger"; and Tina Chanter's chapter, "Irigaray, Heidegger, and the Greeks," in *Ethics of Eros*, 127–169.

47. Gallop, *Thinking Through the Body*, 94.

48. Foucault, *The Hermeneutics of the Subject*, 237.

49. Scott, *The Question of Ethics*, 1.

50. Foucault, "The Return of Morality," 473.

51. Irigaray's most important texts on Levinas include "The Fecundity of the Caress"; and "Questions to Emmanuel Levinas."

52. Chanter, *Ethics of Eros*, 180. Hereafter cited in this chapter as EE.

53. For a recent attempt to systematize eros in Irigaray's work, see Christopher Cohoon, "Coming Together: The Six Modes of Irigarayan Eros," *Hypatia* 26, no. 3 (2001): 478–496. Cohoon highlights Irigarayan eros as a concept of separation and alliance that allows subjectivity and intersubjectivity to emerge as effects of the erotic relation. Importantly, Cohoon argues that through affective, sensuous, subjective, elemental, temporal, and numerical modes, Irigaray situates eros "as the paradigmatic site for ethics" (481).

54. See Huffer, *Mad for Foucault*, especially chapter 5, "A Political Ethic of Eros." On loving and knowing, see Carson, *Eros*, 70.

55. See Foucault, "Lives of Infamous Men," 157–175.

56. See Foucault, *Society Must Be Defended*, 11.

57. Irigaray, *An Ethics of Sexual Difference*, 3. See also Butler, "The End of Sexual Difference?" who insists on the importance of sexual difference in Irigaray as "a persistence whose status is not eternal" (177).

58. The French term Foucault uses for this self-undoing—*se déprendre de soi-même*—means literally to release oneself from oneself. See UP, 15.

59. Foucault, *The Archeology of Knowledge*, 211.

2. There Is No Gomorrah

1. In the West, this tension dates back to the institutionalization of Christianity in the Middle Ages. For a history of the rise of religious moralism in twelfth-century Europe, see Jordan, *The Invention of Sodomy in Christian Theology*. For an analysis of this tension in the contemporary period, see Gayle Rubin's 1984 article, "Thinking Sex." Also see Rubin's interview with Butler, "Sexual Traffic."

2. Colette, *The Pure and the Impure*, 131–32 (translation modified). Hereafter cited in this chapter as PI.

3. For a detailed analysis of this chapter in Colette's *The Pure and the Impure*, see Huffer, *Another Colette*, 71–102.

4. For historical studies of sodomy as a term that constructs sexual norms, see Boswell, *Christianity, Social Tolerance, and Homosexuality*; Fisher, "Queer Money"; Foucault, *History of Sexuality*, vol. 1; hereafter cited in this chapter as HS1; Goldberg *Reclaiming Sodom* and *Sodometries: Renaissance Texts/Modern Sexualities*; and Jordan, *The Invention of Sodomy in Christian Theology*. For a critique of Boswell's normalizing view of gay sexuality, see Dinshaw, *Getting Medieval*. For a feminist critique of medieval and contemporary scholarship on sodomy, see Lochrie, *Covert Operations* and, especially, "Presumptive Sodomy and

Its Exclusions." For an interpretation of contemporary uses of sodomy in the law, see chapter 4, "Queer Victory, Feminist Defeat? Sodomy and Rape in *Lawrence v. Texas*," this volume.

5. It is true that most of what constitutes *The Pure and the Impure* was first published before the war, in 1932, as *Ces plaisirs*. . . . However, as Colette's biographer Judith Thurman points out, the changes made to the 1941 version are significant. Thurman cites the editor of the 1941 edition in the unsigned preface to the book: "She [Colette] has manifested her predilection . . . in making changes and additions important enough for the present edition to be considered, in part, original." See Thurman, *Secrets of the Flesh*, 450. On *Ces plaisirs* and *The Pure and the Impure*, also see Francis and Gontier, *Colette*, 327–337.

6. Genesis 19:24–25. In the *New Oxford Annotated Bible*.

7. In *Bodies That Matter*, Judith Butler asks: "Is it a matter of knowing" (241)? My answer to her question is "yes." As Lyotard shows, the question of knowing is inextricable from ontological and ethical questions. Indeed, Lyotard theorizes the crisis he calls "the postmodern condition" through a "report on knowledge." See Butler, *Bodies That Matter*; and Lyotard, *The Postmodern Condition*.

8. Gallop, *The Deaths of the Author*, 24.

9. See Derrida, "Signature Event Context." As Derrida puts it: "Such iterability—*iter*, again, probably comes from *itara, other* in Sanskrit, and everything that follows can be read as the working out of the logic that ties repetiton to alterity" (7).

10. See especially Adamson, Freadman, and Parker, *Renegotiating Ethics*; Booth, *The Company We Keep*; Caruth, *Unclaimed Experience*; Chow, *Ethics After Idealism*; Felman and Laub, *Testimony*; Garber, Hanssen, and Walkowitz, *The Turn to Ethics*; Keenan, *Fables of Responsibility*; Miller, *The Ethics of Reading*; Newton, *Narrative Ethics*; Nouvet, *Literature and the Ethical Question*; and Nussbaum, *Poetic Justice*. For a useful overview of ethics and literature, see Buell, "Introduction."

11. For important works that have influenced my thinking about feminist and queer ethics see especially Benhabib, *Situating the Self*; Card, *Feminist Ethics*; Champagne, *The Ethics of Marginality*; Cornell, *Beyond Accommodation*; Daly, *Feminist Theological Ethics*; Dean, *Unlimited Intimacy*; Hoagland, *Lesbian Ethics*; Irigaray, *An Ethics of Sexual Difference*; Kaplan, *Sexual Justice*; Kramer, *Reports from the Holocaust*; Mohr, *Gays/Justice*; Tronto, *Moral Boundaries*; Warner, *The Trouble with Normal*; and Young, *Intersecting Voices* and *Justice and the Politics of Difference*.

12. As Michael Warner puts it: "For most people, at least, the ethical response to sexual shame seems to be: more shame" (*The Trouble with Normal*, 3).

13. For example, see Lyotard's critique of Habermas in *The Postmodern Condition*, especially chapter 14. For a classic articulation of the antinormative deconstructive position, see Keenan who, in *Fables of Responsibility*, argues that "the possibility of the ethical lies in its impossibility" (36).

14. Both Benhabib and Newton exemplify this tendency. For a summary of the vexed relationship between narrative, ethics, and politics, see Buell, "Introduction."

15. Paradoxically, when it does arise, the queer call for (good) ethics tends to rely on a liberal humanist discourse of individual rights. For example, Rubin's vision of "true ethics" is based on the liberal ideal of pluralism: "It is difficult to develop a pluralistic sexual ethics without a concept of benign sexual variation" ("Thinking Sex," 15). Similarly, Warner bases his "ethics of queer life" (*The Trouble with Normal,* 33) on the liberal principle of autonomy, "an ethical respect for the autonomy of others" (4).

16. The phrase comes from Nagel. For an important feminist critique of this traditional ethical view, see Bordo, "Feminism, Postmodernism, and Gender Scepticism."

17. Crenshaw, "Demarginalizing the Intersection of Race and Sex," 141.

18. Crenshaw, "Mapping the Margins," 1242.

19. Ibid.

20. Ludvig, "Differences Between Women?"

21. Butler, *Bodies That Matter,* 52.

22. For an important reading of a similar logic in American writing postslavery, see Holland, *Raising the Dead.*

23. Much has been made of Colette's contradictory and even derogatory writings on same-sex eroticism between women. Lillian Faderman, for example, although generally positive in her assessment of Colette's depictions of lesbians, complains that Colette "was not entirely free of the lesbian images of her predecessors" (364). Adrienne Rich is even more critical, asserting that Colette "writes about lesbian existence as if for a male audience" (245). See Faderman, *Surpassing the Love of Men;* and Rich, "Compulsory Heterosexuality and Lesbian Existence." For less condemning readings of eroticism between women in Colette, see Huffer, *Another Colette,* especially chapter 3, and Ladenson, "Colette for Export Only." For biographies that explore Colette's intimate relations with women, see Francis and Gontier, *Colette;* and Thurman, *Secrets of the Flesh.*

24. This figuration of Irigaray, Colette, and Gomorrah as ghosts resonates with Terry Castle's insight into the ghosting of lesbians in literature. See Castle, *The Apparitional Lesbian.*

25. Although there are, in my view, important limits to the Levinasian frame; see, especially, chapter 6, "Queer Lesbian Silence: Colette Reads Proust," this volume. I am indebted to a number of scholars who have drawn on the Levinasian articulation of responsibility to the other in order to develop a concept of relational ethics that takes seriously notions of alterity in the context of narrative. See especially Chanter, *Ethics of Eros;* Eaglestone, *Ethical Criticism;* Felman and Laub, *Testimony;* Newton, *Narrative Ethics;* Robbins, *Altered Reading;* and Wyschogrod, *An Ethics of Remembering.*

26. As Ladenson explains in *Proust's Lesbianism:* "In fact, the tradition that links Gomorrah to lesbianism is a short one, largely a French phenomenon, and almost entirely due to Proust himself. It was Proust who put Gomorrah on the map, as it were, as something more specific than a shadowy sister city destroyed along with Sodom in Genesis: it was Proust who made Gomorrah a recognized euphemism for female homosexuality" (35). See Ladenson, *Proust's Lesbianism.*

27. This allegory also serves to illustrate one of the crucial effects of the feminist/queer split: the erasure of the "lesbian" subject.

28. Miller, *Narrative and Its Discontents*.

29. Butler, "Gender Trouble, Feminist Theory," 339.

30. Butler, "Imitation and Gender Insubordination," 315.

31. Berlant and Warner, "Sex in Public."

32. Although Butler disregards ethics in *Gender Trouble* and *Bodies That Matter*, she begins to address ethical questions in *Excitable Speech*, where she briefly engages ethics by implicitly rethinking performativity in a context that includes temporality and forms of address, both of which are constitutive of narrative structures. As Butler puts it in her argument about injurious speech: "The responsibility of the speaker does not consist of remaking language ex nihilo but rather of negotiating the legacies of usage that constrain and enable that speaker's speech" (27). I would take Butler's point one step further to argue that those "legacies of usage" are specifically transmitted as *narrative* legacies. Similarly, in *The Psychic Life of Power*, Butler theorizes the relationship between subjectivity and narrative, arguing that "the narrative that seeks to account for how the subject comes into being presumes the grammatical 'subject' prior to the account of its genesis" (111). Of course, in Butler's view, to presume a subject prior to its narrativization is "to literalize or to ascribe an ontological status to the grammatical requirement of 'the subject'" (124); indeed, for Butler the subject is no more than "the grammatical place for the subject," something narrative requires as a result of "the narrative itself" (124). Although Butler never explicitly links this notion of subject formation and subjection in narrative with the concept of performativity, the connection remains implicit in her argument. Just as there is no subject prior to narrative, so too "there is no subject prior to their performing" (119).

33. See especially Butler, *Giving an Account of Oneself*, much of which is an ethical meditation on the "constitutive incommensurability" (39) between the "I" and the narrative the "I" tells about itself.

34. Patton, "Tremble, Hetero Swine!" 147–148. Patton alludes to a connection between queerness and narrative in her conclusion as well: "queers are nothing if not good readers. . . . We are constructed both through reading and as a rhetorical effect of reading" (174).

35. This crisis was most famously articulated by Lyotard in 1979, nearly a decade before the advent of "queer theory," as a crisis of "narrative" giving way to the atomizing, efficiency-based forces of "performativity." It is also worth noting that Lyotard explicitly links J. L. Austin's concept of the performative to a more general understanding of *performance* and *performativity*, terms used by Lyotard to describe the measurable efficiency of a system based on the relationship of input to output. Significantly, Lyotard links the rise of performativity in the postmodern age to the legitimation of knowledge claims through systems of force. See Austin, *How to Do Things with Words*,

36. Butler links this misogyny to "the antifeminism accompanying the rise of gay conservatives to power positions within the queer movement" and suggested well over a decade ago that "the 'gayocon' sensibility has arrived in queer

studies" (Butler, "Against Proper Objects," 24). For a related discussion of gay male misogyny in the context of drag, see Tyler,"Boys Will Be Girls." Rubin, on the other hand, has pointed to the hegemony of a "conservative sexual morality" within feminism ("Thinking Sex," 28), regarding the feminist condemnation of gay male sexual practices as "an expression of reconstituted homophobia" ("Sexual Traffic" 82). For another classic example of the queer critique of feminist homophobia, see Anonymous Queers: "You ignore me in public because I bring 'too much' attention to 'my' lesbianism. But then you want me to be your lover, you want me to be your friend, you want me to love you, support you, fight for 'OUR' right to exist" (591). See Anonymous Queers, "Queers Read This." For a queer critique of the sex-phobic moralism of lesbian cultural feminism, see Halberstam, *Female Masculinity*.

37. Butler makes this point much more explicitly in her work on subjection (*assujettissement*): "To literalize or to ascribe an ontological status to the grammatical requirement of 'the subject' is to presume a mimetic relation between grammar and ontology which misses the point, both Althusserian and Lacanian, that the anticipations of grammar are always and only retroactively installed" (*The Psychic Life of Power*, 124). On subjection as *assujettisement*, see especially Foucault, *Discipline and Punish*.

38. As I argue in *Mad for Foucault*, especially chapter 2, the performative subversion of identity in Butler's work is not the same as Foucauldian desubjectivation.

39. See especially Maclean, *Narrative as Performance*. Also see Chambers, *Room for Maneuver*.

40. See especially Newton, *Narrative Ethics*, for a book-length development of this argument.

41. To be sure, this project is not without its own internal contradictions. As Buell points out regarding the Levinasian ethical system: "it is self-contradictory: it insists on antifoundationalism, but it supplies a foundation (interhumanity) to guard against the inference that . . . can be drawn from a purely relativistic conception of ethics" (15).

42. Sedgwick, *Tendencies*, 9.

43. Bersani, *Homos*.

44. It is important to highlight here what Bersani means by sociality. For Bersani, sociality is unthinkable except as oppression; as he puts it in his reading of Genet: "In a society where oppression is structural, *constitutive of sociality itself*, only what society throws off—its mistakes or its pariahs—can serve the future" (*Homos*, 180, emphasis added). My contention, on the other hand, follows Levinas in suggesting that we can only become subjects within an always prior sociality. In positing ethics as "first philosophy," Levinas gives ethics primacy over epistemology and ontology, thereby affirming what Derrida calls "an 'unlimited' responsibility that exceeds and precedes my freedom" ("Adieu" 3). In this context our challenge becomes the double task of undoing those forms of sociality that oppress us while, at the same time, creating and strengthening those forms of sociality and community that promote the flourishing of human

subjects. See Derrida, "Adieu." Also see Levinas, *Totality and Infinity*. On Derrida's essay on the death of Levinas as an example of ethical close reading, see Gallop, *The Deaths of the Author*, 55–83.

45. Muñoz, *Disidentifications*, 34. For his defense of queer utopianism, see Muñoz, *Cruising Utopia*.

46. Derrida, "Adieu" 3.

47. On lesbian invisibility, see Rich, "Compulsory Heterosexuality and Lesbian Existence." On the ontological impossibility of lesbianism within heterosexism, see Wittig, "The Straight Mind." On the critical inability to see lesbianism, or Gomorrah, in Proust, see Ladenson, *Proust's Lesbianism*. On a similar critical inability to see lesbianism in medieval studies of sodomy, see Lochrie, "Presumptive Sodomy and Its Exclusions."

48. Berlant and Warner, "What Does Queer Theory Teach Us About X?"

49. Scott, *Only Paradoxes to Offer*, 29.

50. For a critique of national citizenship based on an exclusionary logic of queer identity, see Fernandez, "Undocumented Aliens in the Queer Nation." Fernandez's early critique will be repeated and expanded in subsequent queer work, especially in Jasbir Puar's critique of homonationalism. See Puar, *Terrorist Assemblages*. For an overview of the politics of Queer Nation see Berlant and Freeman, "Queer Nationality."

51. Schor, "French Feminism Is a Universalism,"40.

52. Berlant and Warner, "What Does Queer Theory Teach Us About X?" 344 (emphasis added).

53. Cohen, "Punks, Bulldaggers, and Welfare Queens."

54. Arendt explicitly links narrative to action as constitutive of history and politics: "That every individual life between birth and death can eventually be told as a story with beginning and end is the prepolitical and prehistorical condition of history, the great story without beginning and end. But the reason why each human life tells its story and why history ultimately becomes the storybook of mankind [*sic*], with many actors and speakers and yet without any tangible authors, is that both are the outcome of action" (184). See Arendt, *The Human Condition*. For uses of Arendt in feminist political theory, see, especially, Honig, *Feminist Interpretations of Hannah Arendt*; and Zerilli, *Feminism and the Abyss of Freedom*. On Arendt's performative politics see Honig, "Declarations of Independence."

55. See Derrida, "Signature Event Context," 7.

56. Austin, *How to Do Things with Words*, 10.

57. Probyn, *Outside Belongings*.

58. As theorized by Muñoz, "disidentification" resists the homogenizing forces of identification without becoming its polar opposite. Drawing on Pêcheux, Fuss, Žižek, and Butler, Muñoz distinguishes between a purely negative concept of "counteridentification" and a more transformative "disidentification." For Muñoz, disidentification describes "the labor . . . of making identity as a process that takes place at the point of collision of perspectives. . . . This collision is precisely the moment of negotiation when hybrid, racially predicated, and deviantly

gendered identities arrive at representation. In doing so, a representational contract is broken; the queer and the colored come into perception and the social order receives a jolt" (*Disidentifications*, 6).

59. Ibid., 200.

60. Ibid.

61. On reproductive futurism, see Edelman, *No Future*. On Sedgwick's critique of "beyond" (and "beneath") see *Touching Feeling*.

62. See Young, *Intersecting Voices*, 44.

3. Foucault's Fist

1. Foucault, *The History of Sexuality*, vol. 1: *An Introduction*, 159. Hereafter cited as HS1.

2. In several interviews, Foucault praises BDSM practitioners for their corporeal inventiveness. In a 1984 interview in the *Advocate*, for example, Foucault celebrates these practices for "inventing new possibilities of pleasure with strange parts of our bodies." See Gallagher and Wilson, "Michel Foucault," 29. More famously, see Foucault's comments in the recently translated 1978 interview with Le Bitoux, "The Gay Science." For a philosophical discussion of BDSM and Foucauldian desubjectivation, see especially MacKendrick, *Counterpleasures*.

3. Jagose, "Counterfeit Pleasures," 522.

4. Margot Weiss explains that BDSM is a relatively recent term that combines three acronyms: "B & D (bondage and discipline), D/S (domination/submission), and SM (sadomasochism). The use of SM (sometimes S/M or S&M) as the inclusive term predates BDSM, but BDSM is fast becoming the acronym of choice" (vii). "Leather," by contrast, is most often used in gay and sometimes lesbian SM communities to describe practices that include leather fetishism and motorcycle clubs. See Weiss, *Techniques of Pleasure*.

5. Gayle Rubin defines fisting as the following: "a sexual technique in which the hand and arm, rather than a penis or dildo, are used to penetrate a bodily orifice. Fisting usually refers to anal penetration, although the terms are also used for the insertion of a hand into a vagina" (121). See Rubin, "The Catacombs." reprinted in *Deviations*, 224–240.

6. For queer theorists on fisting, see, especially, Bersani, *Homos*, 79; Halperin, *Saint Foucault*, 89–92, and "Forgetting Foucault," 26. On gay men, Foucault, HIV, and abjection, see David Halperin, *What Do Gay Men Want? An Essay on Sex, Risk, and Subjectivity* (Ann Arbor: University of Michigan Press, 2007). On fisting as a metaphor for a Jamesian sentence, see Eve Kosofsky Sedgwick, "The Beast in the Closet," in *Epistemology of the Closet*, 208n33. Also see Jagose's review of fisting in her exploration of fake orgasm and counterpleasures in "Counterfeit Pleasures," 517–521.

7. Halperin goes on to say that fist fucking is not the newest pleasure, pointing out that phone sex and fax sex are newer. *Saint Foucault*, 92, hereafter cited in this chapter as SF. Today we could add cybersex to his list. Of course, it's worth

asking if any of these sexual technologies are in fact "new." As Bruce Benderson puts it regarding the Cartesianism of cybersex: "Not since the invention of the printing press has so much disembodied human consciousness been spread so thin" (6). See Benderson, *Sex and Isolation*.

8. Warner, *The Trouble with Normal*, 178.

9. For a different queer view of fisting and BDSM, see "John Waters, Baron of Bad Taste." As Waters puts it in this 2005 interview: "Fisting [is] messy and bad for your health. . . . Gay S&M has a hard time recruiting. Nobody wants to get whipped anymore. Nobody's that guilty about it. No kid wants to wear chaps. Chaps are mortifyingly out of fashion. At the same time, the real bikers, the hardcore bikers, are all old men. There are no young ones. There are no cute ones. They all have potbellies. It's a corny image" (202). Many thanks to Michael Moon for bringing this interview to my attention.

10. Foucault, "Friendship as a Way of Life," 138.

11. Weiss, *Techniques of Pleasure*, 5. For a detailed ethnography of these changes, also see Rubin, "Elegy for the Valley of the Kings" and "The Miracle Mile."

12. Sedgwick, *Touching Feeling*, 12.

13. For a typical example, see Meyer, "Robert Mapplethorpe and the Discipline of Photography." Meyer's article opens with Robert Mapplethorpe's 1978 "Self-Portrait" in which the photographer presents his anus to the camera, penetrated by a bull-whip, with his head wrenched around to confront the viewer's gaze. The shock of the photograph at the beginning of the article is heightened by the linguistic shock of the article's opening paragraph, where "penis piercing, latex bondage, single and double fist-fucking, and anal-penetration with a bull-whip" (360) are evoked. It is worth noting that this article appears in a standard academic "textbook" to be used in courses on gay and lesbian studies. For other examples, see Berlant and Warner's public spectacle of "erotic vomiting" in "Sex in Public"; Bersani's image of the rectum in "Is the Rectum a Grave?"; and even Sedgwick's "Jane Austen and the Masturbating Girl." It goes without saying that the linguistic shock effect of queer theory is the aspect most vilified by the right. See especially Kimball, *Tenured Radicals*, who goes after the "masturbation" in Sedgwick's MLA title. The fact that today such prurience seems quaint is a testament to the success of the queer incitement to speak in the late twentieth century.

14. Didier Eribon highlights the intellectual and political context of *The History of Sexuality*, vol. 1. In Eribon's view, this work on sexuality contradicts the antirepressive arguments developed by Foucault himself over a decade earlier in *History of Madness*, as well as the antirepressive, Reichian ideology that was pervasive in France throughout the 1960s and 1970s. In addition, Eribon argues that *Sexuality One* situates Foucault as a member of a pre-Stonewall, pre–May 1968 generation confronted with a militant gay movement with which he could not identify. As Eribon explains, French writers and activists such as Guy Hocquenghem announced the "coming into being of a 'desirous social struggle'" and a will to challenge "both those forms of civilization that are founded on 'normal' sexuality and whatever forces of repression guarantee that sexuality's normality." Eribon, "Michel Foucault's Histories of Sexuality," 64. Eribon's argument is

developed more fully in his book, *Insult and the Making of the Gay Self,* especially 296–332. Along similar lines, Robert Nye argues that Foucault was caught in a specifically French, postwar trap that allowed him neither the path of gay identity politics nor the traditional family order of French bourgeois society. In this context, Foucault "applied himself to the delicate task of reconfiguring a new kind of identity out of the wreckage of the one he had spent a considerable part of his life trying to escape" (235). See Nye, "Michel Foucault's Sexuality." For a more recent version of sexual utopianism that explicitly links sexuality to political desire, see José Muñoz, *Cruising Utopia: The Then and There of Queer Futurity* (Durham: Duke University Press, 2009).

15. See especially Bersani, "Is the Rectum a Grave?"

16. Michael Warner's introduction to *Fear of a Queer Planet* is representative of the rebellious insertion of queerness into an overly tame academic environment: "For academics, being interested in queer theory is a way to mess up the desexualized spaces of the academy, exude some rut, reimagine the publics from and for which academic intellectuals write, dress, and perform" (xxvi).

17. Muñoz, *Cruising Utopia,* 1.

18. Halperin, "Forgetting Foucault," 26.

19. Ladelle McWhorter, *Bodies and Pleasures: Foucault and the Politics of Normalization* (Bloomington: Indiana University Press, 1999), 135.

20. This logical conclusion to Foucault's argument could explain his reticence to speak of his own pleasures, with the exception of scattered remarks in interviews. As Leo Bersani comments with regard to such pleasures: "I can't help wondering what the pleasures were. . . . Foucault says almost nothing about those pleasures in the interviews I refer to, although he did speak elsewhere at some length, and with enthusiasm, of gay sadomasochistic sex" ("Is the Rectum a Grave?" 79). In the context of the point about the irony of theory, those enthusiastic comments by Foucault might be seen as theoretical "slips."

21. Waters, "John Waters, Baron of Bad Taste," 202.

22. For an interesting feminist philosophical take on this issue, see Grimshaw: "In general, then, Foucault's work on ethics is disappointing. . . . It seems trapped in a highly masculinist view of ethics as the concern of a male elite to stylize their own lives. It sees this stylized aestheticization of life as the only alternative to a morality based on adherence to a rigid or universal code" (70). Along similar lines, Kate Soper remarks: "Foucault, in short, by abstracting as much as he can both from the social context of the ethical codes he is charting, and from the dialectic of personal relations, defines the ethical so as to make it appear a very private—and masculine—affair: a matter primarily of self-mastery and authorial creation." See Soper, "Productive Contradictions," 41. More recently, feminists have begun to articulate the constructive ways in which Foucault's ethical work can be harnessed in the service of feminist projects. See especially Taylor and Vintges, *Feminism and the Final Foucault.*

23. Berlant, *The Queen of America Goes to Washington City.* Hereafter cited in this chapter as QA.

24. Martin, "Feminism, Criticism, and Foucault," 17.

25. Martin, "Extraordinary Homosexuals and the Fear of Being Ordinary," 110.

26. Bersani, "Is the Rectum a Grave?" The literature on Foucault and feminism is extensive, and it is not my purpose to trace it here. For an especially helpful overview of the debates see Sawicki, *Disciplining Foucault*.

27. Foucault, *Discipline and Punish*, 308. Hereafter cited in this chapter as DP.

28. Cooper and Foucault, "Dialogue sur l'enfermement et la répression psychiatrique," 99 (translation mine).

29. MacKinnon writes: "it is very difficult to say that there is a major distinction in the level of sex involved between being assaulted by a penis and being assaulted by a fist, especially when the perpetrator is a man." MacKinnon, *Feminism Unmodified*, 92. Leo Bersani picks up on MacKinnon's point in "Is the Rectum a Grave," agreeing with her claim that "so-called normal sexuality is already pornographic" (214).

30. Davis, "Racialized Punishment and Prison Abolition," 96.

31. Foucault, "Sexual Choice, Sexual Act," 143.

32. Plaza, "Our Damages and Their Compensation," 29.

33. Soper, "Productive Contradictions," 257.

34. Foucault, *History of Sexuality*, vol. 2: *The Use of Pleasure*, 23, 27. Hereafter cited in this chapter as UP.

35. It is important to point out that Foucault himself insisted that his descriptions of Greek and Roman technologies of the self were not to be read as models for more modern forms of corporeal praxis. Foucault: "Not only do I not identify the ancient culture of the self with the Californian cult of the self, but I think they are diametrically opposed." See Foucault, "On the Genealogy of Ethics," 1:271.

36. See, for example, Mahmood's Foucauldian ethnography of the practices of the self of contemporary Egyptian Muslim women, *Politics of Piety*. Also see Taylor and Vintges, *Feminism and the Final Foucault*.

37. Hunt, "Foucault's Subject in *The History of Sexuality*," 83.

38. Foucault, "Friendship as a Way of Life," 136.

39. Berlant and Warner, "Sex in Public," 558.

40. Hunt, "Foucault's Subject in *The History of Sexuality*," 83.

41. Indeed, in "Friendship as a Way of Life" Foucault himself paves the way for Halperin's slippage: "How is it possible for men to be together?" (136). When pressed by the interviewer, Foucault dismisses the possibility that his concept could be relevant for women: "Women have had access to the bodies of other women: they put their arms around each other, kiss each other. Man's body has been forbidden to other men in a much more drastic way" (139).

42. I borrow this term for the denial of self from Carol Lee Flinders. Flinders points out that this spiritual goal of most religious traditions often denies the debilitating selflessness into which many women have already been socialized. See Flinders, *At the Root of This Longing*, 68–69.

43. Plaza, "Our Damages and Their Compensation," 29.

44. Foucault, *History of Sexuality*, vol. 3: *The Care of the Self*, 51.

45. Jean Grimshaw notes that "this sociality or mutuality is hard to detect in the second and third volumes of *The History of Sexuality*," especially since Foucault only concerns himself with "the relation to self of a few elite males." Further, she notes, "those with whom [these males] have relationships seem to be thought of as instruments through which they fashion their own freedom." Thus "although Foucault pays lip-service . . . to the idea of 'the social,' there is no sense whatever of the importance of collective goals or aspirations, or the ways in which individual lives might be lived in the light of something that transcended these" (68). Grimshaw, "Practices of Freedom." James Faubion provides a more complex understanding of this limitation of sociality in Foucault: "For Foucault, ethical practice requires not simply a repertoire of technologies but also an 'open territory,' a social terrain in which a considered freedom might actually be exercised. In ancient Greece, that terrain was largely the province of citizen males; women and slaves had little, if any, access to it. In the panoptic apparatus, it is (by design!) nowhere to be found" (88). Faubion, "Toward an Anthropology of Ethics." However, from the social terrain of ancient Greece to the modern panoptic apparatus, various emancipatory movements (such as the women's movement or the struggle to abolish American slavery) have had as their goal precisely the exercise of freedom that has been denied to women and slaves for much of human history. It is precisely this historical difference in the social terrain that Foucault's interpreters sometimes ignore.

46. Beauvoir, *The Second Sex*.

47. Faubion, "Toward an Anthropology of Ethics," 101.

48. The original French phrase is "se déprendre de soi-même," perhaps more accurately translated as "releasing oneself from oneself." See Foucault, *Histoire de la sexualité*, vol. 2: *L'Usage des plaisirs*, 15.

49. Foucault, "The Ethics of the Concern for Self," 300.

50. "Foucault finally undertakes a description of a truth that he will qualify, in his course, as ethopoietic: a truth as it is read in the pattern of accomplished acts and corporeal postures." Gros, "Situation du cours," 510 (translation mine). For a slightly different but related take on this question, see Faubion's suggestive remarks regarding a Foucauldian ethical pedagogy of autopoiesis, where "the ethical master must devote himself (or herself, as the case may be) . . . to the enhancement and refinement of the reflexive freedom of his students." Faubion, "Toward an Anthropology of Ethics," 97.

51. Foucault, "Sexual Choice, Sexual Act," 151.

52. Bersani, "Pedagogy and Pederasty," 21.

53. In the context of these reflections on gender and queer ways of being, it is significant that Pat Califia is now Patrick Califia. For an autobiographical view of the politics of sexuality and transgenderism, see Califia, *Sex Changes*.

54. Califia, "Handmade."

55. Hollibaugh, "Seducing Women into 'A Lifestyle of Vaginal Fisting,'" 333.

56. Weiss, *Techniques of Pleasure*, 8.

57. For a detailed examination of this point, see ibid.

58. Foucault, "On the Genealogy of Ethics," 1:253.

4. Queer Victory, Feminist Defeat?

1. *Lawrence v. Texas,* 539 U.S. 558 (2003).

2. *Powell v. State,* 510 S.E. 2d 18 (Ga. 1998).

3. Foucault, *The History of Sexuality,* vol. 1: *An Introduction,* 154. Hereafter cited in this chapter as HS1.

4. *Bowers v. Hardwick,* 478 U.S. 186 (1986).

5. *Powell* is cited approvingly as precedent in the briefs of the petitioners, the CATO Institute, HRC and other lesbian and gay rights organizations, constitutional law professors, the American Bar Association, the ACLU, and in Kennedy's Opinion of the Court.

6. Rancière, *Disagreement,* 29.

7. Lyotard, *The Differend,* 9; *Le Différend,* 24–25.

8. Readings, *Introducing Lyotard,* xxxiii.

9. Ibid., 63.

10. Lyotard, *The Differend,* 13; *Le Différend,* 29.

11. *State of Georgia v. Anthony San Juan Powell,* Crim. No. 96-B-3448–6 (Gwinnett Superior Ct. August 8, 1997), at 23–24.

12. Lyotard, "La Phrase-affect," 43 (translation mine).

13. Ibid., 48 (translation mine).

14. Irigaray, *Speculum of the Other Woman.*

15. Puar, *Terrorist Assemblages.*

16. Graff, "The High Court Finally Gets It Right."

17. Gewirtz, "Narrative and Rhetoric in the Law," 2.

18. Matsuda, "Public Response to Racist Speech," 2322.

19. Razack, *Looking White People in the Eye,* 37.

20. Delgado and Stefanic, *Critical Race Theory,* 44.

21. Ibid., 44. As my analysis of *Powell* will show, this practical deployment of the *differend* within the framework of the law by Delgado and Stefanic departs somewhat from Lyotard. While critical race theory tends to view storytelling as a way to repair the *differend* by bringing an outsider perspective into the field of vision of the legal system, for Lyotard the *differend* describes a condition of exclusion that cannot be corrected as the righting of a wrong within the formal legal system. As Gérald Sfez puts it: "To do justice to the differend is not to pretend to repair the wrong." See Sfez, *Jean-François Lyotard,* 83 (translation mine).

22. For an overview of the "law and literature" field, see Myrsiades, "Mining the Law/Literature Enterprise." The earliest articulation of this approach is generally regarded to be White, *The Legal Imagination.* More recent elaborations include Amsterdam and Bruner, *Minding the Law;* Binder and Weisberg, *Literary Criticisms of the Law;* Brooks, "Narrativity of the Law"; Brooks and Gewirtz, *Law's Stories;* Bruner, *Making Stories;* Dershowitz, *The Genesis of Justice;* Felman, *The Juridical Unconscious;* Posner, *Law and Literature;* Williams, *The Alchemy of Race and Rights;* and Yoshino, "The City and the Poet." Also see the journal *Law and Literature,* edited by faculty at the Cardozo School of Law (formerly *Cardozo Studies in Law and Literature,* 1989–2001). In an early article, Robert Weisberg

distinguishes between "law-*in*-literature" and "law-*as*-literature" (Weisberg, "The Law-Literature Enterprise"). Yoshino complicates this conception by distinguishing between "generalizing" and "particularizing" understandings of "literature" ("The City and the Poet," 1837). Following Felman and poststructuralism more broadly, my analysis of the law and literature (in the generalizing sense) "does not merely 'cross the boundaries' between the disciplines; it shifts those boundaries, it challenges both disciplines' epistemological and legal definition" (Felman, *The Juridical Unconscious*, 194n2). Like Felman, "I do not assume that authority (truth, knowledge, facts, reality) is a prerogative of law" (ibid., 194n2).

23. Farber and Sherry, "Telling Stories Out of School," 849.

24. Posner, *Law and Literature*, 355.

25. Ibid., 353.

26. See Nussbaum, *Poetic Justice* and *Upheavals of Thought.*

27. See Puar, *Terrorist Assemblages*, especially chapter 3: "Intimate Control, Infinite Detention: Rereading the *Lawrence* Case."

28. In this reading of affect I both draw on Puar's analysis of biopolitical intimacy in *Lawrence* and, using Lyotard, move in a slightly different direction. While Puar emphasizes the interface between intimacy and biometric data, I draw on *Powell* and Lyotard's concept of the affect phrase to explore intimacies that do not register on the grids of biopolitical surveillance. See Puar, *Terrorist Assemblages*, 114–165; and Lyotard, "La Phrase affect," 43–54.

29. Rancière, *Disagreement*, 29.

30. Foucault, "The Return to Morality," 473.

31. Franke, "The Domesticated Liberty of *Lawrence v. Texas.*"

32. Ruskola, "Gay Rights Versus Queer Theory," 239.

33. Ibid., 242.

34. Eng, *The Feeling of Kinship*, 34.

35. MacKinnon, "The Road Not Taken," 1085.

36. Ibid., 1088. MacKinnon's critique hinges on the privacy grounds of the liberty argument developed in Kennedy's *Lawrence* decision from the due process clause of the Fourteenth Amendment. MacKinnon argues that a decision based on equal protection grounds would have afforded better results. She further asserts that although Justice O'Connor based her concurring opinion on the equal protection clause, even O'Connor elided "the inequality on the face of the statute": that "the Texas law discriminated on the basis of sex" (ibid., 1082).

37. Ibid., 1089.

38. Spindelman, "Surviving *Lawrence v. Texas.*"

39. Cover, "Violence and the Word."

40. As even Posner admits, "law is deficient in fact rather than fiction" (*Law and Literature*, 352). Specifically, it is worth noting here that even the bare "facts" of *Lawrence* are almost certainly a "fiction," particularly with regard to the central scene of the queer "sex" supposedly observed by the arresting officers. For a detailed analysis of the "fiction" of *Lawrence*, see Carpenter, "The Unknown Past of *Lawrence v. Texas.*" For a more detailed telling of the *Lawrence* story that includes the background of the arrests, the night of the arrests, and the meanings of the

arrests' aftermath in the Supreme Court and gay politics, see Carpenter, *Flagrant Conduct.*

41. Kristeva, *Semeiotikè*, 146 (translation mine).

42. Foucault, *The History of Sexuality,* vol. 2: *The Use of Pleasure,* 9.

43. In this context, I view Puar's biopolitical conception of intimacy-under-surveillance as an extension of this long-standing feminist suspicion about an illusory private protected space. At the same time, Puar's antinormative challenges to the governmental and extragovernmental apparatuses through which this surveillance operates place her squarely in a quasi-Foucauldian queer theoretical camp. While her work contributes, in this sense, to the queer feminism I am calling for, I want to push on the ethical implications of her antinormative position. See Puar, *Terrorist Assemblages,* 114–165.

44. On the racialization of sodomy in the early decades of the twentieth century in western North America through the policing of male migrant sociability see Shah, "Policing Privacy, Migrants, and the Limits of Freedom."

45. Harris, "Race and Essentialism in Feminist Legal Theory." The role of black women as victims of rape in American jurisprudence is a classic example of the *differend* where, as Sfez puts it: "the wrong is not only the erasure of the harm, it is the erasure of the wrong itself. . . . The wrong is the wrong that has been silenced" (*Jean-François Lyotard,* 78). On the legal marginalization of black women as victims of rape, see, especially, Crenshaw, "Demarginalizing the Intersection of Race and Sex" and "Mapping the Margins"; Davis, *Women, Race, and Class;* and Wriggins, "Rape, Racism, and the Law."

46. *State of Georgia v. Anthony San Juan Powell,* Crim. No. 96-B-3448–6 (Gwinnett Superior Ct. August 8, 1997), at 11.

47. Eskridge, "The Lawyers and Sodomy Come Out of Their Closets," 65.

48. *Lawrence v. Texas,* 539 U.S. 558 (2003), at 569. It is important to note the influence of queer historiography here, provided by the historians' amicus brief in *Lawrence.* As George Chauncey explains, the brief "sought to correct the historical errors used to bolster the majority's reasoning in *Bowers* by demonstrating the historical variability of sexual regulation and the historical specificity of the antigay hostility animating the Texas law." See Chauncey, ""What Gay Studies Taught the Court.'"

49. Davis, "Rape, Racism, and the Myth of the Black Rapist."

50. For statistics and analysis of the disproportionate incarceration of African American men, see the Sentencing Project, especially "Schools and Prisons."

51. As Foucault puts it: "*parrhesia* is the courage of truth in the person who speaks and who, regardless of everything, takes the risk of telling the whole truth that he thinks, but it is also the interlocutor's courage in agreeing to accept the hurtful truth that he hears." See Foucault, *The Courage of Truth,* 13.

52. *State of Georgia v. Anthony San Juan Powell,* Crim. No. 96-B-3448–6 (Gwinnett Superior Ct. August 8, 1997), at 24.

53. Ga. Code Ann. § 16–6-2 (2005).

54. It is worth pointing out that a similar logic is at work in *Lawrence* where, as Puar points out, the younger black man in the duo, Tyrone Garner, becomes

invisible in the face of citational practices that "will ensure that this case goes down in history with the name of the white gay man involved" (*Terrorist Assemblages*, 119). Tyrone Garner died in 2006, aged thirty-nine, from complications of meningitis. In the wake of his death, Lambda Legal established the Tyron Garner Memorial Fellowship for African American LGBT Rights, an annual paid summer internship with Lamba Legal aimed at increasing the diversity of lawyers within the LGBT movement. For details on Garner's life and death see Carpenter, *Flagrant Conduct*.

55. Sfez, *Jean-François Lyotard*, 73 (my translation).

56. Ibid., 79 (my translation).

57. It is worth noting an affinity between my critical reading of *Lawrence* and Bersani's classic critique of redemptive sex in "Is the Rectum a Grave?"

58. Lyotard, *The Differend*, 65.

59. Lyotard, *The Differend*, 57; *Le Différend*, 92.

60. Ibid.

61. Lyotard, *The Differend*, 138.

62. Ibid., 13.

63. Hunter, "Sexual Orientation and the Paradox of Heightened Scrutiny," 1554.

64. Thomas, "Beyond the Privacy Principle," 1515.

65. Lyotard, *The Differend*, 138.

66. Thomas, "Beyond the Privacy Principle," 1515.

67. Rancière, *Disagreement*, 58.

5. One-Handed Reading

1. For a provocative and incisive critique of the Anglo-American academic construction of "French feminism," see Delphy, "The Invention of French Feminism."

2. Cixous, "The Laugh of the Medusa," 876 (original French emphasis restored to translation). For the French original, see Cixous, "Le Rire de la Méduse," 39.

3. Ibid., 876–877.

4. See, especially, Bersani, "Is the Rectum a Grave?" who celebrates jouissance as ascesis.

5. Cixous, "The Laugh of the Medusa," 883.

6. Barthes, *S/Z: An Essay*, 160 (translation modified). For the French original, see Barthes, *S/Z*, 166.

7. Ibid.

8. Ibid. (translation modified).

9. See Huffer, "Weaving and Seduction."

10. "This is why desire is neither the appetite for satisfaction nor the demand for love, but the difference that results from the subtraction of the first from the second, the very phenomenon of their splitting (*Spaltung*)." See Lacan, "The Signification of the Phallus," 276.

11. Ibid., 280 (translation modified). For the French original, see Jacques Lacan, "La Signification du phallus," 115.

12. Irigaray, *Speculum of the Other Woman*. For the French original, see Irigaray, *Speculum de l'autre femme*.

13. See Koedt, "The Myth of the Vaginal Orgasm." Koedt claims that, despite myths to the contrary, "the position of the penis inside the vagina, while perfect for reproduction, does not necessarily stimulate an orgasm in women" (ibid., 205); men, therefore, are "sexually expendable" (ibid., 205). Koedt concludes that "the establishment of clitoral orgasms as fact would threaten the heterosexual *institution*" (ibid., 206).

14. See Schor, *Breaking the Chain*. In her study of the detail in French realist fiction, Naomi Schor concludes that "the clitoris is coextensive with the detail. The clitoral school of feminist criticism might then well be identified by its practice of a hermeneutics focused on the detail, which is to say on those details of the female anatomy generally ignored by male critics and which significantly influence our reading of the texts in which they appear" (ibid., 159–160).

15. Elizabeth Lloyd examines the conception of female orgasm in evolutionary science to theorize the clitoris as a form of "adaptation." See Lloyd, *The Case of the Female Orgasm*.

16. Irigaray, "When Our Lips Speak Together." For the French original, see Irigaray, "Quand nos lèvres se parlent."

17. Irigaray, "When Our Lips Speak Together," 207.

18. Ibid., 212.

19. Huffer, "*Luce et veritas*," 113.

20. Locey, *The Pleasures of the Text*, 65.

21. For other analyses of sexuality in the work of Violette Leduc, see Brioude, *Violette Leduc*; Courtivron, *Violette Leduc*; Hughes, *Violette Leduc*; Jansiti, *Violette Leduc*; Marson, *Le Temps de l'autobiographie*; and Renard and Hecquet, *Violette Leduc*.

22. See Sheehan, "Victorian Clitoridectomy."

23. See, especially, Foucault, *Abnormal*.

24. Leduc, *La Bâtarde*, 22. Hereafter cited in this chapter as LBE. For the French original, see Leduc, *La Bâtarde*, 37. Hereafter cited in this chapter as LBF.

25. "J'ai promené souvent mes doigts entre mes lèvres; plus tard, j'ai bouclé souvent ma toison avec un doigt avant de m'endormir, en m'éveillant, en lisant au lit. J'ai fait cela sans jouir jusqu'à l'âge de vingt-huit ans. C'était un passe-temps, une vérification. Je respirais mes doigts, je respirais l'extrait de mon être auquel je n'attachais pas de valeur."

26. Jagose, "Counterfeit Pleasures," 530.

27. Ibid., 531.

28. "Sa main légère monta sous ma jupe. Aimé Patureau me ratissait avec la grâce d'un page."

29. "La promenade des doigts me grandissait."

30. "La caresse est au frisson ce que le crépuscule est à l'éclair. Isabelle entraînait un râteau de lumière de l'épaule jusqu'au poignet, elle passait avec le

miroir à cinq doigts, dans mon cou, sur ma nuque, sur mes reins. Je suivais la main, je voyais sous mes paupières une nuque, une épaule, un bras qui n'étaient pas les miens."

31. "La main remonta: elle esquisait des cercles, elle débordait dans le vide, elle élargissait les ondes de douceur autour de mon épaule gauche pendant que mon épaule droite était abandonnée à la nuit que zébraient les respirations des élèves. J'apprenais le velouté dans mes os, l'aura dans ma chair, l'infini dans mes formes."

32. Beauvoir, *Le Deuxième sexe*.

33. Beauvoir, *The Second Sex*, 416.

34. Bergoffen, *The Philosophy of Simone de Beauvoir*.

6. Queer Lesbian Silence

1. Rich, "Cartographies of Silence."

2. As Beauvoir explains: "The relation of the two sexes is not that of two electrical poles: the man represents both the positive and the neutral. . . . Woman is the negative, to such a point that any determination is imputed to her as a limitation, without reciprocity." Beauvoir, *The Second Sex*, 5 (translation modified). For the French original, see Beauvoir, *Le Deuxième sexe*, 1:14.

3. Beauvoir, *The Second Sex*, 5.

4. Ladenson, "Colette for Export Only."

5. Colette, *The Pure and the Impure*, 65. For the French original, see Colette, *Le Pur et l'impur*, 72–73: "une place de spectateur, une de ces places de choix d'où le spectateur, s'il s'enivre, a le droit de s'élancer pour rejoindre, dûment titubant, la figuration active."

6. Ladenson, "Colette for Export Only," 45–46.

7. As I've suggested, Proust holds an especially important place in the work of Eve Kosofsky Sedgwick, who both drew on him extensively in her aegis-creating work, *Epistemology of the Closet*, and devoted much of her last, posthumous book, *The Weather in Proust*, to a study of Proust. As my analysis makes clear, my social reading of alterity in Proust is more aligned with Sedgwick's chapter on Albertine in *Epistemology of the Closet* than it is with her later reading of Proust as a mystic in *The Weather in Proust*.

8. Ladenson, *Proust's Lesbianism*, 11.

9. In Francis and Gontier, *Colette*, 336 (translation mine).

10. Levinas, "The Other in Proust." For the original French, see "L'Autre dans Proust."

11. Levinas, "The Other in Proust," 162.

12. Ibid.

13. Foucault, *History of Sexuality*, vol. 1: *An Introduction*, 101.

14. Levinas, "The Other in Proust," 162.

15. Proust, *Sodom and Gomorrah*, 4:43. For the French original, see Proust, *Sodome et Gomorrhe*, 33: "On laissa s'enfuir tous les Sodomistes honteux, même si, apercevant un jeune garçon ils détournaient la tête, comme la femme de Loth,

sans être pour cela changés, comme elle, en statues de sel. De sorte qu'ils eurent une nombreuse postérité chez qui ce geste est resté habituel. . . . Ces descendants des Sodomistes, si nombreux qu'on peut leur appliquer l'autre verset de la Genèse: "Si quelqu'un peut compter la poussière de la terre, il pourra aussi compter cette postérité," se sont fixés sur toute la terre, ils ont eu accès à toutes les professions, et entrent si bien dans les clubs les plus fermés que, quand un sodomiste n'y est pas admis, les boules noires y sont en majorité celles de sodomistes, mais qui ont soin d'incriminer la sodomie, ayant hérité le mensonge qui permit à leurs ancêtres de quitter la ville maudite."

16. See Genesis 13:16 in the *New Oxford Annotated Bible*.

17. Colette, *The Pure and the Impure*, 139 (translation modified). For the French original, see Colette, *Le Pur et l'impur*, 151: "chétives contrefaçons . . . préoccupées de l'homme, détractrices hargneuses et apocryphes de l'homme."

18. Sedgwick, *Epistemology of the Closet*, 239.

19. Ibid.

20. Proust, *The Captive* and *The Fugitive, In Search of Lost Time* (translation modified). For French original see Proust, *La Prisonnière*, 5:62 and 65.

21. Eagleton, *The Ideology of the Aesthetic*, 28.

7. What If Hagar and Sarah Were Lovers?

1. Williams, *Sisters in the Wilderness*. Hereafter cited in this chapter as SW.

2. For the initial opposition between justice and care, see Gilligan, *In a Different Voice*.

3. Kittay, *Love's Labor*.

4. For a founding articulation of the grounds for rethinking care as vulnerability, see Fineman, "The Vulnerable Subject."

5. Kittay and Feder, *The Subject of Care*, 3.

6. On welfare reform, see Young, "Autonomy, Welfare Reform, and Meaningful Work"; on reproductive rights, see Solinger, "Dependency and Choice"; on neoliberalism and care workers, see Schutte, "Dependency Work, Women."

7. See especially Tronto, "The 'Nanny' Question in Feminism"; Ehrenreich and Hochschild, *Global Woman*; and Enloe, "'Just Like One of the Family.'"

8. See, especially, Butler, *Precarious Life* and *Frames of War*. For an ethics of precarity and vulnerability, see Butler, *Giving an Account of Oneself*.

9. Butler, *Frames of War*, 43.

10. In their introduction to *Global Woman* (2002), Ehrenreich and Hochschild explain this global problem in terms of the gendered division of labor: "[The] global redivision of women's traditional work throws new light on the entire process of globalization . . . [where] a global relationship arises that in some ways mirrors the traditional relationship between the sexes. . . . A division of labor feminists critiqued when it was 'local' has now, metaphorically, gone global" (12).

11. Tronto, "The 'Nanny' Question in Feminism," 47. Referring specifically to the "nanny" question in feminism, Joan Tronto demonstrates that one of the

consequences of second-wave feminism's success in opening up more of the professions to women has been to "increase social and economic inequality between households" (34). Because the gains of professional women require the services of underpaid domestic workers, feminism has directly influenced a general reorganization of the domestic work of "care" that "undercuts basic feminist notions of justice" (35). Tronto, "The 'Nanny' Question in Feminism."

12. Barkley Brown, "'What Has Happened Here,'" 275.

13. Tronto systematically documents the myriad ways in which domestic workers are economically exploited, vulnerable to abuse, and trapped in a system that is inherently racist. Tronto concludes: "For a variety of reasons, then, hiring domestic servants seems an intrinsically unjust practice" ("The 'Nanny' Question in Feminism," 41). For ethnographic studies of domestic workers and their children, see Colen, "'With Respect and Feelings'"; and Romero, "Who Takes Care of the Maid's Children?"

14. Statistics on the redistribution of labor during the last three decades bear this out. As Ehrenreich and Hochschild note, since the 1970s women's employment in the U.S., western Europe, Japan, and Taiwan has increased: 65 percent of mothers of children six and under participate in the paid work force today as compared to 15 percent in 1950. This has produced a "care deficit" in these wealthier countries; during the same period, poor countries have become poorer (*Global Woman*, 8).

15. See Illouz, *Why Love Hurts*. Although Illouz's analysis focuses primarily on women in heterosexual love and remains committed to a self, its sociological exploration of love as social, economic, and technological rather than simply psychological makes some of its conclusions relevant to my analysis here.

16. Hannah Arendt offers a philosophical foundation for this linking of narrative, history, and action: "That every individual life between birth and death can eventually be told as a story with beginning and end is the prepolitical and prehistorical condition of history, the great story without beginning and end. But the reason why each human life tells its story and why history ultimately becomes the storybook of mankind, with many actors and speakers and yet without any tangible authors, is that both are the outcome of action" (*The Human Condition*, 184).

17. This and all subsequent biblical citations are from the new revised standard version of *The Oxford Annotated Bible* (*NRSV*).

18. Bernard W. Anderson, the annotator for Genesis through Deuteronomy in the *NRSV*, asserts in his note on this passage that "Hagar felt superior to Sarai and threatened to take her mistress's place (Prov. 30.23) as the ancestress of Israel" (*NRSV* 20). This interpretation of Hagar's "contempt" toward Sarah is fairly typical, as Teubal points out, citing as an example A. E. Speiser's comments: "Sarah's hatred of Hagar stemmed from the concubine's tactless behavior toward her childless mistress; and Abraham was either unable or unwilling to intervene in the bitter rivalry between two headstrong women" (*Ancient Sisterhood*, 75). Teubal suggests, in contrast to this traditional interpretation, that "Hagar's disposition flouts the laws that Sarah honors" (ibid., 76). This may well be true.

However, it seems equally valid, particularly from an aesthetic perspective, to imagine the emotional reality of Hagar's experience as well and, so doing, to open up a reading of Hagar's reaction from her point of view, not as feelings of superiority or even rivalry for legitimacy within a system that subordinates her. Rather, at least part of Hagar's "contempt" toward Sarah could have been rage at the way this woman has treated her. After ten years of service to Sarah, she is prostituted—at Sarah's behest and against Hagar's will—to a man whose relationship to Hagar becomes that of patriarch to breeder. Hagar's "contempt" might legitimately be read as anger and resistance in the face of an institution that revolves around her subordinate status as a woman and as a slave. In this view, Sarah's subsequent expulsion of Hagar into the desert marks not only Sarah's continuing complicity with an oppressive system but also her willingness to respond to defiance and resistance of that system with harsh punishment. For a slightly different translation and interpretation of the Hebrew Scripture, see Trible, *Texts of Terror.*

19. Obviously I have given only the bare outline of the story's plot. There are a number of different interpretations of key aspects of the Hagar-Sarah story, especially the significance of Hagar's role vis-à-vis Sarah, the meaning of Sarah's laugh when God tells her she will bear a son, and the interpretation of the narrative in a specifically theological context where different priestly writers (J, E, P, and R) edit and retell the story for particular purposes. See especially Teubal, *Ancient Sisterhood;* Trible, *Texts of Terror,* and Williams, *Sisters in the Wilderness* for detailed feminist readings of the Hagar-Sarah story. For a feminist critique of the story of Abraham's faith, see Delaney, *Abraham on Trial.*

20. It is significant here that Williams's reinterpretation of the Hagar story reflects that of the black church generally, thereby demonstrating the collective significance of imaginative rereadings of the given. Williams points out that "it is not unusual on any Sunday morning to hear a black preacher allude in his or her sermon to Hagar and Ishmael" (*Sisters in the Wilderness,* 245n2). Williams also cites Edmonia Lewis, Frances Harper, Paul Lawrence Dunbar, Richard Wright, E. Franklin Frazier, Francis P. Reid, Toni Morrison, John Langston Gwaltney, and Maya Angelou as prominent examples of artists and writers who explicitly invoke the figure of Hagar in their work. Also see Hayes, *Hagar's Daughters;* and Wilson, "Hagar's Daughters."

21. Oliver, *Witnessing,* 2. Oliver uses the notion of witnessing to rethink subjectivity itself, arguing against a Hegelian concept of the subject entrenched in a struggle for recognition. Locating "address-ability" and "response-ability" at the root of subjectivity, Oliver argues for a reconstructed subjectivity based in love rather than hostility. "To love," Oliver writes, "is to bear witness to the process of witnessing that gives us the power to be, together. And being together is the chaotic adventure of subjectivity" (ibid., 224).

22. See especially Plaskow, *Standing Again at Sinai.*

23. For such a critique, see Davis, "(Love Is) The Ability of Not Knowing."

24. The privilege of silence I refer to here parallels Eve Kosofsky Sedgwick's concept of the "privilege of unknowing" in her "Privilege of Unknowing."

25. Young, "Autonomy, Welfare Reform, and Meaningful Work," 53.
26. Lazarre, *Beyond the Whiteness of Whiteness*, 32–33.
27. Maitland, *Angel Maker*, 187.

8. After Sex

For "postqueer" reflections on this chapter's titular notion, see Halley and Parker, *After Sex*.

1. *Baise-moi* (2000), a film by Virginie Despentes and Coralie Trinh Thi, is based on Virginie Despentes's 1994 novel by the same title, hereafter cited in this chapter as BMF. Although Bruce Benderson's English translation of the novel renders the title as "Rape Me," a slightly more accurate translation is "Fuck me." See Despentes, *Baise-moi (Rape Me)*, hereafter cited in this chapter as BME.

2. Linda Williams, "Sick Sisters," *Sight and Sound* 11, no. 6 (July 2001): 8.

3. Despentes, *King Kong Theory*, trans. Stéphanie Benson (London: Profile, 2009), 11. Hereafter cited in this chapter as KKE. For the French original, see Despentes, *King Kong Théorie*, 19. Hereafter cited in this chapter as KKF.

4. Ronell, "The Deviant Payback," 23. Hereafter cited in this chapter as AR.

5. "J'écris de chez les moches, pour les moches, les vieilles, les camionneuses, les frigides, les mal baisées, les imbaisables, les hystériques, les tarées, toutes les exclues du grand marché à la bonne meuf" (KKF 9).

6. Solanas, *SCUM Manifesto*, 45–46. Hereafter cited in this chapter as SM.

7. "J'écris donc d'ici, de chez les invendues, les tordues, celles qui ont le crâne rasé . . . les grosses putes, les petites salopes, les femmes à chattes toujours sèche, celles qui ont des gros bides, celles qui voudraient être des hommes, celles qui se prennent pour des hommes, celles qui rêvent de faire hardeuses, celles qui n'en ont rien à foutre des mecs mais que leurs copines intéressent, celles qui ont le gros cul, celles qui ont les poils drus et bien noirs et qui ne vont pas se faire épiler, les femmes brutales, bruyantes" (KKF 12).

8. "J'en ai rien à foutre de leurs pauvres bites de branleurs et que j'en ai pris d'autres dans le ventre et que je les emmerde. C'est comme une voiture que tu gares dans une cité, tu laisses pas des trucs de valeur à l'intérieur parce que tu peux pas empêcher qu'elle soit forcée. Ma chatte, je peux pas empêcher les connards d'y rentrer et j'y ai rien laissé de précieux" (BMF 57).

9. Frank, "Popping Off Warhol."

10. Ibid., 219.

11. Ibid.

12. *Libération*, February 1, 2005. ["Double péné par 5 degrés C, suivie d'une éjaculation. Couverte de sperme, trempée, morte de froid, personne ne m'a tendu une serviette. Une fois que t'as tourné la scène, tu vaux plus rien"].

13. http://www.2blowhards.com/archives/002811.html.

14. Despentes blog, February 1, 2005 (my translation), http://web.archive.org/web/20050125233241/http://www.20six.fr/Despentes (accessed June 19, 2008): "Les mots vont pas ensemble, celui de ta mort et le souvenir de toi." The blog en-

try is no longer accessible. As Despentes explains in a 2010 interview, she wrote her blog for six years, but stopped after being hacked. For the 2010 interview see http://www.lemonde.fr/livres/article/2010/08/26/virginie-despentes-je-ne-suis-pas-encore-tres-disciplinee-mais-j-essaie 1402874 3260.html (accessed July 19, 2012).

15. See Anderson, *Hard;* and Trinh Thi, *Betty Monde.*

16. Despentes blog, February 1, 2005.

17. Despentes blog, February 1, 2005: "C'est la seule fille que j'ai connue, vraiment son grand rêve c'était d'être femme au foyer. La première fois qu'elle m'a dit ça, j'ai préféré mettre de côté, mais en la connaissant mieux, j'ai compris que ça existait, comme rêve de vie. C'était son truc à elle. On ne fait pas toujours ce qu'on veut."

18. Mühleisen, "Realism of Convention and Realism of Queering," 123.

19. "Le porno, c'est des mecs qui jouissent sur la gueule des filles, la femme qui en prend plein la tronche. *Baise-moi,* c'est le contraire." *Libération,* February 1, 2005 (my translation).

20. These last two phrases, rendered in the French version of the novel in English, refer to lines from the grunge music Nadine listens to on her Walkman. The lines have been omitted in the English translation of the novel.

21. *Collaboratrices* in the French original (KKF 151).

Afterword

1. The initial occasion for this chapter was a request from the Committee on the Status of Women in the Profession of the Modern Language Association to participate on a panel about work-life balance at the annual MLA conference (Philadelphia, December 2010). My objective on that occasion was to bring a queer perspective to a long-standing "women's issue."

2. Foucault, "On the Genealogy of Ethics," 1:256.

3. Weeks, *The Problem with Work,* 231.

4. For a comprehensive overview of the work-life balance problem as it relates to feminism and antiwork politics see ibid. In the popular press, work-life balance still tends to be framed as a feminist issue. For two recent examples, see Allen, "'Mommy Wars' Redux"; and Cantor, "Elite Women Put a New Spin on an Old Debate."

5. Allen, "'Mommy Wars.'"

6. It is important to point out, of course, that for Irigaray "man" and "woman" are not two sexes at all but, rather, permutations of the logic of the same.

7. Weeks, *The Problem with Work,* 1.

8. Ibid., 228.

9. Bersani, "Is the Rectum a Grave?" 222.

10. Weeks, *The Problem with Work,* 235–236n6.

11. Edelman, *No Future,* 3.

12. Halberstam, *In a Queer Time and Place,* 1, 2.

13. In his most recent book, *Gaga Feminism*, Halberstam focuses on families, child raising, and gender-variant parenting in ways that depart from his previous work. See, especially, his chapter on butch fathers. Halberstam, *Gaga Feminism*.

14. Foucault, *Abnormal*. Hereafter cited in this chapter as Ab.

15. Foucault, *History of Sexuality*, vol. 1: *An Introduction*. Hereafter cited in this chapter as HS1.

16. Foucault writes at the end of *History of Sexuality*, volume 1: "The irony of this deployment is in having us believe that our 'liberation' is in the balance" (HS1 159).

Bibliography

Adamson, Jane, Richard Freadman, and David Parker. *Renegotiating Ethics in Literature, Philosophy, and Theory*. Cambridge: Cambridge University Press, 1999.

Alexander-Floyd, Nikol G. "Disappearing Acts: Reclaiming Intersectionality in the Social Sciences in a Post-Black Feminist Era." *Feminist Formations* 24, no. 1 (2012): 1–25.

Allen, Amy. "'Mommy Wars' Redux: A False Conflict." *New York Times*, May 27, 2012. http://opinionator.blogs.nytimes.com/2012/05/27/the-mommy-wars-redux-a-false-conflict/. Accessed July 19, 2012.

Amsterdam, Anthony, and Jerome Bruner. *Minding the Law*. Cambridge: Harvard University Press, 2000.

Anderson, Rafaëlla. *Hard Core*. Paris: Grasset, 2001.

Anonymous Queers. "Queers Read This: I Hate Straights." *The Columbia Reader on Lesbians and Gay Men in Media, Society, and Politics*. Ed. Larry Gross and James D. Woods. New York: Columbia University Press, 1999.

Arendt, Hannah. *The Human Condition*. Chicago: University of Chicago Press, 1958.

Austin, J. L. *How to Do Things with Words*. Ed. J. O. Urmson and Marina Sbisà. Cambridge: Harvard University Press, 1962.

Barkley Brown, Elsa. "'What Has Happened Here': The Politics of Difference in Women's History and Feminist Politics." In Linda Nicholson, ed., *The Second Wave: A Reader in Feminist Theory*, 272–287. New York: Routledge, 1997.

Barthes, Roland. *A Lover's Discourse: Fragments*. Trans. Richard Howard. New York: Hill and Wang, 1978.

——. *S/Z*. Paris: Seuil, 1970.

———. *S/Z: An Essay*. Trans. Richard Miller. New York: Hill and Wang, 1974.

Bartsch, Shadi, and Thomas Bartscherer, "What Silent Love Hath Writ: An Introduction to *Erotikon*." In Shadi Bartsch and Thomas Bartscherer, eds., *Erotikon: Essays on Eros, Ancient and Modern*. Chicago: University of Chicago Press, 2005.

Beauvoir, Simone de. *Le Deuxième sexe*. 2 vols. Paris: Gallimard, 1949.

Beauvoir, Simone de. *The Second Sex*. Trans. Constance Borde and Sheila Malovany-Chevallier. New York: Knopf, 2010.

Bechdel, Alison. *The Indelible Alison Bechdel: Confessions, Comix, and Miscellaneous Dykes to Watch Out For*. Ithaca: Firebrand, 1998.

Benderson, Bruce. *Sex and Isolation and Other Essays*. Madison: University of Wisconsin Press, 2007.

Beemyn, Brett, and Mickey Eliason, eds. *Queer Studies: A Lesbian, Gay, Bisexual, and Transgender Anthology*. New York: New York University Press, 1996.

Bell, Laurie, ed. *Good Girls/Bad Girls: Feminists and Sex Trade Workers Face to Face*. Seattle: Seal, 1987.

Benhabib, Seyla. *Situating the Self: Gender, Community, and Postmodernism in Contemporary Ethics*. New York: Routledge, 1992.

Benhabib, Seyla, Judith Butler, Drucilla Cornell, and Nancy Fraser. *Feminist Contentions: A Philosophical Exchange*. New York: Routledge, 1995.

Berger, Michele Tracy, and Kathleen Guidroz. *The Intersectional Approach: Transforming the Academy Through Race, Class, and Gender*. Chapel Hill: University of North Carolina Press, 2009.

Bergoffen, Debra. *The Philosophy of Simone de Beauvoir: Gendered Phenomenologies, Erotic Generosities*. Albany: State University of New York Press, 1996.

Berlant, Lauren. "Neither Monstrous Nor Pastoral, But Scary and Sweet: Some Thoughts on Sex and Emotional Performance in *Intimacies* and *What Do Gay Men Want?*" *Women and Performance* 19, no. 2 (2009): 261–273.

———. *The Queen of America Goes to Washington City*. Durham: Duke University Press, 1997.

Berlant, Lauren, and Elizabeth Freeman. "Queer Nationality." *Boundary* 2 (1992): 149–180.

Berlant, Lauren, and Michael Warner. "Sex in Public." *Critical Inquiry* 24, no. 2 (1998): 547–566.

———. "What Does Queer Theory Teach Us About X?" *PMLA: Publications of the Modern Language Association* 110, no. 3 (1995): 343–349.

Bersani, Leo. *Homos*. Cambridge: Harvard University Press, 1995.

———. "Is the Rectum a Grave?" *October* 43 (1987): 197–222.

———. "Pedagogy and Pederasty." *Raritan* 5, no. 1 (1985): 14–21.

———, and Adam Phillips. *Intimacies*. Chicago: University of Chicago Press, 2008.

Binder, Gyora, and Robert Weisberg. *Literary Criticisms of the Law*. Princeton: Princeton University Press, 2000.

Black, Joel. "Taking the Sex Out of Sexuality: Foucault's Failed History." In *Rethinking Sexuality: Foucault and Classical Antiquity*, 42–60. Ed. David Larmour, Paul Allen Miller, and Charles Platter. Princeton: Princeton University Press, 1998.

Blackwell Guide to Ethical Theory. Ed. Hugh LaFollette. Oxford: Blackwell, 2000.

Booth, Wayne. *The Company We Keep: An Ethics of Fiction.* Berkeley: University of California Press, 1988.

Bordo, Susan. "Feminism, Postmodernism, and Gender Scepticism." In Linda Nicholson, ed., *Feminism/Postmodernism,* 133–156. New York: Routledge, 1990.

Boswell, John. *Christianity, Social Tolerance, and Homosexuality: Gay People in Western Europe from the Beginning of the Christian Era to the Fourteenth Century.* Chicago: University of Chicago Press, 1980.

Bouchard, Danielle. *A Community of Disagreement: Feminism in the University.* New York: Peter Lang, 2012.

Bowers v. Hardwick, 478 U.S. 186 (1986).

Braidotti, Rosi. "The Ethics of Sexual Difference: The Case of Foucault and Irigaray." *Australian Feminist Studies* 3 (1986): 1–13.

Brioude, Mireille. *Violette Leduc: La Mise en scène du "je."* Amsterdam: Rodopi, 2000.

Brooks, Peter. "Narrativity of the Law." *Law and Literature* 14, no. 1 (2002): 1–10.

Brown, Wendy. "The Impossibility of Women's Studies." In *Edgework: Critical Essays on Knowledge and Politics.* Princeton: Princeton University Press, 2005.

Bruner, Edward M. "Ethnography as Narrative." In *Memory, Identity, Community: The Idea of Narrative in the Human Sciences,* 264–280. Albany: State University Press, 1997.

Bruner, Jerome. *Making Stories: Law, Literature, Life.* Cambridge: Harvard University Press, 2003.

Buell, Lawrence. "Introduction: In Pursuit of Ethics." *PMLA* 114, no. 1 (1999): 7–19.

Butler, Judith. "Against Proper Objects." In Elizabeth Weed and Naomi Schor, eds., *Feminism Meets Queer Theory,* 1–30. Bloomington: Indiana University Press, 1997.

——. *Bodies That Matter: On the Discursive Limits of "Sex."* New York: Routledge, 1993.

——. *Excitable Speech: A Politics of the Performative.* New York: Routledge, 1997.

——. *Frames of War: When Is Life Grievable?* London: Verso, 2009.

——. *Gender Trouble: Feminism and the Subversion of Identity.* New York: Routledge, 1990.

——. "Gender Trouble, Feminist Theory, and Psychoanalytic Discourse." In Linda J. Nicholson, ed., *Feminism/Postmodernism,* 324–340. New York: Routledge, 1990.

——. *Giving an Account of Oneself.* New York: Fordham University Press, 2005.

——. "Imitation and Gender Insubordination." In Henry Abelove, Michèle Aina Barale, and David M. Halperin, eds., *The Lesbian and Gay Studies Reader,* 307–320. New York: Routledge, 1993.

——. *Precarious Life: The Powers of Mourning and Violence.* London: Verso, 2004.

——. "The End of Sexual Difference?" In *Undoing Gender,* 174–203. New York: Routledge, 2004.

——. *The Psychic Life of Power: Theories in Subjection.* Palo Alto: Stanford UP, 1997.

Butler, Judith, Ernesto Laclau, and Slavoj Žižek. *Contingency, Hegemony, Universality.* London: Verso, 2000.

Califia, Pat. "Handmade." In *Diesel Fuel: Passionate Poetry*, 51–54. New York: Masquerade, 1997.

Califia, Patrick. *Sex Changes: Transgender Politics*. San Francisco: Cleis, 2003.

Cantor, Jodi. "Elite Women Put a New Spin on an Old Debate." *New York Times*, June 21, 2012. http://www.nytimes.com/2012/06/22/us/elite-women-put-a-new-spin-on-work-life-debate.html. Accessed July 19, 2012.

Card, Claudia, ed. *Feminist Ethics*. Lawrence: University Press of Kansas, 1991.

Carpenter, Dale. "The Unknown Past of *Lawrence v. Texas.*" *Michigan Law Review* 102, no. 7 (2004): 1464–1527.

Carrette, Jeremy. "Prologue to a Confession of the Flesh." In Jeremy R. Carrette, ed., *Religion and Culture: Michel Foucault*, 1–47. New York: Routledge, 1999.

Carpenter, Dale. *Flagrant Conduct: The Story of Lawrence v. Texas*. New York: Norton, 2012.

Carson, Anne. *Eros: The Bittersweet*. Princeton: Princeton University Press, 1986.

Caruth, Cathy. *Unclaimed Experience: Trauma, Narrative, and History*. Baltimore: Johns Hopkins University Press, 1996.

Castle, Terry. *The Apparitional Lesbian: Female Homosexuality and Modern Culture*. New York: Columbia University Press, 1993.

Chambers, Chambers. *Room for Maneuver: Reading (the) Oppositional (in) Narrative*. Chicago: University of Chicago Press, 1991.

Champagne, John. *The Ethics of Marginality: A New Approach to Gay Studies*. Minneapolis: University of Minnesota Press, 1995.

Chanter, Tina. *Ethics of Eros: Irigaray's Rewriting of the Philosophers*. New York: Routledge, 1995.

——. "Irigaray's Challenge to the Fetishistic Hegemony of the Platonic One and Many." In Elena Tzelepis and Athena Athanasiou, eds., *Rewriting Difference: Luce Irigaray and "the Greeks."* Albany: SUNY Press, 2010.

Chauncey, George. "'What Gay Studies Taught the Court': The Historians' Brief in *Lawrence v. Texas.*" *GLQ: A Journal of Lesbian and Gay Studies* 10, no. 3 (2004): 509–538.

Cheever, Susan. "The Nanny Dilemma." In Barbara Ehrenreich and Arlie Russell Hochschild, eds., *Global Woman: Nannies, Maids, and Sex Workers in the New Economy*, 31–38. New York: Holt, 2002.

Chow, Rey. *Ethics After Idealism: Theory, Culture, Ethnicity, Reading*. Bloomington: Indiana University Press, 1998.

Cixous, Hélène. "Le Rire de la Méduse." *L'Arc* 61 (1975): 39–54.

——. "The Laugh of the Medusa," *Signs: Journal of Women in Culture and Society* 1, no. 4 (1976): 875–893.

Cohen, Cathy. "Punks, Bulldaggers, and Welfare Queens." In E. Patrick Johnson and Mae G. Henderson, eds., *Black Queer Studies: A Critical Anthology*, 21–51. Durham: Duke University Press, 2005.

Colen, Shellee. "'With Respect and Feelings': Voices of West Indian Child Care and Domestic Workers in New York City." In Johnnetta Cole, ed., *All American Women: Lines That Divide, Ties That Bind*, 46–70. New York: Free Press, 1986.

Colette. *Le Pur et l'impur*. Paris: Hachette, 1971.

———. *The Pure and the Impure*. Trans. Herma Briffault. New York: Farrar, Straus, and Giroux, 1966.

"Combahee River Collective Statement." In Linda Nicholson, ed., *The Second Wave: A Reader in Feminist Theory*, 63–70. New York: Routledge, 1997.

Cooper, David, and Michel Foucault, "Dialogue sur l'enfermement et la répression psychiatrique." In Collectif Change, ed., *La Folie encerclée*, 76–110. Paris: Seghers/Laffont, 1997.

Corber, Robert J., and Stephen Valocchi. *Queer Studies: An Interdisciplinary Reader*. Malden, MA: Blackwell, 2003.

Cornell, Drucilla. *Beyond Accommodation: Ethical Feminism, Deconstruction, and the Law*. New York: Routledge, 1991.

Courtivron, Isabelle de. *Violette Leduc*. Boston: Twayne, 1985.

Cover, Robert. "Violence and the Word." In Martha Minow, Michael Ryan, and Austin Sarat, eds., *Narrative, Violence, and the Law: The Essays of Robert Cover*, 203–238. Ann Arbor: University of Michigan Press, 1995.

Crenshaw, Kimberlé. "Demarginalizing the Intersection of Race and Sex: A Black Feminist Critique of Antidiscrimination Doctrine, Feminist Theory, and Antiracist Politics." *University of Chicago Legal Forum* (1989): 139–167.

———. "Mapping the Margins: Intersectionality, Identity Politics, and Violence Against Women of Color." *Stanford Law Review* 43 (1991): 1241–1299.

Cvetkovich, Ann. *An Archive of Feelings: Trauma, Sexuality, and Lesbian Public Cultures*. Durham: Duke University Press, 2003.

Daly, Lois, ed. *Feminist Theological Ethics: A Reader*. Louisville: Westminster John Knox, 1994.

Dangerous Bedfellows et al., eds. *Policing Public Sex: Queer Politics and the Future of AIDS Activism*. Boston: South End, 1996.

Davis, Angela. "Racialized Punishment and Prison Abolition." In *The Angela Davis Reader*, 96–107. Ed. Joy James. Malden, MA: Blackwell, 1998.

———. "Rape, Racism, and the Myth of the Black Rapist." In *Women, Race, and Class*, 172–210. New York: Vintage, 1983.

———. *Women, Race, and Class*. New York: Vintage, 1983.

Davis, Dawn Rae. "(Love Is) The Ability of Not Knowing: Feminist Experience of the Impossible in Ethical Singularity." *Hypatia* 17, no. 2 (2002): 145–161.

Dean, Jodi. *Solidarity of Strangers: Feminism After Identity Politics*. Berkeley: University of California Press, 1996.

Dean, Tim. *Unlimited Intimacy: Reflections on the Subculture of Barebacking*. Chicago: University of Chicago Press, 2009.

Delaney, Carol. *Abraham on Trial: The Social Legacy of Biblical Myth*. Princeton: Princeton University Press, 1998.

Deleuze, Gilles. *Nietzsche and Philosophy*. Trans. Hugh Tomlinson. New York: Columbia University Press, 2006.

Delgado, Richard, and Jean Stefanic. *Critical Race Theory: An Introduction*. New York: New York University Press, 2001.

Delphy, Christine. "The Invention of French Feminism: An Essential Move." In Lynne Huffer, ed., "Another Look, Another Woman: Retranslations of French Feminism," *Yale French Studies* 87 (1995): 190–221.

Derrida, Jacques. "Adieu." *Critical Inquiry* 23, no. 1 (1996): 1–10.

———. "Signature Event Context." *Limited Inc*, 1–23. Evanston, IL: Northwestern University Press, 1988.

Dershowitz, Alan. *The Genesis of Justice: Ten Stories of Biblical Injustice That Led to the Ten Commandments and Modern Law.* New York: Warner, 2000.

Despentes, Virginie. *Baise-moi.* Paris: Florent-Massot, 1994.

———. *Baise-moi (Rape Me).* Trans. Bruce Benderson. New York: Grove, 1999.

———. *King Kong Théorie.* Paris: Bernard Grasset, 2006.

———. *King Kong Theory.* Trans. Stéphanie Benson. London: Profile, 2009.

———, and Coralie Trinh Thi. *Baise-moi*, film. 2000.

Deutscher, Penelope. *A Politics of Impossible Difference: The Late Works of Luce Irigaray.* Ithaca: Cornell University Press, 2002.

———. "Conditionalities, Exclusions, Occlusion." In Elena Tzelepis and Athena Athanasiou, eds., *Rewriting Difference: Luce Irigaray and "the Greeks."* Albany: SUNY Press, 2010.

Dinshaw, Carolyn. *Getting Medieval: Sexualities and Communities, Pre- and Postmodern.* Durham: Duke University Press, 1999.

Dreyfus, Hubert, and Paul Rabinow, eds. *Michel Foucault: Beyond Structuralism and Hermeneutics.* Chicago: University of Chicago Press, 1983.

Duggan, Lisa, and Nan D. Hunter. *Sex Wars.* New York: Routledge, 1995.

Eaglestone, Robert. *Ethical Criticism: Reading After Levinas.* Edinburgh: Edinburgh University Press, 1997.

Eagleton, Terry. *The Ideology of the Aesthetic.* Oxford: Blackwell, 1990.

Edelman, Lee. "Antagonism, Negativity, and the Subject of Queer Theory." *PMLA* 121, no. 3 (2006): 821.

———. "Forum: Conference Debates, the Antisocial Thesis in Queer Theory." *PMLA* 121, no. 3 (May 2006): 819–828.

———. *No Future: Queer Theory and the Death Drive.* Durham: Duke University Press, 2004.

Ehrenreich, Barbara, and Arlie Russell Hochschild, eds. *Global Woman: Nannies, Maids, and Sex Workers in the New Economy.* New York: Holt, 2002.

Elias, Amy J. *Sublime Desire: History and Post-1960s Fiction.* Baltimore: Johns Hopkins University Press, 2001.

Eng, David L. *The Feeling of Kinship: Queer Liberalism and the Racialization of Intimacy.* Durham: Duke University Press, 2010.

———, Judith Halberstam, and José Muñoz, eds. "What's Queer About Queer Studies Now?" Special issue of *Social Text* 84–85 (2005).

Enloe, Cynthia. "'Just Like One of the Family': Domestic Servants in World Politics." In *Bananas, Beaches, and Bases: Making Feminist Sense of International Politics*, 177–194. Berkeley: University of California Press, 1989.

Eribon, Didier. *Insult and the Making of the Gay Self.* Trans. Michael Lucey. Durham: Duke University Press, 2004.

———. *Michel Foucault*. Trans. Betsy Wing. Cambridge: Harvard University Press, 1991.

———. "Michel Foucault's Histories of Sexuality." Trans. Michael Lucey. *GLQ: A Journal of Lesbian and Gay Studies* 7, no. 1 (2001): 31–86.

Eskridge, William. "The Lawyers and Sodomy Come Out of Their Closets, 1986–2001." In *Dishonorable Passions: The Rise and Fall of the Crime Against Nature*. New York: Viking, 2008.

Faderman, Lillian. *Surpassing the Love of Men: Romantic Friendship and Love Between Women from the Renaissance to the Present*. New York: William Morrow, 1981.

Farber, Daniel J., and Suzanna Sherry. "Telling Stories Out of School: An Essay on Legal Narratives." *Stanford Law Review* 45, no. 4 (1993): 807–856.

Faubion, James. "Toward an Anthropology of Ethics: Foucault and the Pedagogies of Autopoiesis." *Representations* 74 (2001): 83–104.

Felman, Shoshana. *The Juridical Unconscious: Trials and Traumas in the Twentieth Century*. Cambridge: Harvard University Press, 2002.

———. *The Literary Speech Act: Don Juan with J. L. Austin, or Seduction in Two Languages*. Trans. Catherine Porter. Ithaca: Cornell University Press, 1983.

———, and Dori Laub. *Testimony: Crises of Witnessing in Literature, Psychoanalysis, and History*. New York: Routledge, 1992.

Ferguson, Roderick. *Aberrations in Black: Toward a Queer of Color Critique*. Minneapolis: University of Minnesota Press, 2004.

———. "Reading Intersectionality," *Transcripts* 2 (2012): 92.

Fernandez, Charles. "Undocumented Aliens in the Queer Nation." *Out/Look* 12 (1991): 20–23.

Fineman, Martha Albertson. "The Vulnerable Subject: Anchoring Equality in the Human Condition." *Yale Journal of Law and Feminism* 20 (2008): 1–21.

Fisher, Walter R. *Human Communication as Narration: Toward a Philosophy of Reason, Value, and Action*. Columbia: University of South Carolina Press, 1989.

Fisher, Will. "Queer Money." *ELH* 66 (1999): 1–23.

Flinders, Carol Lee. *At the Root of This Longing: Reconciling a Spiritual Hunger and a Feminist Thirst*. New York: Harper Collins, 1998.

Foster, Patricia. "Outside the Hive: A Meditation on Childlessness." In Rochelle Ratner, ed., *Bearing Life: Women's Writings on Childlessness*, 92–101. New York: Feminist Press, 2001.

Foucault, Michel. *Abnormal: Lectures at the Collège de France, 1974–1975*. Trans. Graham Burchell. New York: Picador, 2003.

———. "Different Spaces." In *Essential Works of Foucault, 1954–1984*, 2:175–186. Ed. Paul Rabinow. New York: New Press, 1998.

———. *Discipline and Punish: The Birth of the Prison*. Trans. Alan Sheridan. New York: Random House, 1977.

———. "Final Interview." *Raritan* 5, no. 1 (1985): 1–13.

———. "Friendship as a Way of Life." In *Essential Works of Foucault, 1954–1984*, 1:135–140. Ed. Paul Rabinow. New York: New Press, 1997.

———. *Histoire de la folie à l'âge classique*. Paris: Gallimard, 1972.

———. *Histoire de la sexualité*, vol. 2: *L'Usage des plaisirs*. Paris: Gallimard, 1984.

———. *History of Madness*. Trans. Jonathan Murphy and Jean Khalfa. London: Routledge, 2006.

———. "Lives of Infamous Men." In *Essential Works of Foucault, 1954–1984*, 3:157–175. Ed. Paul Rabinow. New York: New Press, 2000.

———. "On the Genealogy of Ethics." In *Essential Works of Foucault, 1954–1984*, 1:253–280. Ed. Paul Rabinow. New York: New Press, 1997.

———. "On the Ways of Writing History." In *Essential Works of Foucault, 1954–1984*, 2:279–296. Ed. Paul Rabinow. New York: New Press, 1997.

———. "Sexual Choice, Sexual Act." In *Essential Works of Foucault, 1954–1984*, 1:141–156. Ed. Paul Rabinow. New York: New Press, 1997.

———. *Society Must Be Defended: Lectures at the Collège de France, 1975–1976*. Trans. David Macey. New York: Picador, 2003.

———. *Surveiller et punir: Naissance de la prison*. Paris: Gallimard, 1975.

———. *The Archeology of Knowledge*. Trans. Alan Sheridan. New York: Pantheon, 1972.

———. *The Courage of Truth: Lectures at the Collège de France, 1983–84*. Trans. Graham Burchell. New York: Palgrave Macmillan, 2011.

———. "The Ethics of the Concern for Self as a Practice of Freedom." In *Essential Works of Foucault, 1954–1984*, 1:281–302. Ed. Paul Rabinow. New York: New Press, 1994.

———. *The Hermeneutics of the Subject: Lectures at the Collège de France, 1981–82*. Trans. Graham Burchell. New York: Palgrave Macmillan, 2005.

———. *The History of Sexuality*, vol. 1: *An Introduction*. Trans. Robert Hurley. New York: Vintage, 1978.

———. *The History of Sexuality*, vol. 2: *The Use of Pleasure*. Trans. Robert Hurley. New York: Vintage, 1985.

———. *The History of Sexuality*, vol. 3: *The Care of the Self*. Trans. Robert Hurley. New York: Vintage, 1988.

———. *The Order of Things: An Archeology of Human Sciences*. New York: Random House, 1970.

———. "The Return of Morality." In *Foucault Live*. Ed. Sylvère Lotringer. New York: Semiotext(e), 1996.

———, with Jean Le Bitoux. "The Gay Science." Trans. Nicolae Morar and David W. Smith. *Critical Inquiry* 37, no. 3 (2011): 385–403.

Francis, Claude, and Fernande Gontier. *Colette*. Paris: Perrin, 1997.

Frank, Marcie. "Popping Off Warhol: From the Gutter to the Underground and Beyond." In Jennifer Doyle, Jonathan Flatley, and José Esteban Muñoz, eds., *Pop Out: Queer Warhol*, 210–223. Durham: Duke University Press, 1996.

Franke, Katherine M. "The Domesticated Liberty of *Lawrence v. Texas*." *Columbia Law Review* 104, no. 5 (2004): 1399–1426.

Freud, Sigmund. *Civilization and Its Discontents*. Trans. James Strachey. New York: Norton, 1961.

Fuss, Diana. *Identification Papers*. New York: Routledge, 1995.

Gallagher, Bob, and Alexander Wilson. "Michel Foucault: An Interview: Sex, Power, and the Politics of Identity." *Advocate* 400 (August 7, 1984): 26–30, 58.

Gallop, Jane. *The Deaths of the Author: Reading and Writing in Time.* Durham: Duke University Press, 2011.

———. *Thinking Through the Body.* New York: Columbia University Press, 1988.

Garber, Marjorie, Beatrice Hanssen, and Rebecca Walkowitz, eds. *The Turn to Ethics.* New York: Routledge, 2000.

Gewirtz, Paul. "Narrative and Rhetoric in the Law." In Peter Brooks and Paul Gewirtz, eds., *Law's Stories: Narrative and Rhetoric in the Law,* 2–13. New Haven: Yale University Press, 1996.

Gilligan, Carol. *In a Different Voice: Psychological Theory and Women's Development.* Cambridge: Harvard University Press, 1982.

Goldberg, Jonathan. *Reclaiming Sodom.* New York: Routledge, 1994.

———, ed. *Sodometries: Renaissance Texts/Modern Sexualities.* Palo Alto: Stanford University Press, 1992.

Graff, E. J., "The High Court Finally Gets It Right." *Boston Globe,* June 29, 2003, D11.

Grimshaw, Jean. "Practices of Freedom." In Caroline Ramazanoglu, ed., *Up Against Foucault: Explorations of Some Tensions Between Foucault and Feminism,* 51–72. London: Routledge, 1993.

Gros, Frederic. "Situation du cours." In Michel Foucault, *L'Hermeneutique du sujet: Cours au College de France. 1981–1982.* 487–526. Ed. Frederic Gros. Paris: Seuil/Gallimard, 2001.

Grosz, Elizabeth. "Irigaray and the Ontology of Sexual Difference." In *Becoming Undone: Darwinian Reflections on Life, Politics, and Art.* Durham: Duke University Press, 2011.

———. "The Hetero and the Homo: The Sexual Ethics of Luce Irigaray." In Carolyn Burke, Naomi Schor, and Margaret Whitford, eds., *Engaging with Irigaray,* 335–350. New York: Columbia University Press, 1994.

Halberstam, J. Jack. *Gaga Feminism: Sex, Gender, and the End of Normal.* Boston: Beacon, 2012.

Halberstam, Judith. *Female Masculinity.* Durham: Duke University Press, 1998.

———. *In a Queer Time and Place.* Durham: Duke University Press, 2005.

———. "The Politics of Negativity in Recent Queer Theory." *PMLA* 121, no. 3 (2006): 824.

Hale, C. Jacob. "Leatherdyke Boys and Their Daddies: How to Have Sex Without Women or Men." In Robert J. Corber and Stephen Valocchi, eds., *Queer Studies: An Interdisciplinary Reader,* 61–70. Malden, MA: Blackwell, 2003.

Halley, Janet. *Split Decisions: How and Why to Take a Break from Feminism.* Princeton: Princeton University Press, 2006.

———, and Andrew Parker, eds., *After Sex: On Writing Since Queer Theory.* Durham: Duke University Press, 2011.

Halperin, David M. "Forgetting Foucault." In *How to Do the History of Homosexuality,* 24–47. Chicago: University of Chicago Press, 2002.

———. *Saint Foucault: Towards a Gay Hagiography.* New York: Oxford University Press, 1995.

Harpham, Geoffrey. *Shadows of Ethics: Criticism and the Just Society.* Durham: Duke University Press, 1999.

Harris, Angela. "Race and Essentialism in Feminist Legal Theory." *Stanford Law Review* 42 (1990): 581–616.

Hayes, Diana L. *Hagar's Daughters: Womanist Ways of Being in the World.* New York: Paulist, 1995.

Hinchman, Lewis and Hinchman, Sandra, eds. *Memory, Identity, Community: The Idea of Narrative in the Human Sciences.* Albany: State University of New York Press, 1997.

Hoagland, Sarah Lucia. *Lesbian Ethics: Toward New Value.* Palo Alto: Institute of Lesbian Studies, 1988.

Hochschild, Arlie Russell. "Love and Gold." In Barbara Ehrenreich and Arlie Russell Hochschild, eds., *Global Woman: Nannies, Maids, and Sex Workers in the New Economy,* 15–30. New York: Holt, 2002.

Hocquenghem, Guy. *Homosexual Desire.* Trans. Danielle Dangoor. Durham: Duke University Press, 1993.

Hodge, Joanna. "Irigaray Reading Heidegger." In Carolyn Burke, Naomi Schor, and Margaret Whitford, eds., *Engaging with Irigaray,* 191–210. New York: Columbia University Press, 1994.

Holland, Sharon. *Raising the Dead: Readings of Death and (Black) Subjectivity.* Durham: Duke University Press, 2000.

Hollibaugh, Amber. "Seducing Women Into 'A Lifestyle of Vaginal Fisting': Lesbian Sex Gets *Virtually* Dangerous." In Dangerous Bedfellows, ed., *Policing Public Sex: Queer Politics and the Future of AIDS Activism,* 321–336. Boston: South End, 1996.

Honig, Bonnie. "Declarations of Independence: Arendt and Derrida on the Founding of a Republic." *American Political Science Review* 85, no. (1991): 97–113.

——, ed. *Feminist Interpretations of Hannah Arendt.* State College: Pennsylvania State University Press, 1995.

Hope, Trevor. "Melancholic Modernity: The Hom(m)osexual Symptom and the Homosocial Corpse." In Naomi Schor and Elizabeth Weed, eds., *Feminism Meets Queer Theory.* Bloomington: Indiana University Press, 1997.

Huffer, Lynne. *Another Colette: The Question of Gendered Writing.* Ann Arbor: University of Michigan Press, 1992.

——. *"Luce et veritas:* Toward an Ethics of Performance." In "Another Look, Another Woman: Retranslations of French Feminism." *Yale French Studies* 87 (1995): 20–41.

——. *Mad for Foucault: Rethinking the Foundations of Queer Theory.* New York: Columbia University Press, 2010.

——. *Maternal Pasts, Feminist Futures: Nostalgia, Ethics, and the Question of Difference.* Palo Alto: Stanford University Press, 1998.

——. "Weaving and Seduction: *Les Chansons de toile."* *Romanic Review* 82, no. 4 (1991): 392411.

——. "Weird Greek Sex: Rethinking Ethics in Irigaray and Foucault." In Elena Tzelepis and Athena Athanasiou, eds., *Rewriting Difference: Luce Irigaray and "the Greeks,"* 119–134. Albany: SUNY Press, 2010.

Hughes, Alex. *Violette Leduc: Mothers, Lovers, and Language*. London: Modern Humanities Research Association, 1994.

Hunt, Lynn. "Foucault's Subject in *The History of Sexuality*." In Domna C. Stanton, ed., *Discourses of Sexuality: From Aristotle to AIDS*, 78–93. Ann Arbor: University of Michigan Press, 1992.

Hunter, Nan. "Sexual Orientation and the Paradox of Heightened Scrutiny." *Michigan Law Review* 102, no. 7 (2004): 1528–1554.

Illouz, Eva, *Why Love Hurts*. Cambridge: Polity, 2012.

Irigaray, Luce. *An Ethics of Sexual Difference*. Trans. Carolyn Burke and Gillian Gill. Ithaca: Cornell University Press, 1993.

———. *Conversations*. London: Continuum, 2008.

———. *I Love to You: Sketch of a Possible Felicity in History*. Trans. Alison Martin. New York: Routledge, 1996.

———. "Quand nos lèvres se parlent." *Ce sexe qui n'en est pas un*, 203–217. Paris: Minuit, 1977.

———. "Questions to Emmanuel Levinas." Trans. Margaret Whitford. In Robert Bernasconi and Simon Critchley, eds., *Rereading Levinas*, 109–118. Bloomington: Indiana University Press, 1991.

———. *Sexes and Genealogies*. Trans. Gillian C. Gill. New York: Columbia University Press, 1993.

———. *Sharing the World*. London: Continuum, 2008.

———. *Speculum de l'autre femme*. Paris: Minuit, 1974.

———. *Speculum of the Other Woman*. Trans. Gillian Gill. Ithaca: Cornell University Press, 1985.

———. "The Fecundity of the Caress." In *An Ethics of Sexual Difference*, 185–217. Trans. Carolyn Burke and Gillian Gill. Ithaca: Cornell University Press, 1993.

———. *The Forgetting of Air: In Martin Heidegger*. Trans. Mary Beth Mader. Austin: University of Texas Press, 1999.

———. "The Return." In Elena Tzelepis and Athena Athanasiou, eds., *Rewriting Difference: Luce Irigaray and "the Greeks*," 259–272. Albany: SUNY Press, 2010.

———. *The Way of Love*. Trans. Heidi Bostic and Stephen Pluhácek. London: Continuum, 2002.

———. "When Our Lips Speak Together." In *This Sex Which Is Not One*, 205–218. Trans. Catherine Porter. Ithaca: Cornell University Press, 1985.

Jagose, Annamarie. "Counterfeit Pleasures: Fake Orgasm and Queer Agency." *Textual Practice* 24, no. 3 (2010): 517–539.

———. "Feminism's Queer Theory." *Feminism and Psychology* 19, no. 2 (2009): 157–174.

———. *Lesbian Utopics*. New York: Routledge, 1994.

———. *Queer Theory: An Introduction*. New York: New York University Press, 1996.

Jansiti, Carlo. *Violette Leduc*. Paris: Grasset, 1999.

Jordan, Mark D. *The Invention of Sodomy in Christian Theology*. Chicago: University of Chicago Press, 1997.

Kaplan, Morris. *Sexual Justice: Democratic Citizenship and the Politics of Desire*. New York: Routledge, 1997.

Keenan, Thomas. *Fables of Responsibility: Aberrations and Predicaments in Ethics and Politics*. Palo Alto: Stanford University Press, 1997.

Kimball, Roger. *Tenured Radicals: How Politics Has Corrupted Higher Education*. New York: Harper and Row, 1990.

King, Thomas. "M/S, or Making the Scene: An Erotics of Space." http://www .ars-rhetorica.net/Queen/Volume11/Articles/King.htm.

Kittay, Eva Feder. *Love's Labor: Essays on Women, Equality, and Dependency*. New York: Routledge, 1999.

Kittay, Eva Feder, and Ellen K. Feder, eds. *The Subject of Care: Feminist Perspectives on Dependency*. Lanham, MA: Rowman and Littlefield, 2002.

Koedt, Ann. "The Myth of the Vaginal Orgasm." In Anne Koedt, Ellen Levine, and Anita Rapone, eds., *Radical Feminism*, 198–207. New York: Quadrangle, 1973.

Kramer, Larry. *Reports from the Holocaust: The Story of an AIDS Activist*. New York: St. Martin's, 1994.

Kristeva, Julia. *Semeiotikè: Recherches pour une sémanalyse*. Paris: Seuil, 1969.

Lacan, Jacques. "La Signification du phallus." *Ecrits II*. Paris: Seuil, 1971.

——. "The Signification of the Phallus." *Ecrits: A Selection*, 271–280. Trans. Bruce Fink. New York: Norton, 2002.

Laclau, Ernesto. "Identity and Hegemony: The Role of Universality in the Constitution of Political Logics." In Judith Butler, Ernest Laclau, and Slavoj Žižek. *Contingency, Hegemony, Universality*, 44–89. London: Verso, 2000.

Ladenson, Elisabeth. "Colette for Export Only." In Brigitte Mahuzier, Karen McPherson, Charles A. Porter, and Ralph Sarkonak, eds., "Same Sex/Different Text? Gay and Lesbian Writing in French." Special Issue. *Yale French Studies* 90 (1996): 25–46.

——. *Proust's Lesbianism*. Ithaca: Cornell University Press, 1999.

Laqueur, Thomas. "Orgasm, Generation, and the Politics of Reproductive Biology." In Roger N. Lancaster and Micaela di Leonardo, ed., *The Gender/Sexuality Reader: Culture, History, Political Economy*, 219–243. New York: Routledge, 1997.

——. *Solitary Sex: A Cultural History of Masturbation*. New York: Zone, 2003.

Lauretis, Teresa de. "Introduction." *Differences: A Journal of Feminist Cultural Studies* 3, no. 2 (1991): iii–xviii.

Lawrence v. Texas, 539 U.S. 558 (2003).

Lazarre, Jane. *Beyond the Whiteness of Whiteness: Memoir of a White Mother of Black Sons*. Durham: Duke University Press, 1996.

Leduc, Violette. *La Bâtarde*. Paris: Gallimard, 1964.

——. *La Bâtarde*, Trans. Derek Coltman. New York: Farrar, Straus, and Giroux, 1965.

Levinas, Emmanuel. "L'Autre dans Proust." *Deucalion* 2 (1947): 117–123.

——. "The Other in Proust." In *The Levinas Reader*, 160–165. Ed. and trans. Seán Hand. Oxford: Blackwell, 1989.

——. *Totality and Infinity: An Essay on Exteriority*. Trans. Alphonso Lingis. Pittsburgh: Duquesne University Press, 1979.

Lloyd, Elizabeth A. *The Case of the Female Orgasm: Bias in the Science of Evolution.* Cambridge: Harvard University Press, 2005.

Locey, Elizabeth. *The Pleasures of the Text: Violette Leduc and Reader Seduction.* Lanham, MA: Rowman and Littlefield, 2002.

Lochrie, Karma. *Covert Operations: The Medieval Uses of Secrecy.* Philadelphia: University of Pennsylvania Press, 1998.

———. "Presumptive Sodomy and Its Exclusions." *Textual Practice* 13.2 (1999): 295–310.

Love, Heather. "'Oh, the Fun We'll Have': Remembering the Prospects for Sexuality Studies." *GLQ: A Journal of Lesbian and Gay Studies* 10, no. 2 (2004): 258–261.

Ludwig, Alice. "Differences Between Women? Intersecting Voices in a Female Narrative." *European Journal of Women's Studies* 13, no. 3 (August 2006): 249.

Lyotard, Jean-François. "La Phrase-affect (D'un supplément au *Différend*)," *Misère de la philosophie,* 43–54. Paris: Galilée, 2000.

———. *Le Différend.* Paris: Minuit, 1983.

———. *The Differend: Phrases in Dispute.* Trans. Georges Van Den Abbeele. Minneapolis: University of Minnesota Press, 1988.

———. *The Postmodern Condition: A Report on Knowledge.* Trans. Geoffrey Bennington and Brian Massumi. Minneapolis: University of Minnesota Press, 1984.

McCall, Leslie. "The Complexity of Intersectionality." *Signs: Journal of Women in Culture and Society* 30, no. 1 (2005): 1771–1800.

MacIntyre, Alasdair. *After Virtue.* Notre Dame: University of Notre Dame Press, 1981.

MacKendrick, Karmen. *Counterpleasures.* Albany: State University of New York Press, 1999.

MacKinnon, Catharine A. *Feminism Unmodified: Discourses on Life and Law.* Cambridge: Harvard University Press, 1987.

———. "The Road Not Taken: Sex Equality in *Lawrence v. Texas.*" *Ohio State Law Journal* 65 (2004): 1081–1096.

Maclean, Mary. *Narrative as Performance: The Baudelairean Experiment.* London: Routledge, 1988.

McWhorter, Ladelle. *Bodies and Pleasures: Foucault and the Politics of Sexual Normalization.* Bloomington: Indiana University Press, 1999.

———. *Racism and Sexual Oppression in Anglo-America: A Genealogy.* Bloomington: Indiana University Press, 2009.

Mahmood, Saba. *Politics of Piety: The Islamic Revival and the Feminist Subject.* Princeton: Princeton University Press, 2004.

Maitland, Sara. *Angel Maker: The Short Stories of Sara Maitland.* New York: Holt, 1996.

Marinucci, Mimi. *Feminism Is Queer: The Intimate Connection Between Queer and Feminist Theory.* London: Zed, 2010.

Marson, Susan. *Le Temps de l'autobiographie: Violette Leduc ou la mort avant la lettre.* Saint-Denis: PUV, 1998.

Martin, Biddy. "Extraordinary Homosexuals and the Fear of Being Ordinary." In Naomi Schor and Elizabeth Weed, eds., *Feminism Meets Queer Theory*, 109–135. Bloomington: Indiana University Press, 1997.

———. *Femininity Played Straight: The Significance of Being Lesbian*. New York: Routledge, 1996.

———. "Feminism, Criticism, and Foucault." *New German Critique* 27 (1982): 3–30.

Matsuda, Mari J. "Public Response to Racist Speech: Considering the Victim's Story." *Michigan Law Review* 87 (1989): 2320–2381.

Meyer, Richard. "Robert Mapplethorpe and the Discipline of Photography." In Henry Abelove, Michèle Aina Barale, and David M. Halperin, eds., *The Lesbian and Gay Studies Reader*, 360–380. New York: Routledge, 1993.

Miller, D. A. *Narrative and Its Discontents: Problems of Closure in the Traditional Novel*. Princeton: Princeton University Press, 1989.

Miller, J. Hillis. *The Ethics of Reading: Kant, de Man, Eliot, Trollope, James, and Benjamin*. New York: Columbia University Press, 1987.

Mohr, Richard. *Gays/Justice: A Study of Ethics, Society, and Law*. New York: Columbia University Press, 1988.

Moi, Toril. *What Is a Woman? and Other Essays*. Oxford: Oxford University Press, 1999.

Mortensen, Ellen. "Woman's Untruth and *le féminin*: Reading Luce Irigaray with Nietzsche and Heidegger." In Carolyn Burke, Naomi Schor, and Margaret Whitford, eds., *Engaging with Irigaray*, 211–228. New York: Columbia University Press, 1994.

Mühleisen, Wencke. "Realism of Convention and Realism of Queering: Sexual Violence in Two European Art Films." *Nordic Journal of Women's Studies* 13, no. 2 (2005): 115–125.

Muñoz, José. *Cruising Utopia: The Then and There of Queer Futurity*. New York: New York University Press, 2009.

———. *Disidentifications: Queers of Color and the Performance of Politics*. Minneapolis: University of Minnesota Press, 1999.

———. "Thinking Beyond Antirelationality and Antiutopianism in Queer Critique." *PMLA* 121, no. 3 (2006): 825–826.

Myrsiades, Linda. "Mining the Law/Literature Enterprise." *College Literature* 30, no. 1 (2003): 169–179.

Nagel, Thomas. *The View from Nowhere*. Oxford: Oxford University Press, 1986.

Nash, Jennifer C. "Re-thinking Intersectionality." *Feminist Review* 89 (2008):1–15.

New Oxford Annotated Bible with the Apocrypha: New Revised Standard Version. Ed. Michael D. Coogan, Marc Z. Brettler, and Carol A. Newsom. Oxford: Oxford University Press, 2001.

Newton, Adam Zachary. *Narrative Ethics*. Cambridge: Harvard University Press, 1995.

Nietzsche, Friedrich. *Daybreak: Thoughts on the Prejudices of Morality*. Trans. R. J. Hollingdale. Cambridge: Cambridge University Press, 1997.

———. *On the Genealogy of Morals*. Trans. Walter Kaufmann. New York: Vintage, 1969.

Nouvet, Claire, ed. "Literature and the Ethical Question." Special Issue. *Yale French Studies* 79 (1991).

Nussbaum, Martha C. *Poetic Justice: The Literary Imagination and Public Life.* Boston: Beacon, 1995.

———. *Upheavals of Thought: The Intelligence of the Emotions.* New York: Cambridge University Press, 2001.

Nye, Robert. "Michel Foucault's Sexuality and the History of Homosexuality in France." In Jeffrey Merrick and Bryant T. Ragan, eds., *Homosexuality in Modern France,* 225–241. New York: Oxford University Press, 1996.

Oliver, Kelly. *Witnessing: Beyond Recognition.* Minneapolis: University of Minnesota Press, 2001.

Owens, Craig. "Outlaws: Gay Men in Feminism." In Scott Bryson, Barbara Kruger, Lynne Tillman, and Jane Weinstock, eds., *Beyond Recognition: Representation, Power, and Culture,* 218–238. Berkeley: University of California Press, 1992.

Patton, Cindy. "Tremble, Hetero Swine!" In Michael Warner, ed., *Fear of a Queer Planet: Politics and Social Theory,* 143–177. Minneapolis: University of Minnesota Press, 1993.

Pêcheux, Michel. *Language, Semantics, and Ideology.* New York: St. Martin's, 1982.

Pippin, Robert. *Nietzsche, Psychology, and First Philosophy.* Chicago: University of Chicago Press, 2010.

Plaskow, Judith. *Standing Again at Sinai: Judaism from a Feminist Perspective.* New York: Harper and Row, 1990.

Plato. *The Republic: The Complete and Unabridged Jowett Translation.* New York: Random House, 1991.

Plaza, Monique. "Our Damages and Their Compensation. Rape: The Will Not to Know of Michel Foucault." *Feminist Issues* 1, no. 3 (1981): 25–35.

Posner, Richard. *Law and Literature: A Misunderstood Relation.* Cambridge: Harvard University Press, 1998.

Powell v. State, 510 S.E.2d 18 (Ga. 1998).

Probyn, Elspeth. *Outside Belongings.* New York: Routledge, 1996.

Proust, Marcel. *La Prisonnière. A la recherche du temps perdu,* vol. 5. Paris: Gallimard, 1988.

———. *Remembrance of Things Past.* Trans. C. K. Scott Moncrieff and Terence Kilmartin. New York: Random House, 1981.

———. *Sodom and Gomorrah: In Search of Lost Time.* Trans. C. K. Scott Moncrieff and Terence Kilmartin, revised by D. J. Enright. New York: Random House, 1992.

———. *Sodome et Gomorrhe. A la recherche du temps perdu,* vol. 4. Paris: Gallimard, 1988.

Puar, Jasbir. "'I would rather be a cyborg than a goddess': Intersectionality, Assemblage, and Affective Politics." *Transversal* (2001). http://eipcp.net/transversal/0811/puar/en. Accessed June 20, 2011.

———. *Terrorist Assemblages: Homonationalism in Queer Times.* Durham: Duke University Press, 2007.

Rajchman, John. *Truth and Eros: Foucault, Lacan, and the Question of Ethics.* New York: Routledge, 1991.

Rancière, Jacques. *Disagreement: Politics and Philosophy.* Trans. Julie Rose. Minneapolis: University of Minnesota Press, 1999.

Razack, Sherene H. *Looking White People in the Eye: Gender, Race, and Culture in Courtrooms and Classrooms.* Toronto: University of Toronto Press, 1998.

Readings, Bill. *Introducing Lyotard: Art and Politics.* London: Routledge, 1991.

Reich, Wilhelm. *The Invasion of Compulsory Sex-Morality.* New York: Farrar, Strauss, and Giroux, 1971.

Renard, Paul, and Michele Hecquet, eds. *Violette Leduc.* Lille: Université Charles-de-Gaulle, 1998.

Rich, Adrienne. "Cartographies of Silence." *Dream of a Common Language: Poems, 1974–1977.* New York: Norton, 1993.

———. "Compulsory Heterosexuality and Lesbian Existence." In Henry Abelove, Michèle Aina Barale, and David M. Halperin, eds., *The Gay and Lesbian Studies Reader,* 227–254. New York: Routledge, 1993.

Robbins, Jill. *Altered Reading: Levinas and Literature.* Chicago: University of Chicago Press, 1999.

Rodríguez, Juana María. *Queer Latinidad: Identity Practices, Discursive Spaces.* New York: New York University Press, 2003.

Romero, Mary. "Who Takes Care of the Maid's Children? Exploring the Costs of Domestic Service." In Hilde Lindemann Nelson, ed., *Feminism and Families,* 151–169. New York: Routledge, 1997.

Ronell, Avital. "The Deviant Payback: The Aims of Valerie Solanas," 1–31. In Valerie Solanas, *SCUM Manifesto.* London: Verso, 2004.

Rotello, Gabriel. *Sexual Ecology: AIDS and the Destiny of Gay Men.* New York: Dutton, 1997.

Rubin, Gayle. *Deviations: A Gayle Rubin Reader.* Durham: Duke University Press, 2011.

———. "Elegy for the Valley of the Kings: AIDS and the Leather Community in San Francisco, 1981–1996." In Martin Levine, Peter Nardi, and John Gagnon, eds., *Changing Times: Gay Men and Lesbians Encounter HIV/AIDS,* 101–144. Chicago: University of Chicago Press, 1997.

———. "The Catacombs: A Temple of the Butthole." In Mark Thompson, ed., *Leatherfolk: Radical Sex, People, Politics, and Practice,* 119–141. Boston: Alyson, 1991.

———. "The Miracle Mile: South of Market and Gay Male Leather in San Francisco, 1962–1996." In James Brook, Chris Carlsson, and Nancy Peters, eds., *Reclaiming San Francisco: History, Politics, Culture,* 247–272. San Francisco: City Lights, 1998.

———. "Thinking Sex: Notes for a Radical Politics of Sexuality." In Henry Abelove, Michèle Aina Barale, and David M. Halperin, eds., *The Lesbian and Gay Studies Reader,* 1–44. New York: Routledge, 1993.

Rubin, Gayle, with Judith Butler. "Sexual Traffic: Interview." In Naomi Schor and Elizabeth Weed, eds., *Feminism Meets Queer Theory,* 68–108. Bloomington: Indiana University Press, 1997.

Rumi. "Birdwings." In *The Essential Rumi,* 174. Trans. Coleman Barks. Edison, NJ: Castle, 1997.

Ruskola, Teemu. "Gay Rights Versus Queer Theory: What Is Left of Sodomy After *Lawrence v. Texas?*" *Social Text* 84–85 (2005): 25–250.

Salamon, Gayle. *Assuming a Body: Transgender and Rhetorics of Materiality*. New York: Columbia University Press, 2010.

Sawicki, Jana. *Disciplining Foucault: Feminism, Power, and the Body*. New York: Routledge, 1991.

Schor, Naomi. *Breaking the Chain: Women, Theory, and French Realist Fiction*. New York: Columbia University Press, 1985.

———. "French Feminism Is a Universalism." *differences: A Journal of Feminist Cultural Studies* 7, no. 1 (1995): 15–46.

———, and Elizabeth Weed, eds. *Feminism Meets Queer Theory*. Bloomington: Indiana University Press, 1997.

Schroeder, William R. "Continental Ethics." In *The Blackwell Guide to Ethical Theory*, 375–399. Ed. Hugh LaFollette. Oxford: Blackwell, 2000.

Schutte, Ofelia. "Dependency Work, Women, and the Global Economy." In Eva Feder Kittay and Ellen Feder, eds., *The Subject of Care: Feminist Perspectives on Dependency*, 138–159. Lanham, MA: Rowman and Littlefield, 2002.

Scott, Charles. *The Question of Ethics: Nietzsche, Foucault, Heidegger*. Bloomington: Indiana University Press, 1990.

Scott, Joan Wallach. *Only Paradoxes to Offer: French Feminists and the Rights of Man*. Cambridge: Harvard University Press, 1996.

Sedgwick, Eve Kosofsky. *Epistemology of the Closet*. Berkeley: University of California Press, 1990.

———. "Jane Austen and the Masturbating Girl." In *Tendencies*. Durham: Duke University Press, 1993, 109–129.

———. "Privilege of Unknowing: Diderot's *The Nun*." In *Tendencies*, 23–51. Durham: Duke University Press, 1993.

———. *Tendencies*. Durham: Duke University Press, 1993.

———. *The Weather in Proust*. Ed. Jonathan Goldberg. Durham: Duke University Press, 2011.

———. *Touching Feeling: Affect, Pedagogy, Performativity*. Durham: Duke University Press, 2003.

———, and Adam Frank. "Shame in the Cybernetic Fold: Reading Silvan Tomkins." In *Shame and Its Sisters: A Silvan Tomkins Reader*, 1–28. Ed. Eve Kosofsky Sedgwick and Adam Frank. Durham: Duke University Press, 1995.

Sentencing Project. "Schools and Prisons: Fifty Years After *Brown v. Board of Education*." May 2004. http://sentencingproject.org/pdfs/brownvboard.pdf. Accessed July 18, 2012.

Sfez, Gérald. *Jean-François Lyotard: La Faculté d'une phrase*. Paris: Galilee, 2000.

Shah, Nayan. "Policing Privacy, Migrants, and the Limits of Freedom." *Social Text* 84–85, nos. 3–4 (2005): 275–284.

Sheehan, Elizabeth. "Victorian Clitoridectomy: Isaac Baker Brown and His Harmless Operative Procedure." In Roger N. Lancaster and Micaela di Leonardo, eds., *The Gender/Sexuality Reader: Culture, History, Political Economy*, 325–334. New York: Routledge, 1997.

Sheth, Falguni. "The War on Terror and Ontopolitics: Concerns with Foucault's Account of Race, Power, Sovereignty." *Foucault Studies* 12 (October 2011): 51–76.

———. *Toward a Political Philosophy of Race*. Albany: SUNY Press, 2009.

Signorile, Michelangelo. *Life Outside: The Signorile Report on Gay Men: Sex, Drugs, Morals, and the Passages of Life*. New York: Harper Collins, 1997.

Solanas, Valerie. *SCUM Manifesto*. London: Verso, 2004.

Solinger, Rickie. "Dependency and Choice: The Two Faces of Eve." In Eva Feder Kittay and Ellen Feder, eds., *The Subject of Care: Feminist Perspectives on Dependency*, 61–87. Lanham, MA: Rowman and Littlefield, 2002.

Soper, Kate. "Productive Contradictions." In Caroline Ramazanoglu, ed., *Up Against Foucault: Explorations of Some Tensions Between Foucault and Feminism*, 29–50. London: Routledge, 1993.

Spindelman, Marc. "Surviving *Lawrence v. Texas*." *Michigan Law Review* 102, no. 7 (2004): 1615–1657.

Spivak, Gayatri. "Can the Subaltern Speak?" In Cary Nelson and Lawrence Grossberg, eds., *Marxism and the Interpretation of Culture*, 24–28. London: MacMillan, 1988.

State of Georgia v. Anthony San Juan Powell, Crim. No. 96-B-3448-6 (Gwinnett Superior Ct. August 9, 1997).

Stengers, Jean, and Anne Van Neck. *Masturbation: The History of a Great Terror*. Trans. Kathryn Hoffman. New York: Palgrave, 2001.

Stockton, Kathryn Bond. *God Between Their Lips: Desire Between Women in Irigaray, Brontë, and Eliot*. Stanford: Stanford University Press, 1994.

Stryker, Susan, and Stephen Whittle, ed. *The Transgender Studies Reader*. New York: Routledge, 2006.

Sullivan, Nikki. *A Critical Introduction to Queer Theory*. New York: New York University Press, 2003.

Taylor, Dianna, and Karen Vintges, *Feminism and the Final Foucault*. Urbana: University of Illinois Press, 2004.

Teubal, Savina J. *Ancient Sisterhood: The Lost Traditions of Sarah and Hagar*. Athens: Ohio University Press, 1990.

Thomas, Kendall. "Beyond the Privacy Principle." *Columbia Law Review* 92 (1992): 1431–1516.

Thurman, Judith. *Secrets of the Flesh: A Life of Colette*. New York: Knopf, 1999.

Trible, Phyllis. *Texts of Terror: Literary-Feminist Readings of Biblical Narratives*. Philadelphia: Fortress, 1984.

Trinh Thi, Coralie. *Betty Monde*. Vauvert: Au diable vauvert, 2002.

Tronto, Joan. *Moral Boundaries: A Political Argument for an Ethic of Care*. New York: Routledge, 1993.

———. "The 'Nanny' Question in Feminism." *Hypatia* 17, no. 2 (2002): 34–51.

Turner, William. *A Genealogy of Queer Theory*. Philadelphia: Temple University Press, 2000.

Tyler, Carole-Anne. "Boys Will Be Girls: The Politics of Gay Drag." In Diana Fuss, ed., *Inside/Out: Lesbian Theories, Gay Theories*, 32–70. New York: Routledge, 1991.

Van Leeuwen, Anne. "An Examination of Irigaray's Commitment to Transcendental Phenomenology in *The Forgetting of Air* and *The Way of Love*," *Hypatia*, early view, Dec. 19, 2011. DOI: 10.1111/j.1527-2001.2011.01257.x.

Warner, Michael, ed. *Fear of a Queer Planet: Queer Politics and Social Theory*. Minneapolis: University of Minnesota Press, 1993.

———. *The Trouble with Normal: Sex, Politics, and the Ethics of Queer Life*. New York: Free Press, 1999.

Waters, John. "John Waters, Baron of Bad Taste from Baltimore, Is Obsessed with Michael Jackson's Polka Dot Penis." In Jop van Bennekom and Gert Jonkers, eds., *Butt Book: The Best of the First Five Years of Butt Magazine*, 197–206. Hong Kong: Taschen, 2006.

Weber, Samuel. *Institution and Interpretation*. Stanford: Stanford University Press, 2001.

Weed, Elizabeth. "The More Things Change." In Naomi Schor and Elizabeth Weed, eds., *Feminism Meets Queer Theory*, 266–291. Bloomington: Indiana University Press, 1997.

Weeks, Kathi. *The Problem with Work: Feminism, Marxism, Antiwork Politics, and Postwork Imaginaries*. Durham: Duke University Press, 2011.

Weisberg, Robert. "The Law-Literature Enterprise." *Yale Journal of Law and Humanities* 1 (1988–1989): 1–68.

Weiss, Margot. *Techniques of Pleasure: BDSM and the Circuits of Sexuality*. Durham: Duke University Press, 2011.

Weston, Kath. *Long Slow Burn: Sexuality and Social Science*. New York: Routledge, 1998.

White, Hayden. *The Content of Form: Narrative Discourse and Historical Representation*. Baltimore: Johns Hopkins University Press, 1987.

White, James Boyd. *The Legal Imagination: Studies in the Nature of Legal Thought and Expression*. Boston: Little, Brown, 1973.

Wiegman, Robyn. "'Dear Ian.'" *Duke Journal of Gender, Law, and Policy* 11 (2004): 93–120.

———. "Heteronormativity and the Desire for Gender." *Feminist Theory* 7 (2006): 89–103.

———. *Object Lessons*. Durham: Duke University Press, 2012.

Willett, Cynthia. *The Soul of Justice: Social Bonds and Racial Hubris*. Ithaca: Cornell University Press, 2001.

Williams, Bernard. *Ethics and the Limits of Philosophy*. Cambridge: Harvard University Press, 1985.

Williams, Delores. *Sisters in the Wilderness: The Challenge of Womanist God-Talk*. Maryknoll, NY: Orbis, 1993.

Williams, Linda. "Sick Sisters." *Sight and Sound* 11, no. 6 (July 2001): 28–29.

Williams, Patricia J. *The Alchemy of Race and Rights: Diary of a Law Professor*. Cambridge: Harvard University Press, 1991.

Wilson, Judith. "Hagar's Daughters: Social History, Cultural Heritage, and Afro-U.S. Women's Art." In *Bearing Witness: Contemporary Works by African American Women Artists*. New York: Rizzoli International, 1996.

Winnubst, Shannon. "Exceeding Hegel and Lacan: Different Fields of Pleasure Within Foucault and Irigaray." *Hypatia* 14, no. 1 (1999): 13–37.

———. *Queering Freedom*. Bloomington: Indiana University Press, 2006.

Wittig, Monique. "The Straight Mind." *The Straight Mind and Other Essays*, 21–32. Boston: Beacon, 1992.

Wriggins, Jennifer. "Rape, Racism, and the Law." *Harvard Women's Law Journal* 6 (1983): 103–141.

Wyschogrod, Edith. *An Ethics of Remembering: History, Heterology, and the Nameless Others*. Chicago: University of Chicago Press, 1998.

Yoshino, Kenji. "The City and the Poet." *Yale Law Journal* 114, no. 8 (2005): 1835–1896.

Young, Iris Marion. "Autonomy, Welfare Reform, and Meaningful Work." In Eva Feder Kittay and Ellen Feder, eds., *The Subject of Care: Feminist Perspectives on Dependency*, 40–60. Lanham, MA: Rowman and Littlefield, 2002.

———. *Intersecting Voices: Dilemmas of Gender, Political Philosophy, and Policy*. Princeton: Princeton University Press, 1997.

———. *Justice and the Politics of Difference*. Princeton: Princeton University Press, 1990.

Yuval-Davis, Nira. "Intersectionality and Feminist Politics." *European Journal of Women's Studies* 13, no. 3 (August 2006): 193–209.

Zerilli, Linda. *Feminism and the Abyss of Freedom*. Chicago: University of Chicago Press, 2005.

Žižek, Slavoj. *The Sublime Object of Ideology*. New York: Verso, 1991.

Index